BLOOD & BOUNDARIES

THE

MENAHEM STERN JERUSALEM

LECTURES

BRANDEIS UNIVERSITY PRESS

HISTORICAL SOCIETY OF ISRAEL

STUART B. SCHWARTZ

Blood & Boundaries

THE LIMITS OF

RELIGIOUS AND RACIAL

EXCLUSION IN EARLY

MODERN LATIN AMERICA

BRANDEIS UNIVERSITY PRESS

Waltham, Massachusetts

Historical Society of Israel

Brandeis University Press

© 2020 Stuart B. Schwartz

All rights reserved

Manufactured in the United States of America

Designed by Richard Hendel

Typeset in Garamond Premier Pro by Tseng Information Systems, Inc.

For permission to reproduce any of the material in this book,
contact Brandeis University Press, 415 South Street,
Waltham MA 02453, or visit
http://www.brandeis.edu/press

CIP data appears at the end of the book

5 4 3 2 1

To my colleagues and friends,
Fernando Bouza Álvarez
and Jean-Frédéric Schaub

And to the memory of
Joaquim Romero Magalhães
and António Manuel Hespanha

Tot hostes, quot exclusi [everyone excluded is an enemy].

MATEO LÓPEZ BRAVO

(*De rege et regendi ration*)

There are no more than two lands in the world:
The land of the good and the land of the bad. All the good,
whether they be Jews, Moors, gentiles, Christians,
or some other sect, are of the same land, the same household,
the same blood; and the same can be said of the bad.

FADRIQUE FURIÓ CERIOL

(*Del Consejo y consejeros del principe*)

CONTENTS

FOREWORD
Yosef Kaplan

As a twelve-year-old student at the Hebrew gymnasium in his hometown of Bialystok, Poland, the young Menahem Stern decided he would become a historian when he grew up. In the gymnasium's rich library, he developed his great love for books and the habit of reading in libraries. This habit endured until his very last day, June 22, 1989 — the day he was murdered as he walked along his regular route from his house on Tchernichovsky Street to the National Library in Jerusalem. With every fiber of his being, Stern was tied to this institution, established by Josef Chazanowitch (another native of Bialystok). Almost every day Stern would cross the valley that leads to the National Library on the Hebrew University's campus in Givat Ram. Many of us still remember seeing him sitting in the Jewish Studies Reading Room, or in the corner next to the classical literature shelves in the General Reading Room. One could also see him there walking briskly to the periodicals room, carrying a bundle of proof sheets of the periodical *Zion*, the Hebrew quarterly of the Historical Society of Israel of which he was an editor from 1975 until 1989. Stern was a unique scholar, a historian who left behind a monumental research project. His writings are an essential asset of the historiography on the Jews in the Hellenistic and Roman periods.

"Animus facit nobilem [the spirit ennobles man]," wrote Seneca. And indeed Stern was one of the noblest of spirit among us — generous and kind to young scholars at the beginning of their academic careers, with an excellent sense of humor and a witty, playful, and captivating irony without a hint of arrogance. In 1993, four years after his murder, the Historical Society of Israel decided to establish the Menahem Stern Jerusalem Lectures Series in his memory. We set ourselves the goal of inviting each year a historian, prominent by virtue of his or her unique contribution to historical research, to give a series of three lectures. Since 1993, we have been privileged to host twenty-three historians who are among the shapers of the historical discipline of the last generation, renowned experts in a wide variety of fields and historical periods.

It was a great honor for the Historical Society of Israel to host Professor Stuart Schwartz, the George Burton Adams Professor of History at Yale University, during January 2019. Schwartz is among the most important historians of Latin America during the colonial period, and he is considered the leading historian of Brazil of our generation. He has left his mark on the study of the transatlantic empires of Spain and Portugal, on Native American history, and on world history.

He has written and edited approximately twenty books. *Sugar Plantations in the Formation of Brazilian Society: Bahia 1559–1835*, published in 1985, is a monumental study spanning the history of the sugar economy and the peculiar development of plantation society over a three-hundred-year period in Bahia. In 1992, four years after Brazil marked the centennial of the abolition of slavery, Schwartz published *Slaves, Peasants, and Rebels*, a fascinating and exhaustive study about the history of slavery in Brazil, which was the last country in the Western Hemisphere to abolish it.

In 2016, he published *Sea of Storms: A History of Hurricanes in the Greater Caribbean from Columbus to Katrina*. This impressive book is a tour de force by a multifaceted historian, who excels in working with a wide variety of sources and draws from them original and daring conclusions. In *Sea of Storms*, he taught us how the cultures that developed and crystallized in the Caribbean were as much shaped by the hurricanes that struck the area as they were by diplomacy, trade, and colonial heritage. Schwartz studied in depth how Caribbean societies reacted to the dangers of hurricanes and how these devastating storms affected the region from the days of Columbus to the present. For this book, he received the Gustav Ranis award for the best book on an international topic by a Yale faculty member.

From the preface of Schwartz's splendid book *All Can Be Saved:*

Religious Tolerance and Salvation in the Iberian Atlantic World, we learn how it germinated:

> This book was conceived in bed. I remember laughing out loud while reading Carlo Ginzburg's *The Cheese and the Worms* one winter night in Minneapolis and thinking how tolerant and modern its protagonist, the free-thinking Friulian miller Menocchio, seemed when he told his inquisitors in 1584 that no one really knew which religion was best; and that while he was, of course, a Catholic, if he had been born among the Turks, he would have lived in their religion and thought it best. . . . A decade later, while working in the records of the Spanish Inquisition, . . . I began to encounter the cases of individuals whose attitudes toward other religions seemed quite close to those of Menocchio . . . they expressed ideas of religious relativism and tolerance, often summed up in a common expression: *Cada uno se puede salvar en su ley* (each person can be saved in his religion).

Thus was born *All Can Be Saved*, which was published in 2008 and soon became one of the most important studies ever written about the world of beliefs and ideas in early modern Spain, Portugal, and their colonies in America. The book has won many important prizes, and reviewers have gone out of their way to praise Schwartz's remarkable achievement.

All Can Be Saved connects Schwartz with Ginzburg, who was the first historian to deliver a Menahem Stern lecture. And in many ways it also links us to the topic of the Stern lectures that Schwartz gave in Jerusalem in January 2019. The Ibero-American society in which some individuals—among them conversos, Moriscos, and Old Christians—dared to claim that each person could be saved in his or her religion was a world ruled by the Inquisition and the statutes of purity of blood.

This situation was extremely different from the one that prevailed in Spain and Portugal during the Middle Ages, an era that saw a fruitful and vital encounter among Christians, Muslims, and

Jews that had far-reaching social and cultural consequences. However, during the fifteenth century, and especially under the rule of the Catholic monarchs Ferdinand and Isabella, a dramatic reversal occurred: the change in the attitude of the monarchy toward the Muslim and Jewish minorities put an end to the long-standing policy of *convivencia*, which had characterized the Iberian kingdoms since the time of the *reconquista*. The imposition of Catholicism on the Jews and Muslims, the establishment of the Inquisition in Spain and Portugal, the expulsions, and the application of the laws of purity of blood to the descendants of converts from the two religions all marked the beginning of a new age in the history of the two Iberian monarchies, which were becoming worldwide colonial empires.

Mustering his impressive expertise in the details of the history of Spain and Portugal and their colonies in the New World, Schwartz described and analyzed the processes that affected the two Catholic kingdoms in the period when they attained the height of their political power and colonial achievements. It is to be expected that this book, too, which presents the contents of Schwartz's three fascinating lectures with admirable clarity, will make an impression similar to that of his earlier works.

ACKNOWLEDGMENTS

I am most grateful to Professor Yosef Kaplan and the Israeli Historical Society for the invitation to present the Menachem Stern Lectures of 2019, which have provided the foundation of this book. I also thank the audience that attended and participated in the discussions, especially Elisheva Baumgarten, Miriam Eliav-Feldon, Alex Kerner, Amos Megged, Rene Levine Melamed, Moshe Sluhovsky, and Claude Stuczynski — all of whose hospitality and guidance made my first visit to Jerusalem a memorable experience.

During the writing and editing of these essays I have been fortunate to have received advice, encouragement, and criticism from a number of "frank and fearless" friends and colleagues. James Amelang, Mercedes García-Arenal, Fernando Bouza Alvarez, Franco Borja Llopis, Ignacio Chuecas Saldías, Bruno Feitler, Antonio Feros, Richard Kagan, Iris Kantor, Kris Lane, David Nirenberg, Juan Ignacio Pulido Serrano, Joanne Rappaport, Macarena Sánchez, Jean-Frederic Schaub, Jonathan Schorsch, David Sorkin, Claude Stuczynski, Hernan Taboada, Francesca Trivellato, Bernard Vincent, and Angela Xavier all read chapters or versions of the full text. I also received advice, suggestions, and research leads from, Pedro Cardim, Pilar Gonzalbo Aizpuru, Martin Nesvig, Fernanda Olival, Joanne Rappaport, Tatiana Seijas, and Daviken Studnicki-Gizbert. I also wish to thank C.L. Stopford Sackville and Irma Mèndez of the Museo de Historia Mexicana (Monterrey, Mexico) for facilitating the reproduction of various images in this book. My wife, María Jordán Arroyo, has been a constant interlocutor, colleague, informant, critical reader, and companion. Finally, I would like to recognize the contribution to my thinking about the themes of this book over the years made by my coauthors, collaborators, teachers, and interlocutors: Guillaume Boccara, Herbert

Klein, Elizabeth Kuznesof, James Lockhart, Robert McCaa, Magnus Mörner, Stanley Stein, Nathan Wachtel, Charles Wagley, Anita Novinsky, and Frank Salomon. I am indebted to all of them for their generosity, support, and help.

BLOOD & BOUNDARIES

INTRODUCTION

Great empires like those of Rome, the Mughals, or the Ottomans brought peoples of different languages, ethnicities, and faiths under imperial rule. They ruled by establishing hierarchies of differentiation, but they allowed differences in practices, customs, and belief. The empires of early modern Spain and Portugal, both of which justified their expansion by spreading the Roman Catholic faith, departed from this imperial model by imposing whenever possible a uniformity of religion and law, although sometimes granting limited acceptance of cultural and ethnic differences.[1] Both these empires—born in the late Middle Ages, consolidated in the sixteenth century, and motivated by millenarian dreams of a universal Christian monarchy—enforced policies of religious intolerance as the most effective way to ensure the conformity and loyalty of their subjects. Common membership in the community of Christendom would mute or overcome cultural and linguistic differences and ensure unity.

Spain and Portugal, motivated by the ideal of "one flock, one shepherd, one monarch, one empire, one sword," promoted religious unity by converting and assimilating their internal others (Jews and Muslims) or, eventually, by expelling them.[2] But this drive for religious unity at home was complicated by the roughly contemporaneous creation of overseas empires. Warranted and legitimated by papal authority to spread the faith among myriad peoples of other cultures and beliefs, the monarchs of both Portugal and Castile viewed their Christian missionary activity as a principal justification of empire and as a basis of their legal claims to sovereignty. As the chronicler Diogo de Couto noted approvingly, Portugal's kings had always believed that temporal and spiritual power "should never be exercised one without the other."[3] Conversions, which had been done in Granada and Lisbon with Muslims and Jews, now became

1

a great missionary enterprise as these empires created New Christians around the globe from the Canary Islands, to the Kongo kingdom, coastal Brazil, Mexico, the Philippines, India, and Japan.[4] In various areas of contact such as Portuguese Goa prior to 1540, or in Spanish America in general, there was some experimentation with juridical plurality and allowance of cultural and religious diversity, somewhat akin to the way in which Jews and Muslims had lived under their own law in medieval Christian Iberia, but such concessions were short-lived or remained mostly theoretical.[5]

In the Americas, although levels of religious syncretism varied with time, place, and the policies of various missionary orders or individual bishops, the general tendency over time was to define indigenous beliefs and practices as superstition and to extirpate any religious alternatives that were clearly outside of the Catholic tradition. In Spain's overseas "kingdoms" (the term "colony" came into use only in the eighteenth century) although the newly converted Native Americans were exempted from the jurisdiction of the Inquisition, missionaries, episcopal courts, and separate inquisitorial-style tribunals sought to maintain Indian orthodoxy. Africans — most of whom arrived in the Americas as slaves — enjoyed no such exemption from the Inquisition, and once baptized they and their descendants fell under the jurisdiction of the Holy Office, which vigorously suppressed African rituals, practices, and beliefs as superstition or witchcraft. The Church sought to channel African and Afro-American religiosity into lay confraternities, the cults of particular saints, and other more orthodox beliefs, but African continuities and syncretism flourished despite these efforts, and peoples of African descent (both enslaved and free) used the approved organizations and practices to protect and advance their own interests.[6]

However, empires have always had more than a religious dimension. Rather quickly the processes of conquest, colonization, sexual exploitation, and contact engendered in the Iberian empires new social divisions based on ethnicity, comportment, appearance, and a variety of other characteristics and conditions that supposedly determined not only a person's civic obligations, rights (*fueros*), and privileges, but also her or his life opportunities and place in the social order.

In the Iberian Americas, the inclusion of Europeans, Amerindians, Africans, some peoples from Asia, and neoteric populations of mixed origins produced a new and complex social hierarchy based on a variety of cultural, ethnic, social, and physical characteristics. How this social order came into being and changed over time, from the moment of Columbus's landfall in 1492 to the independence of Latin America in the 1820s, provides the framework for the following chapters. They will examine how the principles of incorporation or exclusion shifted in emphasis from religious affiliation, ethnic origins, or some moral or social deficiency to phenotype — or what some scholars have called racial discrimination.

To do this, I have not concentrated on the Native American populations or on the large numbers of Africans brought as slaves. Instead, I have focused on three minority categories of people — Muslims, Jews, and mestizos — whose place in Spanish and Portuguese colonial societies or exclusion from them defined the peculiar ordering that distinguished the Iberian from other colonial enterprises in the Americas. Conquest, alliances, barter, and violence neutralized Native American resistance, and all of the European colonies either eliminated indigenous peoples or incorporated them as a dependent or subject population. Africans came to all the European colonies, usually as slaves, and everywhere they and their descendants (even when free) were placed near the bottom of the social ladder. The Iberians shared in those experiences and, in fact, had been the forerunners of the fusion of Amerindians and Africans into colonial society. However, the Spaniards and Portuguese also introduced a hierarchy not only based on ethnic or phenotypical differences, but one that also incorporated elements such as reason and religion. In Spain and Portugal various categories of people and groups at different times suffered discrimination or legal disadvantage — Gypsies, homosexuals, Protestants, religious dissidents, witches, the mentally ill, and beggars, to mention just a few. Moriscos (converts from Islam) and conversos (converted Jews) were two minority groups that were denigrated and disadvantaged in Spain and Portugal and were eventually prohibited from migrating to or residing in the New World. Even after conversion, they and their descendants were disadvantaged and discriminated against, based not necessarily on what they did but on who they were.[7] This made lineage and blood a model for dealing with ethnic and cultural or religious alterity that influenced the shaping of social hierarchies of Latin America. There, sexual contact with the indigenous peoples began to produce a population of mixed heritage that rather quickly became a challenge to the existing social and juridical categories. Of course, people of mixed parentage (mestizos, *mamelucos*, métis, half-breeds, and so on) existed in all the European American colonies, but probably nowhere did their numbers or importance rival those of the Iberian colonies. "Mestizo" was a term that originally meant simply the offspring of European and Indian unions, but eventually it usually implied illegitimacy as well. The word was also sometimes used generically to include the offspring of any mixed union, so over time it became used interchangeably with terms like *casta* (caste) in Spanish America or *pardo* in Brazil—both of which had pejorative connotations because they encompassed persons of African descent and thus implied servile origins. Like Morisco and converso, *mestizo* was a label that underlined genealogical thinking and the importance of lineage, and thus it suggested the presence of *mala sangre* (bad blood) and the defects it was thought to transmit to anyone whose lineage included Africans, heathens, heretics, or people of ignoble birth or occupation.[8] Although there were some parallels with the other European colonies in the Americas, especially in the case of the mestizos, these three minorities seemed dangerous and destabilizing to the society because they were so difficult to physically distinguish from the Old Christian population of European descent, and thus they are a key to understanding the role of race and other forms of social difference in these colonial regimes.[9]

The following chapters will examine the reasons for and the results of the exclusion of and discrimination against these categories of people. However, my focus is not so much on the laws and institutions that sought to enforce the exclusions and reinforce the social hierarchy or on the discourse and patterns of genealogical thinking that sought to distinguish between purity and infection, but rather on the experience of those whose lived under these constraints, and on how and why the attempts to marginalize them were limited, modified, ignored, or evaded — not only by the victims of the exclusions but also by other groups and individuals in their society, and at times even by the state or by ecclesiastical institutions as well.

To some extent by concentrating on the resistance, negotiation, or evasion of the restrictive laws and the dominant social ideology, I am following a path I began to travel in my book *All Can Be Saved*, which explored surprising sentiments of religious tolerance or at least indifference to orthodox dogma in the Iberian world as expressed by common people in Spain, Portugal and their overseas territories in the Americas.[10] In these chapters I draw on that work, but I seek to broaden my scope from religious considerations to social and political ones as well. As a historian of colonial Latin America, I have often written about the impact that the intersection of color, religion, class, and gender has had on that region's social organization.[11] There may be no topic in early Latin American history that has generated more interest and debate than the issue of race and racial identity — including that identity's characteristics, terminology, effects, history, and hierarchies. This historiography is extensive and rich.[12] Since the middle of the twentieth century, generations of historians have examined the origins, structure, and vocabulary of the exclusionary laws and practices, as well as their effects on the people they affected. Over time, historians have concentrated on differing aspects of this history. In the 1970s and 1980s many scholars, often employing quantitative methodologies, sought to determine the extent to which race was more important than social class or wealth in structuring Latin American societies.[13] By the 1990s there had been a perceptible shift in emphasis to questions about the degree to which people identified with these racial categories and the extent to which that identity shaped their collective behavior. There was also a continuous preoccupation with the impact of gender on the system of exclusions and incorporations, and the degree to which gender affected social status in these societies.[14]

Many of these studies made clear that these New World Iberian colonies were in various ways extensions of their founding European metropoles, and that to understand the social systems in America, it was necessary to place them within the context of the original Iberian societies. However, doing that was complex and daunting, since in the historiography of medieval and early modern Spain and Portugal there may have been no topic that had generated more scholarly writing or more heated debate than their religious and ethnic plurality before the sixteenth century and their religious exclusivity thereafter, as their Muslim and Jewish populations either converted voluntarily or by force or were expelled.[15] One aspect of those debates carried out by two Spanish medievalists, Américo Castro and Claudio Sánchez Albornoz, and their respective supporters was about the extent to which Hispanic culture itself was a result of cultural plurality (Castro) or was essentially and positively forged in the rejection of its non-Christian elements (Sánchez Albornoz). Their exchanges about these two opposing visions of Spanish history and culture, and especially of the role of the Jews and Muslims in that history, had a broad impact and generated renewed interest in Spain and its multicultural past. It was also a stimulus to the scholars of Judaism and Islam, who now saw the Iberian experience as a crucial moment in a broader history. By the 1960s, Hispanists and those interested in Spain's and Portugal's role in that broader history had begun to pose new questions and shift their areas of interest and interpretations.[16] Some of them still followed Castro's approach but dropped his essentializing of "Jewish" character traits and ways of thinking. They found in the social and cultural histories of Spain and Portugal a hopeful model of an at least practical religious tolerance and a productive cultural exchange among Muslims, Jews, and Christians, the so-called *convivencia* of the Hispanic medieval period. However, in early modern Iberian history and in the forced conversions and exile of the minorities, others found the origins of modern racism, religious discrimination, and (in the methods of the Inquisition) even the technologies of the modern totalitarian state.[17]

Underlying much of this historiography was a concern with the origins of racism and the extent to which it, or something like it, existed prior to the nineteenth century. Even before World War II, some scholars had seen clear parallels to contemporary racial thinking in the Iberian treatment of Jews and Jewish converts, and after the war, other scholars even sought to find a direct link between Nazi policies and racial ideology and such Hispanic precedents.[18] Particularly troubling was the late Iberian medieval idea that culture and rejection of Christian attitudes could be genealogically transmitted, so that certain Jewish characteristics were carried in the blood and were genetic. This was the thinking upon which a series of regulations requiring purity of blood (*limpieza de sangre*) had rested. The first of these regulations had appeared in Toledo in 1449 in the midst of a power struggle in which the opponents of newly converted Jews sought to limit them as competitors by excluding anyone who had a Jewish ancestry from public office and other positions of distinction or authority. These restrictions — eventually expanded to exclude anyone whose lineage included Muslims, heretics, or relatives punished by the Inquisition — quickly spread throughout Spain and later Portugal and were adopted by cathedral chapters, religious orders, municipalities, universities, and other institutions. Although contested on theological and practical grounds and never fully incorporated into royal or ecclesiastical law, these restrictions effectively served to discriminate against and potentially disadvantage anyone who could not claim to be "pure." They had the effect of creating a new social division in a society no longer simply divided between gentlemen (hidalgos) and commoners (*pecheros*), but now separated as well by the purity of their genealogy. Limpieza created a new kind of nobility that even a most humble person like Don Quixote's companion Sancho Panza could claim as a way to set himself above those lacking in this regard. As an anonymous seventeenth-century observer wrote, "it is more prestigious to be a gentleman than to be a 'clean' commoner, but more disgraceful to be lacking in that quality because in Spain we value far more a 'clean' commoner than a hidalgo who is not."[19]

Early historical considerations of the exclusion of or discrimination against certain ethnicities or categories of people had used the concept of race (*raza*) in very general terms or had avoided it all together, claiming that prior to the development of scientific racism in the nineteenth century, that use of the term was probably erroneous and surely anachronistic. However, much recent scholarship has questioned that previous avoidance, with considerable emphasis placed by medievalists on the perception and mistreatment of Jews and Africans as evidence that racial theories (some of them based on the "sciences" of those times, like astrology, the Hippocratic medical theory of bodily humors, Aristotelian natural science, and demonology) and discrimination easily merged with other forms and principles of hierarchy and distinction well before the nineteenth century and the birth of "scientific" racism.[20] Other scholars, however, are still cautious, and some are not at all inclined to employ that term.[21] For those who do use it, Catholic Iberia's treatment of its religious or ethnic minorities (Jews and Muslims) was a key factor in and a crucial step toward the development of racialist thinking.[22] In contrast, some North American scholars — perhaps influenced by the movement for civil rights in the United States and the legacy of black slavery in the Atlantic world — tended to see racism mostly in terms of its modern association with skin color. They also found the Iberian world a logical starting point and began to search for the origins of racism in the extensive presence of African slaves and the color hierarchies of colonial Latin America, but they sometimes paid little or no attention to the well-established literature on the Hispanic exclusionary policies toward the Jews and conversos and, to a lesser extent, Muslims.[23]

In the following chapters I have accepted the argument that aspects of the purity of blood restrictions and the beliefs of the inheritability of cultural and moral characteristics have a similarity to modern racism, but I also believe that the system of social organization and hierarchy of early modern Spain, Portugal, and their empires importantly incorporated concepts such as nobility, honor, legitimacy of birth, occupation, education, and accomplishment in ways that were quite unlike more modern forms of racial thinking. Whatever the specific cause of their origins, limpieza statutes were directed not only against religious or ethnic minorities and heretics but also against persons of illegitimate and thus dishonorable birth and those who worked with their hands in so-called vile occupations.[24] These regulations reflected genealogical thinking and a belief in the essentialism of character traits and behaviors that was not an exclusively Iberian problem. Medieval Western Europe had broadly accepted a juridical division of society into nobles, commoners, and members of the clergy that had never encompassed social and political reality (and that was probably never intended to do so) but that did provide a basic grammar of social standing and expectations of behavior associated with each corporate estate. The distinctions between nobles and commoners often were supported by implications of inherited ethnic or racial difference. For example, in France, to have been among the "companions of Clovis" provided a patina of age and ethnic distinction to noble lineages that justified the concept of *noblesse naturel* that separated commoners from people of quality.[25]

The concept of nobility permeated European societies, and Iberia was no exception. The nobles imposed their conception of life and social order on society as a whole.[26] Despite the many gradations and subranks in each estate, the division into nobles and commoners ordered society. It made nobility (*hidalguía*), with its privileges, precedence, and access to power, a status to which almost all aspired and that, in fact, became increasingly accessible through military, bureaucratic, or financial service to the monarch—a process that opened the door to many people of non-noble origins, although not without objections from those families that wished to maintain their exclusive control of privilege based on blood.[27] What I hope to show in the following chapters is that along with this traditional importance of nobility, the division of society after the fifteenth century based on a family's religious purity created in Spain, Portugal, and their empires a new kind of privileged or noble status based on religious affiliation—and when that was combined with *hidalguía*, it became a potential passport to success but simultaneously created a kind of diminished status that was intended to restrict and disadvantage those who bore the stains of impurity. When carried to the Iberian American colonies, these social divisions were adapted to a new social environment in which the mass of the Native American population in Spanish America was required to pay a tribute or perform labor and, in effect, it became a new taxpaying class. Simultaneously, all Spaniards, or those so considered, were freed of those obligations and thus enjoyed what had been the privileges and honor of hidalgo status in Spain and, mutatis mutandis, in Portugal. The famous German scientist Alexander von Humboldt observed in his 1803 visit to New Spain, "In America, every white man is a gentleman."[28] Those who gained access to Indian labor — or, in some places like Brazil — to African slaves could live without recourse to manual labor, one of the principal characteristics of a noble lifestyle. But the transfer of traditional social divisions of the society of estates was not without complications and transformations. Throughout the Americas, people sought to better their position, avoid their corporate status and its obligations, and erase or forget their supposed lack of honor or purity. That process, combined with miscegenation and manumission, eventually created large populations of persons who did not easily fit into either the medieval corporate categories or the new colonial ethnic or color divisions. Eventually, by the later eighteenth century, a pigmentocracy emerged, but its incorporation of many elements like religious purity, education, occupation, and honor rather than a dependence only on genealogy and color distinguished it from more recent forms of racism. In any case, the principal objective of the following chapters is explain how the system of exclusions that operated not only to set the parameters of life for marginalized groups, but also to show that when seen through the life experiences of families or individuals, the restrictions and disadvantages were repeatedly circumvented, negotiated, ignored, and ultimately failed as policies of social marginalization — even though they were relatively successful in weakening those groups as corporate actors with political interests. Given the clear asymmetry of power between the institutions or groups in authority and those who were objects of their control, it is not an easy task to find the appropriate interpretative balance between agency and authority. However, to ignore the roles of agency and of individual and familial actions and strategies, as has too often been the case, is to lose an important dimension of how the societies of Latin America took shape.

Finally, I am aware that in the following chapters I touch on only a few of the themes that involved these marginalized peoples, all of which have been the subject of extensive scholarship. I have tried to read broadly in those literatures, but I realize both that my concentration on social and political aspects has not addressed the cultural, religious, and identity issues that have motivated much of the scholarship about them, and that understanding the relationship between their inner life and their political and social strategies or actions is a task that still remains to be accomplished. I also recognize that by limiting these chapters chronologically to the early modern era, and geographically to Latin America, they are incomplete and probably also misleading. The questions of civil status or identity did not cease to be asked in 1830, and the shadow of racial designations and disadvantages continued in many places into the nineteenth century alongside the questions of slavery and abolition, or how indigenous peoples would be integrated into the new nation-states of Latin America. Fine studies of Cuba, Puerto Rico, Bolivia, and Mexico have made it clear that *calidad* (quality), the early modern conception of what elements defined a person's status or race, continued to be used long after the end of the colonial era. Similarly, I am well aware that Spain, and especially Portugal, did not limit their overseas empires to the Americas, so that attitudes about other religions and ethnicities were shaped not only by experiences in the Americas but also by contacts with peoples in Africa, the Indian Ocean, East Asia, and the Pacific islands.[29] Although excellent studies have appeared on some of those areas, very few scholars of Latin America (and I count myself among them) have accepted the challenge to address in depth the history of ethnic and religious contact and interchange on that global scale and to question how the variety of experiences in different areas of the world affected each other. Nevertheless, I believe that the history of Spain's and Portugal's experiences with religious and racial minorities in Latin America continues to be a crucial key to understanding not only that area of the world, but also the global history of empire and race. With an academic career that spans the era of the civil rights movement to the present moment of new state-sponsored attempts at discrimination and exclusion in my own country and elsewhere, I find this topic sadly relevant and contemporary, but I take heart in what the following chapters reveal about the resilience of those who found the means to avoid, contest, and struggle against the many obstacles created to limit, exclude, and demean them.

Moriscos

Real, Occasional, and
Imaginary Muslims

High in the Andes, each year in celebration of the day of Santiago (the patron saint of the great silver rich mining center of Potosí), the town council of that city unfurled a faded silk banner. Supposedly, this flag had been carried by the troops of the Catholic monarchs, Ferdinand of Aragon and Isabella of Castile, when Muslim Granada had fallen to them in 1492. It had subsequently been transferred to the Indies, where the companions of Francisco Pizarro carried it in the conquest of Peru, later in the battles of the civil wars that followed, and then again in the final victories of conquest. Its possession had been disputed by three cities, but the flag had been awarded finally to Potosí, and in the seventeenth century its citizens took great pride in the image of Santiago, the Moor slayer, that had seemingly miraculously survived on the threadbare standard. The banner symbolized the triumph of the faith and the continuity of the reconquest of Iberia from the Muslims to the conquest of the Indies from its native infidels. Santiago *matamoros* (Moor killer) had become Santiago *mataindios* (Indian killer), a transformation that was often represented in colonial Andean art.[1] See images 1 and 2 in the insert. History, religion, and political reality had transformed Muslims (moros) and eventually former Muslims baptized in the Church (Moriscos) into the archtypical enemy of Christian Iberia.[2]

This was a trope and a symbol of enmity that was carried to the New World, where it was reinforced continually from pulpits; in religious processions; and in street performances of *moros y cristianos*—folk enactments, dances, and parades brought from Andalucia to celebrate and commemorate past victories, and to serve as examples as well as entertainment.[3] But even in these presentations, the messaging was always a complex mixture of animosity and admiration. The Moors were often depicted as chivalric and noble adversaries, and variants of the performances emphasized not their defeat, but their conversion to and acceptance by the Church. In America, the complexities intensified in the parallel dances of the conquest, which represented the combat between Indians and Spaniards, and in both forms indigenous participants often took part and played the central roles, subverting behind their masks and costumes whatever may have been the original didactic intent or messages of these festive displays.[4] Decoding the message of the *moros y cristiano* has long challenged scholars in a number of fields, but the ambivalence inherent in them is in some ways also a reflection of the ambivalent attitudes about moros and Moriscos in early modern Latin America.[5]

From the moment of Columbus's arrival in the New World, the perception of Muslims and of Islam juxtaposed reality, prophetic expectations, and analogies that in most times and places far exceeded the actual presence of Muslims or former Muslims. Still, that perception often shaped attitudes, missionary activities, and governmental policies. Over the course of three centuries, the threat of Islam and the attitude toward Muslims did not remain unchanged but vacillated between the negative perception of an eternal enemy and respect for a civilized and powerful rival, according to the reality of the threat and the predominant cultural fashion of the time. During the early modern era, opposition to Islam and the so-called Turk played a central role in various Christian millenarian projects to reestablish a world united under the cross, but commerce, diplomacy, and personal contacts had also generated a less hostile vision at various times. By the mid-nineteenth century, Hispanic orientalism could present Islamic culture either in terms of a romanticized Alhambra or as the quintessential model of despotism and moral laxity.[6]

In some ways, such ambiguity had existed long before the fall of Granada in 1492, but thereafter the first concern of Ferdinand

and Isabella was to ensure the unity of faith in all their territories, including the newly claimed "islands and mainlands in the Ocean Sea."[7] As early as 1501, the Catholic monarchs instituted a religious exclusionary policy that prohibited Muslims, Jews, heretics, those punished by the Church, and anyone recently converted (*reconciliados*) from migrating to the New World.[8] Occasionally royal licenses were sought that permitted the arrival of Moriscos — for example, during the sixteenth century when Bishop Juan de Zumárraga, New Spain's first prelate, tried to start a silk industry using Morisco specialists but was prevented from doing so by peninsular silk producers.[9] Despite opposition in that case, until 1578 licenses could be obtained to circumvent these restrictions under certain conditions. Further legislation followed throughout the sixteenth century, especially during the reign of Carlos V, and subsequently the specific prohibition against importing slaves bought in the Mediterranean or Africa who might introduce Islam made that policy even more restrictive.[10]

But policy was one thing and reality another, and as we know, restrictions against the emigration of the prohibited groups like *judeo*conversos were often more honored in the breach than in the observance. In fact, such exclusionary practices against prohibited categories of people designed in Spain were not always welcomed in the Indies. In April 1545, the *audiencia* (appeals court) of Santo Domingo wrote to the king that it had received both the order prohibiting the reading of "printed books of profane stories like that of Amadis de Gaula" and the restrictions on slaves and free persons converted from Islam, as well as their descendants.[11] But there was a local negative reaction to both. In a city like Santo Domingo which had some 100 male and female Barbary slaves to say nothing of those in the countryside, the city council reported many people complained that such a restriction on moros or Moriscos might be justified in New Spain or Peru where there were lots of Indians who might be influenced by the Islamic heresies, but since there were hardly any Indians left in Española, the presence of moros had never caused any problem. Moreover, the North African (*Berberisco*) and moro slaves had come with royal licenses, and their children who were now free had become masons or carpenters, and other trades-men useful to everyone. The citizens of Santo Domingo felt that these laws were harmful, they asked the audiencia to express their discontent. The judges asked the crown for further royal instruc-tion.[12] This incident underlines the existence of a certain dichotomy between the detested and feared moros or Moriscos as the tradi-tional enemy of Spain and the reality of those moros who lived and worked within Christian society and alongside Christians.[13] This was a tension that troubled Hispanic societies in both Iberia and America from the fall of Granada in 1492 to long after the ex-pulsion of the Moriscos from Spain in 1609–14, and it generated heated theological and political debates between those who viewed Muslims and their descendants as an unassimilable domestic enemy whose negative character was carried in their blood (thus represent-ing a cyst in the Christian body politic) and those who believed that the Moriscos had much to offer, true conversion was possible, and expelling Moriscos to non-Christian lands would condemn true Christians to perdition.[14]

Inquisition cases in the American tribunals of Lima; Mexico City; and Cartagena, Colombia, reveal that crypto-islamism was rare, and that while some moros and Moriscos certainly did reach the Indies, until the late eighteenth and early nineteenth cen-turies — when the slave trade began to bring in large numbers of Muslim captives from West Africa — converts from Islam coming from Iberia seem to have been far fewer than the converts from Judaism and their descendants.[15] Nevertheless, in a careful review of the administrative history of the restrictions on Morisco emi-gration, the French scholar Louis Cardaillac directly questioned the effectiveness of the exclusionary policies. More recent scholarly work has also carefully documented the limitations and inconsis-tency of the prohibitions and has identified a few hundred indi-viduals who were able to evade the restrictions.[16]

They turn up at times in unexpected places and situations. Estebanico (Mustafa Azemmouri) the Moorish companion of Alvar Nuñez Cabeza de Vaca who traveled across the southwest-ern borderlands of Texas and New Mexico and eventually died at

Zuni pueblo, is a famous case in point. However, in the early conquest period there are others with fascinating tales — including a few who, like Cristóbal de Burgos and Francisco de Talavera among Pizarro's men in the conquest of Peru, later became *encomenderos* (holders of grants of Indians who were required to pay tribute to them in the form of money, goods, or labor) despite the probably true rumors about their Morisco origins. A number of Moriscos, especially women, who arrived as "white slaves" accompanied the conquest expeditions. Some of the women bore their master's children, and one — Beatriz de Salcedo — married her master on his deathbed and inherited his grant of Indian laborers in Peru.[17] In in a somewhat parallel case in Chile, Juana de Lezcano, a former Morisca slave, bore her owner's child who was legitimized and inherited his father's *encomienda* (grant of indigenous laborers) on the frontier. As guardian of her son, de Salcedo had to defend his interests against a lawsuit in 1563 by another *encomendero*, who claimed that the boy's Morisco blood invalidated his claim to the grant.[18]

Still, we can never be too sure of the dimension of the presence of moros or Moriscos in colonial society. Being a Morisco or moro (or a member of any other social category, for that matter) was always a matter of more than lineage: it depended on self-perception and identification as well as the perception and definition imposed or attempted to be imposed by others. A negative image of Muslims and Moriscos formed during the era of the reconquest and intensified by their various rebellions against forced assimilation during the first decades of the sixteenth century had become an integral aspect of popular culture in Spain, although always with some ambiguity.[19] The religion, dress, language, food, character, and blood of the Moriscos all became subjects of distain, disgust, and distrust in popular refrains and learned treatises, and these attitudes were carried to the New World.[20] Because the most common deprecatory accusations were to call someone a converso or Morisco, or a *perro judío* or *perro moro* (Jewish dog or Muslim dog), such accusations were often part of the constant personal and political squabbling that often marked the period of the conquest, as well as of life thereafter. Suggestions of Muslim or Jewish origin or behavior could be used as an insult against any group or person.[21] One could sink no lower than to be a Turk or a moro. As the Catalans said during their rebellion in the seventeenth century, it was preferable "to be a vassal of the Turk and to live with the Moors than to live with the Castilians."[22] In the Indies a similar use was made of the Moors as a measure of disrespect or criticism. For example, secular authorities in Santo Domingo complained about the resident clergy—who, they claimed, "go about very freely, exempt [from control] like a "*moro* without a king." In a bitter legal dispute between Juan Suárez de Peralta, the Mexican *criollo* author and chronicler of New Spain, and the Gómez family, the latter accused the former and his relatives of being Jews, while they retaliated by claiming that their opponents were recent converts from Islam.[23]

As noted above, the epithet "moro" or "Morisco" was a common weapon in disputes and conflicts, and it generated lawsuits, complaints to the Inquisition, and personal violence from Potosí to New Spain. We have a number of colorful colonial examples of such denunciations—including that of Pedro Ruiz Delgado, a doctor and tax collector in Puerto Rico, who in 1567 ran afoul of the grandson of Ponce de León, the former governor; and the case of the *encomendero* Diego Romero in New Granada, both of whom were accused by their political rivals of being Moriscos.[24] These cases involved questions of limpieza de sangre (purity of blood) and of *vox publica* (hearsay) and of defenses emphasizing services to the king. In both cases the accusations aimed at denigrating these men as moros—whether factually true or not—failed to be upheld, but such indictments were always a useful tool against rivals or enemies. Thus, while historians in the past certainly erred in assuming that the exclusion of those excluded (*prohibidos*) was generally effective, the new generation of historians, anxious to uncover a Muslim presence in the New World, must be wary of accepting every identification or accusation of Muslim background as valid evidence.

This was a challenge not only for modern historians, but also for Old Christian Spaniards and Portuguese at the time. Once the cultural markers, language, and dress of the Muslims had been prohibited and the expulsions had taken place, determining who was or was not a Muslim became something of an ethnographic test that sometimes involved cultural confusion and faux ethnography.[25] An interesting example is that of a black man called Pedro Moreno, who in 1640 showed up on a ship in the southeastern Spanish province of Murcia.[26] Moreno was denounced to local inquisitors because he was *retajado* (circumcised), which in Murcia immediately implied that he was either a Muslim or a renegade Christian who had converted to Islam.[27] Moreno denied the charge. He explained that he was a native of Nabangongo in Angola and had been captured by other Africans and eventually been sold as a slave to a Portuguese ship captain, who had converted him to Christianity.[28] Later, the ship on which he sailed had been captured by the Moors. But although he had lived among them, he had never swayed from his Christian faith. He insisted that his circumcision dated from his youth, saying that "the gentiles of Angola circumcised their sons when they were born."

To decide if he was a Muslim or a renegade depended on an ethnological understanding not only of African practices, but also of Christian customs far from Spain. The inquisitors called for witnesses. Someone who had sailed to Angola was called to testify, but he seemed to miss the point that Moreno had been born to pagan parents, so his testimony that Christians in Angola did no such thing and baptized their children as Catholics did everywhere — and, therefore, that Moreno must be a Jew or a *moro* — was unconvincing. Other informants were needed. Three more witnesses testified, two of them Angolan slaves who could give much more specific information. The final witness was a Spaniard who argued that although in the Kongo kingdom and Luanda (where all were Christians) everyone was baptized according to the "usages of Spain," in "the kingdom of Ndongo and other coasts of Guinea as far as the Cape of Good Hope, they are all inhuman gentiles without law, and they eat human flesh, and when they are children they are circumcised as in Barbary, and later as captives they become Christians and are baptized."[29] Thus while Moreno was *retajado*, that did not mean that he was a renegade. The ethnography was defective, but however biased or wrong it was, the argument about his missing foreskin won Moreno's release by defining him as a member of the community and not as a Muslim "other" — and for many Christians that was enough.

American Fears of Moros and Islam

Early Spanish conquerors and missionaries had seen many resemblances and parallels between the culture and practices of the indigenous peoples of the New World and Christian Iberia's ancient Muslim enemies. Perhaps for that reason, they feared that any contact between Muslims and Native Americans could have terrible consequences for the evangelical goals of the colonial project. The justification for the exclusionary policies was always the protection of the nascent faith of the newly converted indigenous populations, but there was also a geopolitical dimension to these restrictions. Foreigners, even Catholics, were always considered suspect and dangerous. Thus at various moments, other ethnic groups such as the French and the Greeks were added to the list of suspicious categories — the French as potential Protestants, and the Greeks as schismatics and subjects of the Ottoman Turks.

Sometimes such fears ran wildly ahead of realities. In 1573, rumors spread along the Pacific coast of Nueva Galicia in New Spain that a fleet of ten "Turkish or *moro*" ships had been sighted, although investigators found no evidence of them.[30] The danger of *hay moros en la costa* (a common expression in modern Spanish, meaning "watch out, situation dangerous!") joined other parallel fears of religious enemies. In the 1590s, officials worried that the Protestant Dutch might land in Chile and join forces with the native Araucanians to spread the pernicious doctrine of freedom of conscience throughout the Indies, and after 1640 there was an exaggerated fear that the rebellious Portuguese (always suspected as Judaizers) might provoke the slaves of Peru to revolt.[31]

But underlying such exaggerated fears was always the real menace of Islam and the Turks. The Muslim threat was not simply imaginary. Ottoman expansion into the western Mediterranean and North Africa, even after its disruption at the battle of Lepanto in 1571, remained an Iberian concern, and Muslim corsair actions against Spanish shipping and occasional raiding on the Spanish and Portuguese coasts were a reality. Between 1580 and 1602, Ahmad al Mansur — the sultan of Morocco, who was well aware of the wealth of the Americas and anxious to contest the power of Philip II — negotiated with Elizabethan England and Dom Antonio, the exiled pretender to the throne of Portugal, to mount a joint attack against Spanish interests. While England was more interested in moving against Spain itself, the sultan favored an expedition against the Spanish Indies and even suggested that his subjects, more accustomed to warm climes than the English were, could be used to settle the conquered territories.[32] Although no invasion took place, it is clear that the New World Iberian colonies were not beyond consideration in the Islamic world.

The threat of Islam was deep in Spanish consciousness. Authors like Miguel de Cervantes, who had been a captive in Algiers for five years (1575–80) before he was ransomed, made the plight and tribulations of Christian captives in the Mediterranean well known to Spanish society through plays and narratives, and particular missionary orders like the Mercedarians that were dedicated to the ransoming of Christian captives, constantly reminded that society of the threat of Islam.[33] Andrew Hess pointed out long ago that the shadow of Muslim power remained a preoccupation well into the seventeenth century and in fact played an important role in the arguments for the expulsion of the Moriscos as a potential "fifth column" of collaborators who might join with the Turks or Protestants against Catholic Spain.[34] Then, too, in contrast to the perceived threat of other enemies or other religions, Spaniards had a long history of military confrontation with Islam — before 1492 on the peninsula; afterward in Oran, Berbería, and the Mediterranean; and eventually in the Philippines.[35] The Portuguese also had a long history of confrontation. It was two and a half centuries shorter than Spain's on the Iberian peninsula, but it extended more robustly in their Moroccan interventions and outposts like Ceuta and Mazagão and expanded greatly after 1498 in the Indian Ocean as the Portuguese battled with new Muslim opponents.[36] As Mercedes García-Arenal has emphasized, the conquest of Granada in 1492 and the taking of Oran in 1509 stimulated Spanish millennial expectations of the spread of a universal Christendom and the defeat of Islam that would lead eventually to the retaking of Jerusalem and the integration of the world within the Church. These expectations carried over into the conquest of the New World and Iberian understandings of, and practices in, dealing with other peoples.[37]

Early conquistadors and missionaries both found precedents and parallels in the Iberian experience with Muslims for their relations with the native peoples of the Americas.[38] The well-known use of terminology from Mediterranean conflicts and contacts with Islam to describe New World phenomena was a practice that revealed the enduring impact of the long history of contact. The letters of Hernán Cortés and other early accounts of Yucatan and Mexico often made references to that Mediterranean experience and terminology. Early Franciscan missionaries in New Spain and Jesuits in Brazil both drew on Old World experience with Islam in addressing the challenges of dealing with native peoples in the Americas, and those usages and analogies persisted as the conquests expanded to new frontiers. For example, the use of terms such as *mezquitas* (mosques) for Aztec temples, *mamelucos* (Mamalukes) for mestizos in Brazil, and *genízaros* (janissaries) for detribalized Native Americans under Spanish control in the northern borderlands of New Spain all revealed perceptions, past experience, and expectations that drew from Mediterranean precedents and sought to transform the native peoples and cultures into an "other" equal to the traditional opponent. The religion of the Indians, said Suárez de Peralta, was like that of Muslims and other infidels because they all had the same teacher (*maestro*): the devil.[39]

Such comparisons and analogies were not limited to areas of high civilization in the New World. In the Caribbean, for example, the state of warfare with and the taking of prisoners by the Caribs invoked Mediterranean comparisons. As one report complained, "these Indians come so continually with their armadas to this island that they are like Turks, and they have carried off so many captives that many parts of the island are abandoned."[40] Reports from Puerto

Rico often noted the Caribs' taking of Spanish captives, who were given the same treatment as "the Muslims do to Christians."[41] The Mediterranean model was made very clear following the Morisco rebellion of Alpujarras (1568–71) in Spain, when the audiencia of Santo Domingo wrote to the king in 1572 about the need for the inhabitants of the island to enslave hostile Caribs from neighboring islands "according to the regulations and order that Your Majesty has commanded for the rebel Muslims of the kingdom of Granada."[42] In debates about the enslavement of new peoples, what constituted just war, and the best methods for conversion, theologians, missionaries, bureaucrats, and soldiers on Iberian colonial frontiers all turned to Mediterranean precedents and constantly compared their relations to Caribs, Chichimecas, Quechua speakers, and Araucanians to similar relations in situations that had involved Muslims or converts from Islam.[43] In 1608, the Council of the Indies wrote to the king that while rebellious Araucanians on the Chilean frontier could be enslaved, indigenous boys (younger than ten and a half years) and girls (younger than nine and a half) could not—and they should be removed to peaceful areas where they would serve until they were twenty years old, while being "Christianly taught and instructed as was done with the Moriscos in the kingdom of Granada, and under the same conditions."[44] The degree to which these comparisons and parallels simply sprang readily to mind or were just a useful tactic in gaining the attention and support of the king and peninsular interests by presenting easily recognizable analogies remains to be seen. However, as I will argue below, their use continued into the nineteenth century, although their valence changed over time.[45]

Thus, contacts and conflicts with the traditional enemy, Islam, became and remained a colonial Iberian preoccupation, even though other potential enemies like English and Dutch interlopers or pirates of many nationalities were far more of an actual threat. In the sixteenth and seventeenth centuries, the immediate danger was usually associated first with real moros—North Africans or black West Africans like the Jollofs or Fula, who might be introduced into the Indies as slaves—or with Moriscos whose rebellion in the

mountains of Granada (1568–71) against their enforced accultura-
tion had led to their enslavement. Their status or appearance often
set them apart, and they were feared as both traditional enemies and
potential collaborators with the Ottomans. Of lesser danger were
those Moriscos and the occasional moro who simply arrived surrep-
titiously as free people seeking to make their fortune in the Indies.
Still, their perceived cultural or religious instability added to the
danger they seemed to imply, even when their status or appearance
did not clearly set them apart. These were people like Juan Antonio
Valentín, whose original name was Ahmed Crasi. Born in Jerusalem to Muslim parents about 1678, he was captured by the Knights
of Malta in a Turkish ship and served as a galley slave for two years
before escaping. Traveling to Catalonia and Cádiz, he eventually
sailed in a French vessel into the Pacific. He deserted ship in Valparaiso, where he eventually married. When arrested in 1718 by the
Inquisition and charged with having been baptized twice, he con-
fessed that instead he had always followed the law of Mohammad.
Whether this was a confession of real belief or simply a clever way
of evading the Inquisition's jurisdiction is difficult to determine.[46]

Of course, studies of other groups such as conversos and Protestants have also revealed surprisingly unstable religious affiliations
and sentiments, but many of the Morisco testimonies underline a
theological or personal insecurity about belief and identity.[47] Take,
for example, Manuel Francisco Zapata, who was tried and convicted
by the Inquisition of Cartagena de Indias in 1716. His story is a
strange mix of anger and denial. Zapata, a married man and a mason
(albañil), was the slave of Doña María Carranza. He was said to be
a native of Mesquines, in North Africa, but in his testimony he revealed that his parents were Jollofs who had brought him to Mesquines—where he had become a Muslim. He had gone into the
world of pirating (corso) between Ceuta and el Peñon but had been
captured and sentenced to the galleys. He was eventually bought by
Don Francisco Navarro, a merchant, who took him to Madrid. He
told the inquisitors that if he was in his own land living as a pirate
as he had, he would have "killed that white man who had captured
him and sought vengeance for the many tribulations that he had

suffered." Asked if he was a Christian, he admitted that he had accepted baptism, but only to avoid being called a moro, and that he had never believed in Christian precepts. The inquisitors admonished him that he should be grateful to have been saved from error, but Zapata would none of it, saying that they could burn him if they wanted, but that he would not believe in bulls and edicts and other *porquerías* (crap). Now came the real shock: Under further questioning, Zapata told his inquisitors that he was not a Christian or a Muslim, and that for him the only true law was that of his former masters who had been burned as Judiaizers. He believed in "the true God, the God of Israel, the God of Jacob." And then, raising his eyes to the heavens, he said, "Blessed be your name."[48]

Zapata knew his way around the inquisitorial process, having been arrested before with his master in Seville. He had been accused of showing disrespect to a religious image and was sentenced to work as a water carrier in Osuna before he had been taken to Cartagena de Indias and then to the island of Trinidad and finally to Panama. Now in serious trouble, his anger having subsided, he turned to the usual strategies of defense in these cases. He claimed to be a good Christian and that he had spoken against Christianity only because he was drunk. However, a number of witnesses said that he never drank. He said that while imprisoned in Seville he had heard from a Jew the remarks he had made about the God of Jacob. Then he referred to the Jews as excrement. The expression of such invective and the fact that he had left piracy of his own will earned him some leniency, and he received a sentence of a public auto-da-fé, ten years of exile from Panama, and various religious obligations.

Renegades: Sometimes Moros, Sometimes Not

In the Iberian Americas, there was another category of potential moros who also came with their own peculiar characteristics and generated a considerable sense of distrust and insecurity, although they usually lacked physical or cultural attributes that made them easily recognizable. These people were what had been called in the Mediterranean world *moros por profesión* (Muslims by choice), to distinguish them from *moros por naturaleza* (born Muslims). Since the publication of Bartolomé Bennassar and Lucille Bennassar's *Les Chrétiens d'Allah* and similar studies of the Inquisition in Italy and Portugal, we have had access to the stories of a few thousand Christians who deserted to, or were captured and enslaved by, Muslims in the Mediterranean or the Indian Ocean and converted to Islam.[49] They came from all parts of Christian Europe (from Russia and Scandinavia to Iberia and Italy) and also included "Abyssinians of Prester John, Indians from Portuguese India, from Brazil, and from New Spain," in the words of a Portuguese friar who was a captive in Algiers (and whose account was later edited by the nephew of a bishop of Palermo, who went in the early seventeenth century to North Africa to examine the condition of the Christians in captivity).[50] We know a good deal about those who returned to Christendom because they were questioned about their apostasy, but they account for only a small and highly selected sample of the many people who crossed the porous cultural and religious boundaries between Islam and Christianity on the margins of empire. Most of those who never returned to their original culture were, as the Portuguese chroniclers recognized, lower-class, faceless men, and although there were some whose lives and exploits can be documented, most of those who remained part of their new cultures have been lost to the historical record.[51]

Situational circumstances contributed to this cultural and religious shape-shifting. Enslaved prisoners after long captivity converted — sometimes to better their condition or status and sometimes out of religious conviction — but there was also much crossing of the cultural and religious frontiers by fugitives from justice, military deserters, adventure seekers, and those who battered by a love affair gone sour or a family feud and had decided to "turn Turk (mi faccio turco)."[52] Critics often believed that the major attraction of Islam was carnal — the ability to have many wives or to live in liberty (that is, without sexual constraints). In some places, economic advantage was a driving motive. In the Indian Ocean, for example, opportunities in areas beyond Portuguese control and the seasonality of the Portuguese pepper route and Portuguese military operations left thousands of young mariners and soldiers (some estimates are over 20,000) without employment for much of the year. This prodded them to offer their skills to Asian rulers, a situation that provoked more than one chronicler to complain about the instability of the imperial margins. Those who served Hindu or Buddhist princes were simply considered *chatins* (mercenaries), but those who served Muslims were usually considered traitors and *renegados*, even though the chroniclers sometimes celebrated their exploits while lamenting their apostasy.[53]

In the Mediterranean, the Americas, or the Indian Ocean, for those who crossed cultural or religious boundaries but later returned to Catholic Christendom there was usually only one path back: reconciliation through the Inquisition. Everyone knew the sort of story that had to be told to return: "I converted because of mistreatment," "it made my escape easier," or "I fell in love" (a kind of madness), "but in my heart of hearts, I never left the Church of my parents." These were the standard tales, and in many ways they paralleled the stories and trajectories of those Iberian conversos who sought to return to Spain or Portugal.[54] We have the transcripts of hundreds of these renegade cases. Despite the formulaic and repetitive nature of the testimony, some aspects of the renegades' lives and stories are worthy of further analysis and comment because of what they reveal about attitudes toward Islam and those who followed it.

The renegade profiles collected by inquisitors reveal characteristics of those who crossed of religious and cultural frontiers between the Luso-Hispanic world and Islam. Although they returned to the so-called true faith, many renegades—despite their reconciliation with the Church and their previous mistreatment as captives—later expressed various degrees of respect for or toleration of Islam, or at least contested the usual denunciations of Muslims. Former renegados were denounced for saying things like "the Moors are very charitable," "they too have holy men," "they pray five times a day," and even (as I have written elsewhere) "they too can be saved in their own law." This was a religious relativism that easily led to suspicions about their Christian orthodoxy and to denunciations to the Inquisition.

In the Luso-Hispanic Mediterranean world, former renegados always bore a certain stigma of suspicion. The time of honorable Christian military service for Muslim princes like El Cid had long passed, and in the final decades of the war against Granada, Castilian law usually treated *tornadizos* or *elches* (former Christians siding with the Moors) with exemplary cruelty (they were sometimes used for target practice by the *ballesteros* (crossbowmen).[55] The Spanish rulers tended to include renegados along with conversos and Moriscos as a category of people who were prohibited from emigrating to or serving in the Indies because of their potential threat to orthodoxy. But like members of other prohibited groups, they came just the same.

We run across them in the American Inquisition records. They included men like the Neopolitan carpenter Mestre Andrea, who was arrested in Panama about 1579 for saying that the Moors also believed in God and could be saved according to their law. He had spent many years in captivity and knew about Muslim religiosity, but when challenged, he retracted his statements and said that he did not believe that the law of the Turks, Moors, or Indians was valid and that they could be saved only if they believed in Jesus Christ.[56] In the same year, the Lima Inquisition arrested another former renegade, a man who had taken holy orders. The Toledan Sebastian Herrera, a parish priest, had gone to North Africa as a young man and had served as a mercenary for Muslim rulers, fighting for pay against both Christians and Muslims. There he fell in love with a *mora* who had convinced him to renounce his faith. Later he had fallen in love with a Jew (*una judía ynfiel*)" whom he greatly loved," and her father—known as "the Jew of Ganso," who was like a rabbi—had read to them. How he had left that life and taken orders is not explained in the surviving documents, but he had become a priest (*doctrinero*) in Peru, where he worked with the indigenous population. There he was accused of celebrating the mass and blessing the deceased ancestors of the "indios yngas"—in other words, of honoring the cult of the ancestors that was so important in Andean culture. Father Herrera claimed that these charges were false and stemmed from an argument he had had with the dean of the City of La Plata, but he did not deny having told people about his adventures and love affairs in Berbería. The question remains whether his early experiences had made him more accepting of other ways or whether the charges against him were false but believable because he was a former renegade.[57] A similar but even more adventurous saga of religious confusion or pretense is that of Fernando Ramírez de Arellano, the son of a professional soldier. He was born in Oran and kidnapped at the age of five (so he claimed) and taken to Algiers, later traveling to Constantinople and eventually becoming involved in corsair raiding. He turned himself over to the authorities in Sardinia, where his conversion was forgiven because of his youth and the prestige of his family. But by 1679 he was telling a different story to the inquisitors in Seville, admitting that he had lived with his family until age fifteen, had gone to Algiers on his own, and had lived for nine years as a Turk before his return. He had taken orders as a Franciscan in 1677, but he admitted that he had also had contact with conversos and had been attracted to their kabbalah and other teachings. He eventually sailed to the Indies under the pretext of raising funds to ransom his brother, then a captive in Algiers, but he was arrested by the Inquisition in Cartagena and finally returned for imprisonment in Seville.[58] All of these cases seem to justify the distrust of the religious commitment of the returning Mediterranean renegades, especially in the context of the Indies—where so many souls still new to the faith might be endangered by their influence.

The instability of Christian identity among the renegades added to the discomfort they generated. That cultural suspicion or distrust increased when they were also foreigners. In this regard, the Greeks and other eastern Christians were a major concern.[59] Of course, not all of those who came to the Americas were renegades, nor were all of the Greeks Eastern Orthodox Christians. Various Venetian outposts like Crete had confronted the Ottomans in the eastern Mediterranean in the sixteenth century, so the region had a varied religious background, and there were some Greeks and Christians among the Ottomans who recognized papal authority. Many Greeks served in the ranks of the Spanish armies that conquered the New World. Perhaps the most famous was Pizarro's companion and chief of artillery, Pedro de Candia, who eventually headed a contingent of Greeks—some of them trained in the Venetian Scuola de Bombardieri, where by 1500 many Greeks (especially Cretans) were being trained.[60] The Greeks had circulated widely in the western Mediterranean in late medieval times, but especially after the Ottoman expansion in the late fifteenth and early sixteenth centuries, their presence in Iberia had become common. Among foreigners, the Greeks came behind only the Italians and Portuguese in terms of their numbers in the conquest of the Indies. Over fifty Greeks came to Peru between 1532 and 1560, and they played an important role in the conquest and subsequent civil wars. Their skills as mariners and soldiers were valued, but they always remained suspect as slaves of the Turks and schismatics, and they were often thought to be too cosmopolitan and untrustworthy in terms of dogma, so they were regularly under scrutiny by the Inquisition.[61] Many cases could be cited, but a few examples will suffice. Constantino, from Negroponte, had been a janissary and had arrived in southern Spain after service in Spanish campaigns in Italy. In 1577, like a number of other Greeks, he had gotten into trouble for believing and saying that sex between unmarried people was no sin. Jorge Griego, a former captive of the Turks who spoke Turkish, had been tattooed and was accused by his neighbors on Mallorca in 1583 of bathing in the Moorish manner. Juan Nicolas from Corfu doubted the existence of purgatory and thought that the pope lived too well. He was a man who had seen the world, having visited Constantinople, Cairo, and Jerusalem, and he had eventually arrived in Cartagena de Indias—where in 1683 his words got him arrested. Juan de Rodas was a mariner from Rhodes. As a captive, he had served a highly placed Turk in Constantinople for a dozen years. Rodas eventually converted to Islam but was able to escape before he had been circumcised. He ended up in Huanuco, Peru, where the Inquisition took an interest in his beliefs.[62] The Greeks in general, and particularly Greek and other foreign renegades, underlined both the utility but also the danger that presented by people with a history of contact with Islam.

_____

Moros by Analogy

In many ways the Spanish and Portuguese experience with Islam in Iberia and then in North Africa and Mediterranean created a background of understandings and expectations against which their experience in the Americas on new cultural frontiers could be measured or shaped.[63] Renegades and others who came from those previous contact zones carried with them not only a certain suspicion about their religious inconstancy, but also a familiarity with and opinions about Islam that were not entirely negative. Moreover, with their frontier experience, former captives and renegades from the Mediterranean world also offered a model for understanding and categorizing the parallel experiences on the frontiers of the colonial establishments in the Indies. Europeans who by intention (desertion), accident (captivity), or command (placement by colonial authorities) became cultural brokers or intermediaries among native American societies also seemed to present a danger to the stability of orthodoxy and the social order, as well as to the maintenance of the cultural and technological advantages of colonial society—although gender had a marked influence on the degree to which former cultural boundary crossers were accepted back in their original societies.[64]

Of course, the foundational and classic example of the American renegade was Gonzalo Guerrero, the semifictional Spanish castaway among the Maya, who preceded Cortés's arrival in Yucatan. Guerrero (in the earliest accounts, he was called Morales) refused to join his countrymen when Cortés arrived in 1519, although Jerónimo de Aguilar, his former companion and another castaway, became Cortés's translator. The failure to bring Guerrero back supposedly led Cortés to worry that he could later cause trouble, and in the subsequent difficult struggle to conquer Yucatan that lasted into the 1540s, Guerrero was said to have been an important figure in the Maya resistance. As Rolena Adorno has shown, the story of

Guerrero was constructed and embellished by a number of authors over a long period who seem to have conflated the lives of a number of Spaniards who had joined in the Maya resistance.[65] In a sense, Guerrero and Aguilar became the embodiments of the renegade and the captive, two roles that Mediterranean Christendom knew very well. Thus Aguilar, a captive, was described as a man of solid Christian faith who had kept a tattered book of hours throughout his captivity and had eventually returned to help his own people.[66] However, the depictions of Guerrero, varied. Some painted him as a man so moved by passion for a woman, love for his children, and shame about his tattoos and perhaps piercings and Maya appearance that he could not return.[67] In other words, favorable accounts explained his decision with the usual excuses offered by returning apostates seeking reconciliation, and later commentators who tried to explain his choice emphasized those affective motives and argued that he had never abandoned his faith or fought against his former compatriots. However, others saw him as an unredeemed renegade. The chronicler Gonzalo Fernández de Oviedo even suggested that he must have been of low social class and probably of Morisco or converso origin, and thus predisposed by blood to traitorous anti-Christian behavior.[68]

The story of Guerrero as the classic Hispanic American renegade closely parallels the Mediterranean precedents. Oviedo's essentialist social or religious explanation of Guerrero's choice to abandon Christ and his king was based on the author's belief that an inclination to alterity, inconstancy, or traitorous behavior based on ethnic origin, social status, or religious belief could be inherited. This idea had played a role in the development of the concept of limpieza de sangre, which excluded the descendants of Muslims, Jews, and eventually mulattoes and blacks—as well as people of peasant or mechanic or artisan origins—from honors and offices.[69] Despite theological and practical objections to these limitations and exclusions, these disabilities were widely accepted in Spanish and Portuguese society. It was a protoracial interpretation of behavior based on lineage and inherited characteristics passed on through blood or mothers' milk, and it was a principal argument among those who had advocated the Morisco expulsions. In the Americas, similar arguments based on the defects of birth would eventually be made about the mestizos, mulattoes, and Africans and Afro-Americans who were often found among the Spanish and criollo renegades in frontier regions like northern New Spain, southern Chile, and the Argentine pampa. In many ways, as a category, mestizos (in Spanish America) and mamelucos (in Brazil), as well as Africans and their descendants, often filled the social niches of alterity that conversos or Moriscos had held in Spain and Portugal, a position justified by the defects of birth.

Going native created real dangers. The idea that Guerrero later became a leader in the stubborn Maya resistance also fit with the usual Iberian belief that renegades had knowledge and military skills useful to Christendom's enemies. In this belief, the analogy with the world of Islam, with its janissaries and renegade corsairs, was strong. That is why Cortés had been preoccupied with Guerrero's refusal to return. And on the frontiers of the Indies, in places like Nueva Vizcaya, New Mexico, or Chile where native peoples acquired access to horses, firearms, and a knowledge of European tactics, this became a constant concern. When in 1615 a Peruvian viceroy asked the Inquisition to exonerate Christians who had fled to the Chiriguanos and had served as leaders of their raids to encourage them to return to colonial society, he was recognizing the danger that they represented and the necessity of neutralizing their potential threat.[70] That hazard was made particularly clear in the 1660s in the picaresque case of Pedro Bohórquez, the Spanish soldier who some said was a Morisco and who tried to claim the crown of the Incas for himself in a restorationist movement among the Calchaquíes in Tucumán—and who ended on the gallows.[71] In this fear of the transfer of military knowledge and technology to the Indians, persons of mixed race were particularly distrusted, since in many places they had the reputation as being not only disorderly and criminal but also the best fighters. One 1590 project for Brazil suggested sending five hundred mamelucos as solders to Angola as a way to both free Brazil from their bad habits and take advantage of their skills in warfare since "they were raised in it"—and almost identical statements were common in many regions of Spanish America.[72]

Similar tales of so-called white Indians could be found on all the frontiers of European settlement in the Americas, where captivity, commerce, flight, and opportunity created the conditions of cultural interaction and crossing.[73] The justifications or defenses people who sought to return to so-called civilized life and be reconciled with the Church, as well as those who were arrested for their cultural or religious inconstancy, were much like those of the Old World renegades: They had departed from Christian society and faith because of captivity or force, or out of necessity, love, or moral failings, but they usually gave as an excuse that in their hearts they had never been apostates. For example, the testimony of the Portuguese settlers and mamelucos — some of whom had spent long periods living with tribes in the backlands (*sertão*) — who had joined a Brazilian millenarian indigenous movement called Santidade of the 1580s has a familiar ring to it.[74] Their testimony before the Inquisition often seems theologically confused or uninformed, although that stance may have been a defensive strategy. They were men and a few women attracted by the seeming lack of sexual or religious constraints (men were able to have as many wives as they wanted), or by the ability to eat meat on Fridays. A few were attracted by millenarian hopes. But for the most part they were marginal people — mamelucos or poor whites who saw opportunities for advancement in indigenous societies, sometimes because of their technological knowledge (regarding firearms) or their linguistic skills. They had conformed with the requirements of their adopted societies and had indelibly marked their bodies — not by circumcision like the converts to Islam, but with tattooing like Guerrero. Notably, among the Tupi, such marking signaled having killed an enemy in combat, and perhaps feasting on him as well. As noted above, some renegades admitted that they had been attracted by the liberties of the backlands. In fact, the idea of freedom from constraints and the order of their original societies often emerges in unguarded moments both among the American cultural crossovers and their Mediterranean and Indian Ocean counterparts. That desire was often a principal accusation of their prosecutors, who saw in leisure and libertinism the principal motives of anyone who would risk eternal damnation by abandoning salvation and civilization for barbarism. Nevertheless, after their return, the American renegades were sometimes able to use their experience to advantage. In contrast, in the Mediterranean—except for some opportunities in the North African outposts like Oran, Mazagão, or Ceuta—where the renegados seemed to offer little utility to their original societies. Often socially marginal and disadvantaged before their conversion, they remained so after their return. However, the former captives and frontiersmen (they were mostly men) on the American frontiers had skills, linguistic abilities, and sometimes fictive and blood kinship ties that made them particularly useful to colonial governments. *Comancheros* (those who traded with the Comanches) on the northern border of New Spain or former captives settled on the banks of the Bío-Bío River in Chile could be of inestimable utility as negotiators, guides, informants, and translators. In the latter case, the recent work of Ignacio Chuecas Saldías on the Chilean region called the Isla de Lajas shows how former Hispanic captives among the Mapuche became a frontier elite, rewarded with lands and labor grants for their hardships (*servicios*) and able to use their relations and kinship ties to important chiefs (*ulmen*) to bargain, trade, and negotiate with indigenous peoples across the frontier.[75] The transformation and social elevation of cultural boundary crossers makes clear that renegade status and reacceptance depended not only on theological concerns or degrees of liminality, but also on the objective military, cultural, and diplomatic contexts in which they were inserted. Cultural boundary crossing always implied moral or religious dangers and decisions about who would be considered "other," but such decisions were also made using practical criteria.

By the mid-eighteenth century, references to Muslims and their threat had diminished, due to changing historical circumstances in the Mediterranean; the intensification of Spanish cultural orientalism in the court of Charles III of Spain; the effects of the expulsions of Jews, Muslims, and Moriscos from Spain and Portugal; and the reduction of a direct threat from moros as invaders or immigrants in those countries or their American colonies.[76] Moreover, unlike the conversos—who, as powerful urban financiers and merchants, had generated sentiments of great envy and dislike—the Moriscos (many of whom had been rural workers or artisans) did not seem to engender the same level of concern, especially after their expulsion. In the Spanish Indies allusions to them and the use of analogies about Islam and Muslims became far less common in the most densely populated regions or in the centers of viceregal authority. However, in fringe areas, especially on militarized frontiers, the Mediterranean analogies and metaphors proved more tenacious. The parallel situations of the two regions had, in fact, become intertwined when the Mercedarian religious order dedicated to the ransoming of Christian captives from Muslims began to depend heavily on funds raised in America. The Spanish crown had long prohibited the use of such funds to free captives in the Americas, but in 1786 it ended that restriction, recognizing that on the frontiers of empire the numbers and conditions of captives were analogous to the Mediterranean experience.[77]

On some frontiers, this situation had developed in a long historical process. This was especially the case on the Chilean frontier along the Bío-Bío River—where, after 1598, both the Spanish and the Araucanians (later called the Mapuche) continually raided and took captives, creating a situation akin to that of the military frontiers of the Mediterranean. By the eighteenth century, the raids (malones) of Mapuche groups had spread across the Andes into areas of the Argentine pampa. On these militarized frontiers, there was a considerable amount of cultural contact. To be sure, this was often hostile, but at times it included trade, missionary efforts, diplomacy, and alliances. This was a frontier world of violence, self-sufficiency, shifting identities, fugitives, captives, ransom, and renegades who responded to their social and cultural environment. In the lapidary phrase of the Argentine historians Carlos Mayo and Amalia Latrubesse, citing the case of a former captive woman who after being rescued returned to her children and Indian husband, her decision was attributed to "the call of the frontier, the living frontier of yearning to be other and [to seek] a new destiny."[78] Here the analogies with the Mediterranean experience had a new utility. References to Indian raiders as corsairs and to Hispanized persons who lived in their indigenous villages as renegades, even if there had been no actual conversion, recalled the vocabulary of the confrontation with Islam. Colonial officials referred to the broad and underpopulated region between Buenos Aires and Mendoza that the Araucanian-related bands called Mamil Mapu as a "hidden Algiers" (*Argel disimulado*), an area where colonial control was weak and indigenous raids were common—a zone of renegades, *malones*, and violence.[79] It was the same metaphor that the Chilean soldier-chronicler Jerónimo de Quiroga had used a century before to explain why the great Araucanian leader, Lautaro, a stable boy raised by the Spanish invaders, "had returned to barbarism and left the company of Christians, like the renegade corsairs of Algiers."[80] However, Quiroga directed his ire at the renegades whom he called "the most iniquitous barbarians in these provinces. Today there are many whiter than us, and almost all of them are captains of the arms against us; they are genízaros and mestizos, which is enough to make one think about it."[81] By the late eighteenth century on the Argentine pampa, the analogy of the threat of Islam still persisted. From Carmen de Patagones, the southernmost town of Buenos Aires Province, the viceroy of the Río de la Plata received this denunciation of the renegades among the indigenous tribes:

They are apostates from our Holy Faith, opponents of the state and traitors to their homeland. They have accustomed themselves to the libertinage of the Indians, denigrating the religion that they professed, and I do not know if they or those [in Barbary] who became Muslims committed the worse crime. . . . The Indians would not be as bad or as opposed to us if they did not have these fugitive people at their side to induce them to hate and distrust us.[82]

From Analogy to Reality

The cultural and religious frontier of the Mediterranean persisted in the Americas as an analogy that placed the liminal situation of mestizos and other groups of mixed origins, as well as the desertion of marginalized Europeans and American-born Creoles, in an understandable if negative context. The fear of military action by hostile Muslims in the Indies — always somewhat fantastical — had subsided to a distant concern in the seventeenth century, and for most people in Spanish and Portuguese America, the only moros who touched their daily lives were those in the legends of the sensual *moura encantada* (enchanted Mooress), expressions such as "to work like a Moor (*mourejar*)," the masked dancers in *moros y cristianos*, the Corpus Christi processions, and the staged jousts of the *juegos de canas* (in which Spanish gentlemen dressed as moros to show off their military and equestrian skills for the applause of the crowds).[83] See image 3 in the insert.

In an ironic twist of history, the imagined Muslim threat finally became a reality in the early nineteenth century as a result of the internal politics of West Africa and the emergence of a movement to limit or end the Atlantic slave trade. Throughout much of the eighteenth century, Islamicized Africans had been carried in the slave trade to the European colonies in North America, the West Indies, Spanish America, and Brazil, but after 1804 their numbers had greatly swelled as a result of state formation, political alliances, jihads, and religious repression among groups such as the Fulani, Bornu, Hausa, and Yoruba in the areas of Nigeria and Dahomey.[84] The fall of the Oyo empire, the formation of the Sokoto caliphate in 1809, and the expansion of the kingdom of Dahomey threw thousands of people into this turmoil, and those on the losing sides were often sold into the slave trade.[85] By the 1820s, because of both the restrictions on the slave trade imposed by the British abolitionist movement and growing antislavery sentiment in the newly independent nations of the United States, Haiti, and Latin America, the vast majority of these captives arrived at the Cuban port of

Havana or the Brazilian port of Salvador, in Bahia.[86] The Haitian Revolution (1792–1804) had destroyed the sugar industry in that former French colony, and the sugar plantation economies of Cuba and Brazil, expanding to meet an increased demand, were booming and anxious to receive African slaves—while neither the slave traders nor the planters were preoccupied with the religion of the new workers. Between 1800 and 1850 over 400,000 men, women, and children from various ethnicities—including Muslim Hausas, Fon, and Yoruba speakers (called Lucumís in Cuba and Nagô in Brazil)—were transported from ports in the Bight of Benin to the cane fields, tobacco farms, and cities of the New World.[87]

Thousands of West Africans, many of them Muslims and many of them formerly employed as soldiers in the dynastic and regional conflicts of their homelands, arrived in the Americas. Between 1807 and 1845, the Spanish colony of Cuba and the Portuguese colony of Brazil (which was an independent country after 1822) experienced over fifty risings or plots, many of which involved the leadership or participation of Muslims.[88] While there is still controversy over the extent to which these movements were religiously motivated or drew primarily on ethnic solidarities or other factors, there is little doubt that Muslims—most of whom were born in Africa and some of whom had previous military experience—were a major element in these movements.[89]

By the mid-nineteenth century, analogy had become reality. The ancient quintessential enemy of Christian Iberia had finally arrived: not Ottoman Turks or Barbary corsairs, but the many Muslims among the West Africans who came as slaves and then did not seek to raise minarets, contest Christianity, or (for the most part) respond to the revolutionary political slogans of the age, but who used their ethnic and religious associations to end their captivity and in some ways to maintain their cultures and beliefs.

{ 2 }

Conversos

The Mestizos of Faith

If the Muslim presence in or threat to the Iberian Americas was mostly a matter of fantasy and analogy, the presence of conversos — the other quintessential "other" — was far more of a reality, and one that openly and persistently challenged the guiding principles of social order and hierarchy in Spain and Portugal. We should remember that by the fifteenth century, Jews in Iberia had been burdened by a series of restrictions and humiliations that limited their social and sexual contacts with Christians, imposed the use of distinguishing clothing or other markers, prohibited them from following certain occupations, demanded a tax, and sought to isolate that community and in various ways to restrict its members' social and physical mobility.[1]

The basis of this discrimination was supposedly religious, although by the sixteenth century, a protoracial discourse about lineage, so-called bad blood, and transmitted inherent faults of character or morality had already begun to take hold. Although similar quasi-racial justifications had long been used in Iberia and elsewhere in Europe by the theorists of nobility to justify social disparities and hierarchy, these concepts proved readily adaptable to religious differences — despite some theological resistance. When these concepts of social distinction and hierarchy were eventually carried to the Indies — where concerns with nobility were pervasive, and officials often complained that on stepping onto land, every person of European origins pretended to be a hidalgo and a descendant of the Goths — they were all too easily applied to ethnic or phenotypical differences.

From Jews to Conversos in Iberia and Its Empires

The expulsion of the Jews in 1492 from Castile and Aragon and their forced conversion or exile from Portugal in 1497 radically transformed the rationales and practices of exclusion or assimilation. Some evidence suggests that many of the converts to Christianity following the massacres and forced conversions of 1391 in Spain had been assimilated, but the expulsion and forced conversion of the end of the fifteenth century changed the religious landscape. By 1500 a publicly professing religious community of Jews no longer existed in Spain or Portugal. In its place were thousands of individuals and lineages that were ostensibly Christian in religion but that remained ethnically and culturally linked to the Hebrew nation — both in their own sense of identity and in the perception of their Christian neighbors. In the Middle Ages occasional legislation had prohibited ridiculing or offending converts, but by the sixteenth century that was no longer the case.[2] Although some theologians raised their voices to emphasize the equality of all baptized people within the Church and objected to discrimination against the newly converted, after 1550 an ever increasing number of ecclesiastical and secular institutions adopted rules insisting on limpieza de sangre.[3] In regard to conversos, this discourse and line of argument had developed to prevent the full assimilation of people who were ostensibly baptized Christians and to eliminate the Jewish culture and practices related to it.[4] When a Christian society that had dedicated centuries to the conversion and assimilation of its religious minorities finally met with success, it imposed barriers to prevent that very conversion and assimilation.

To some extent, these restrictions based on blood and descent were designed to replace the hats, or badges, or other types of clothing that had formerly made legible the religious minorities legible and separated them from the general population.[5] As the policy of Christian proselytization and conversion (even by force) succeeded, it undercut the former policies of marking and separating the minority religions. Medieval representations of Muslims and Jews in Christian Iberia had used caricatures of physical features and distinctive dress as visual markers of difference.[6] Once those markers were removed, the fear of religious contamination intensified. As the French scholar Jean Pierre Dedieu has put it:" The converso in all external aspects had been assimilated with the Old Christian. You could not see the lack of purity of blood in his face."[7] Certainly by the second generation, the conversos looked like the rest of the population, and in the few visual representations we have of them — even when they are depicted committing acts of sacrilege, they are notable for their unremarkable appearance and dress. See image 4 in the insert. Even in a canvas like that by Francisco Camilo of the famous desecration of the crucifix of the Paciencia, there is nothing that distinguishes the conversos from the general population. They were made to appear less "other" than moros or Moriscos, who continued to be seen in the popular imagination and shown in painting, engravings, on the stage, and in street performances with distinctive clothing, weapons, or turbans.[8] The normality of conversos' appearance may have made them seem to be an even more dangerous potential enemy as an internal "other," but it also emphasized that there was little in terms of costume, custom, or language to separate them from the rest of the population. Thus, attaching to them an indelible *mancha* (stain) of lineage and blood became a seemingly necessary step to make the conversos "legible" and maintain the social order.[9] What is notable, however, is that to take this step, their supposed moral, behavioral, and spiritual deficiencies had to be made genetic. The basis of discrimination was not, as Yosef Yerushalmi has reminded us, the purity of their religion (*limpieza de fe*) but that of their blood (limpieza de sangre), and thus the elements of a discourse of essentialism and inherited traits of character were created.[10] The wife of the English ambassador Richard Fanshaw reported being told in a Portuguese nunnery in the 1660s of a fourteen-year-old girl who was taken from her imprisoned converso mother at birth, raised in a convent, and was finally burned as a *judaizante* (a baptized Christian who had reverted to Judaism) because — despite knowing nothing of Judaism — she "did daily scratch and whip the crucifixes" and refused to "adore that God." [11] Her inclinations and heresy had been inherited. Perfidy and a hatred of Christ were in her blood.

This belief in the power of blood and inherited characteristics negated or at least diminished the possibility of ever-changing status, order, or estate. Conversion might make a Jew or Muslim into a Christian, and a king might elevate a commoner into knighthood or the nobility, but despite the prerogatives of rulers or the desire to create a universal church, such alterations — which were common enough — threatened to upset the existing order of rank, privilege, and interests. Thus, they generated a vigorous opposition. A Muslim or Jew by nature or birth who was now a Christian was for many people an unnatural creature, or hybrid because of having moved between what were assumed to be fixed categories. [12] Limpieza statutes were created to exclude them. Old Christians, in defense of their collective dignity, saw themselves as the inheritors of Christ's sacrifice and thus entitled to salvation and privileges, and they could not imagine that the descendants of nonbelievers or heretics (no matter how sincere their professions of a new faith were) would similarly be saved or should be also entitled to similar honors, offices, or privileges. In fact, many Old Christians saw in the conversos a threat to society as a whole. The Old Christians believed that the conversos' "bad blood" was a danger to the family, the individual's body, and the body politic, which explained the need to label and exclude them and their descendants despite contrary theological arguments or the fiscal and financial interests of local and royal authorities. [13] These exclusionary practices based on religious or ethnic origins served as precursors for the discrimination and phenotypical ordering by color that would emerge from the process of miscegenation in the Americas. [14] They may also have had the unintended result of ensuring the persistence of a converso identity, and thus instead of suppressing the vestigial remnants of a fading tradition, they may have "amplified it and perpetuated social disunion." [15]

We need not recount in detail the saga of the conversos following the expulsion of the Jews from Castile and Aragon in 1492 and the flight of perhaps as many as some 70,000 of those who refused to convert across the border to Portugal.[16] In that country harsh measures that were imposed on them, followed in 1497 by forced conversion — accompanied, however, by a policy of no inquiry into their Catholic orthodoxy for an extended period.[17] During the following century their ability to travel and trade was facilitated the subsequent dispersion of conversos and the Portuguese New Christians across the Mediterranean into Italy and the Ottoman empire as well as to southern France, Hamburg, Antwerp, Amsterdam, and other northern European cities — as well as by their subsequent return to Spain after the Hapsburg incorporation of Portugal from 1580 to 1640. By that time, they had already become involved in the colonial trades of the Spanish and Portuguese empires, so that their networks included Goa, Malacca, Lima, Vera Cruz, and Bahia.[18]

Policies toward them in Iberia, however, were always ambivalent. The Castilian and Portuguese rulers banned Jews and conversos — like Muslims and Moriscos — from traveling to or residing in the newly discovered lands across the Atlantic. Nonetheless, there was always a contradiction in the process created by the conflicting goals of religious purity and those of matters of reasons of state, such as effective colonization or the financial needs of the rulers. The result was both periods of hiatus in the restrictions, or intervals of a studied negligence in their enforcement, and a continuing disregard or avoidance of the limitations by the excluded groups themselves.

The Portuguese crown had first used places like Cape Verde and São Tomé as places of penal exile and had even infamously taken Jewish children from their anguished parents on the eve of Passover in 1497 to colonize São Tomé. But in the Indian Ocean, in the first decades after Vasco da Gama's voyage, large numbers of New Christians had journeyed to the East on their own accord as soldiers and merchants, and the crown — always anxious for colonists — accepted them. By 1520, there were already complaints about a New Christian presence, calls for more colonists with so-called clean genealogies, and restrictions on New Christian service in municipal governments. Portugal created an Inquisition tribunal in Goa in 1560 to correct and punish departures from Christian orthodoxy, but it made recent New Christians of the nation its principal target.[19] By

1600 it had condemned to the flames eighty-four of them and publicly punished another forty. Still the trade opportunities and distances from authority continued to attract the New Christians, and despite prohibitions against their presence, they continued to arrive. For about the first three decades of the seventeenth century, to compensate for its own problems in maintaining a profitable trade with Asia, the Portuguese crown actually turned to the extensive New Christian trade network across Asia, and as it did, the attention of the Goa Inquisition turned away from the prosecution of conversos to the repression of *gentilismo*, the residual traces of Brahmanic or other faiths among its new converts in Asia.[20]

In the Portuguese Atlantic, Brazil was something of an anomaly in this story of converso exclusions. Almost immediately after the first moment of Portuguese contact in 1500, the king had granted a contract for the private development of the dyewood trade to Fernão de Noronha, a New Christian merchant in Lisbon, and during the first three or four decades after 1500 — the period just before the Portuguese Inquisition began to function — the king exercised little control over who went to the colony, as long as the people proved useful. New Christians seized this opportunity and immigrated in considerable numbers. Attempts to restrict New Christian emigration by law in 1532 and 1567 were ineffective. Moreover, in an attempt to find sufficient settlers for the new colony, Brazil also became a dumping ground for orphan girls and civil and ecclesiastical penal exiles of various sorts — including, in a seeming contradiction, New Christians who, after the establishment of the Inquisition in Portugal in 1536, were condemned now for Judaizing.[21]

For the New Christians, the subsequent creation of the Inquisition of Goa in 1560 and the growth of a Brazilian sugar plantation economy in the following decade made that colony an even more attractive destination, especially since in its multiethnic society their religious deficiencies were more than compensated for by their white European origins. By the end of the sixteenth century, perhaps 10–14 percent of the Portuguese population of the principal sugar regions of Pernambuco and Bahia were New Christians — with many of them involved in the sugar trade, and some owning sugar mills.[22] In 1631, an ecclesiastical investigator complained from Bahia that the "people of the Nation confess that since the creation of the world there has been no better place to live and do business" than Brazil.[23] He believed that the majority of them were practicing Jews. We do not know if that was true, but curiously, Brazil became a land of hope and expectation both for the Jesuit missionaries who yearned to bring native peoples into the Church and for New Christians, some of whom at least longed to live outside the Church.[24] Manuel Themudo, canon of the cathedral of Bahia, reported that the local New Christians mocked those who remained in Portugal under the eye of Inquisition, saying that "those who stay [t]here and do not live in Brazil where they would be at their liberty are stupid."[25] By the 1620s, even the governors of Portugal believed that the New Christians in Brazil were so many and so influential that the security of the whole colony was in doubt.[26] Despite such concerns and considerable pressure from the crown, institutional rivalries, costs, and perhaps New Christian influence in the colony combined to prevent the creation of a permanent Inquisition tribunal in Brazil.[27]

In Spanish America, although the percentage of conversos among the immigrants was probably lower, the attractions were much the same. In the roughly contemporary early Spanish Caribbean settlements, conversos began to arrive with Columbus's second voyage in 1493, but as was the case with Muslims, the practice and habit of denigrating rivals or enemies with the term *judío* or converso was so common that it is difficult to separate immigrants from insults. You can see that plainly in the 1498 rebellion in Hispaniola against Columbus. He claimed that the rebels were "conversos, enemies of Your Majesties' prosperity, and that of Christians."[28] However, Francisco Roldán, leader of the rebels, denounced Columbus for exactly the same fault of converso origins. In fact, for the first decade there were no legal barriers on immigration, but as I have noted above, beginning in the early sixteenth century, the crown issued prohibitions against the immigration to the Indies "of a variety of people of untrusted religious orthodoxy," and these early restrictions usually included the children and grandchildren of these categories as well — prohibitions that emphasized bad blood, or the genealogical danger of religious impurity. Despite these restrictions there continued to be a steady stream of complaints about a converso presence and continual circumventions of restrictions, which were sometimes allowed for a payment and sometimes performed illegally. Conversos turn up in all the conquests, from Nueva Galicia in New Spain (Mexico) to Chile, and sometimes in prominent roles as *encomenderos*.[29] This process took place throughout the Spanish Indies. New Spain had perhaps 10,000 conversos by the end of the sixteenth century, and in 1570 the inquisitor general in Lima could speak of the many *confesos* (another term for converts) and their children and grandchildren in the colony and remark that given the size of the Spanish population in the colony, there was a high probability that the percentage of conversos was greater in Peru than in Castile.[30] It was precisely that concern about their presence and the possible contagion they supposedly represented to newer New Christians — the masses of newly converted Indians — that led to the creation of tribunals of the Inquisition in Mexico City (1569) and Lima (1570), where previously the bishops had exercised inquisitorial powers.

If the numbers of conversos in the Indies had troubled Spanish authorities during the period of the conquest, the situation became far more threatening after 1580, with Philip II's incorporation of Portugal into the composite monarchy of the Spanish Hapsburgs. By that time, the Portuguese, both Old and New Christians, had been penetrating Spain's Atlantic possessions for almost a century. Now as subjects of the same ruler, they were less constrained by restrictions on foreigners and began to arrive in even greater numbers, some with permission, but most without it.[31] The Portuguese were attracted by access to the silver, slave, and other trades and by the multiple contraband opportunities of the Indies, and their numbers swelled. By the 1630s they made up 13 percent of the *vecinos* (citizens) of Cartagena de Indias and about 25 percent of those in Buenos Aires.[32] In Mexico City by 1641 there were over 400 Portuguese male heads of household, which suggests that the Portuguese made up perhaps 20 percent of the 8,000 European residents.[33] As

Luis de Lima told inquisitors in the 1630s, "Peru for the Portuguese was the promised land, there one could find, wealth, honor, and esteem."[34]

The Portuguese—especially those in commerce or maritime occupations—tended to concentrate in urban areas, specifically in neighborhoods near the central markets or close to the ports. But not all of the Portuguese were New Christians, nor were all of the New Christians *hombres de negocio* (large-scale merchants, bankers, or government contractors). The artisans, muleteers, tradesmen, and farmers among them lived scattered in small rural towns, mining camps, and frontier outposts, sometimes with surprising outcomes. In and around Ixquimilpan in the Mezquital region of New Spain, for example, a small but successful group of Portuguese conversos settled. Some of them married indigenous Otomí women, learned their language, and became prominent and respected members of these communities.[35]

How many of the Portuguese who arrived in the Spanish Indies were New Christians and how many of those were crypto-Jews remain mysteries. Still, the possibility that they were crypto-Jews continuously preoccupied Spanish authorities, whose fears were usually both political and religious. The Inquisition and anticonverso interest groups always tended to see the conversos as a homogeneous category in terms of their inherent moral defects, if not entirely because of their insincerity of belief.

Contagion and Discrimination

Concerns that Indians and Jews might somehow be related and that conversos would corrupt the recently converted native populations and sponsor rebellion among the African slaves, or—as they had supposedly done in the Dutch capture of Salvador, Brazil, in 1624—collaborate with hostile powers continuously haunted Iberian policy makers and affected their decisions.[36] There were even fears that the Jews might provoke internal unrest by introducing the destructive concept of freedom of conscience or by agitating among slaves or native peoples.[37] After 1640 the long-standing suspicion of conversos became indistinguishable from the political distrust of all Portuguese in general. The level of concern was unrealistic. The viceroy of Peru, the Marquis of Mancera, worried that since the Portuguese were often involved in the African slave trade and gave the slaves their first religious instruction, their attempts to stimulate rebellion might be effective because they were so loved by the slaves.[38]

We get some inkling of Spanish perceptions of the threat from a report of Fray Antonio de Chinchilla, a commissary of the Inquisition in the Caribbean. In the mid-seventeenth century he recalled that around 1600, a ship that people called the *barco iudaíco* had arrived in the Caribbean, full of fugitive families from Portugal that had then distributed themselves and multiplied throughout the districts of Puerto Rico, Caracas, and Margarita Island. These people had secured occupations and positions of honor, but this official believed that they could never erase the stain on their status or forget their Jewish practices.[39] In an area as large and fractionalized as the Caribbean — where English, French, and Dutch contrabandists might spread Protestantism and where large numbers of pagan African slaves who knew the mysteries of poisons and witchcraft were being introduced — the official believed that the conversos presented an immediate threat. Many Portuguese New Christians had been involved in contraband and the slave trade to the region before the union, and after 1587 New Christian merchants held the *asiento* (a royal contract) to supply slaves directly from Africa to Spanish America.[40] That legal role and their increasing numbers made the danger of the conversos only too clear. It is no wonder, then, that a third American tribunal of the Inquisition with jurisdiction over the islands and mainlands of the Caribbean was established at Cartagena de Indias in 1610.[41]

Curiously, as I have noted above, no permanent tribunal was created in Brazil — a region where the New Christians seemed to have thrived and that now became a springboard for their arrival in the Spanish empire. The same held true in the Rio de la Plata, where access to the silver of Potosí and, as in the Caribbean, contraband and illegal slaving had brought many Portuguese New Christians as *peruleros* (people involved in usually illegal trade with Spanish South America) to the region by way of Brazil.[42] In the Rio de la Plata, however, local interests discouraged the establishment of a tribunal. Thus, when in 1610 a new tribunal was created in Cartagena, only a resident agent of the Lima tribunal was established in Buenos Aires.[43]

Despite exclusion and repression, the conversos flourished in the American colonies of Spain and Portugal for a half-century (1580–1630), as did Jews in general within the Atlantic world. In some ways, this seeming Sephardi success was not an anomaly. It should be seen as part of the general reversal of the medieval Jewish exclusions throughout Europe, as mercantilism, trade in general, and considerations of state had moved princes and towns in varying degrees to allow Jewish settlement, worship, freedom of movement, and civil inclusion—especially in port towns and cities that welcomed merchant communities.[44] From Salonica to Hamburg, Venice, Livorno, Bordeaux, and Amsterdam, the process took place with variations in the terms of residence, limits on worship, or civil status. However, as David Sorkin has noted, those states with colonies frequently proved more generous, and "mercantilist policy was often at its most magnanimous in the distant colonies."[45] Of course, these openings and policies of tolerance always had opponents, and in some places and at some times—under pressure of local interests or unsympathetic popes like Paul IV (1555–59)—liberties were rescinded and persecution reinforced. Overall the tendency was in the direction of limited acceptance, although, as the historian Jaime Contreras reminds us about Spain and Portugal, "no matter how generous the permissiveness, always beneath the surface nested the anti-Jewish *fantasmas* [ghosts]."[46] In Portugal, in fact, preventing any royal concessions to conversos and magnifying the threat of Judaism became the battle cry of the Church and the Inquisition, and eventually it also became a principal justification for resistance to Hapsburg rule and the reestablishment of national sovereignty.[47]

In the Hispanic world in general, Jewish worship remained forbidden, Jews' residence was restricted, and the threat of inquisitorial persecution of those who had converted and their descendants continued. However, Lima, Mexico City, Vera Cruz, Salvador, Recife, Cartagena, and Buenos Aires were added to the web of connective points in the global networks of familial, cultural, and mercantile relations of what was often referred to as *hombres de la nación* (the men of the nation), or what in Spanish America were simply called "the Portuguese."

The Conversos in America

Much of what we know about the inner world of the conversos and their lives in general in the New World has been gleaned or surmised from the extensive trial records generated first by inquisitorial *visitas* (investigations) made in Brazil in 1591–93 and 1618–19 and then by the waves of repression and persecution in Spanish America that began in the mid-1630s in Lima and extended into the tribunals in Cartagena and Mexico City until the 1650s. The sad story of this persecution has been extracted from the extensive trial records produced by those inquests.[48] Historians have used these materials to great advantage and have reconstructed in detail the saga of the individuals and families victimized in the repression, as well as the effects on their communities, identities, and *mentalité* (way of thinking).[49]

The question I would like to pose is different. It is not about the wave of repression and its effects, but rather about the conditions of conversos' life and their position in society during the sometimes long chronological interstices between the inquisitorial campaigns. The threat of denunciation or arrest was always present, but sometimes converso life went on normally for extended periods. As I have noted above, in many places in the Indies the percentage of conversos in the Hispanic population was significant. Families with the so-called stain of Jewish origins were not clandestine: many people knew who they were. Despite the restrictions and disabilities imposed by limpieza de sangre regulations and restrictions, some conversos had obtained positions of leadership and high office (even governorships and positions of municipal authority) or had become commercially successful, and a few of them were very wealthy.[50] How was this possible in a social and legal regime intentionally structured to impede conversos' integration, social mobility, education, and acceptance into certain occupations?[51] And in America, how were the disabilities and discrimination imposed on the conversos affected or modified in a social system structured by ethnic and phenotypical categories and the traditional juridical divisions of a society of orders?

Recent research in Spain has opened a window into this question by distinguishing between the formal legal and institutional restrictions on individuals who bore the stain of Jewish or Muslim background and the quotidian reality tempered by common sense, *raison d'état*, good connections, and above all money.[52] Under Phillip II, discrimination in Spain had become institutionalized by the cleanliness of blood statutes. Although the restrictions never became royal law, many institutions and corporate organizations like universities, lay brotherhoods, and guilds had adopted them — despite the forceful objections by both theologians arguing for the equality of all baptized in the Church and policy proponents (*arbitristas*) like Duarte Gomes Solis or Martín González de Cellorigo, "cardiologists" of the country's political and economic ills whose writings sought to bring the conversos and their commercial talents back to Spain.[53] Although Portugal was slower to adopt these restrictions, by the late sixteenth century it had also instituted them.[54] Nevertheless — despite the seeming triumph of the purity of blood statutes — the sale of public offices, the rise of the *letrados* (men with university training, usually in law) as a professional bureaucratic class and their utility as state employees, and the crown's constant need for money combined to create an environment that not only facilitated but also promoted avoidance and circumnavigation of the restrictions on conversos. Individuals from all walks of life falsified thousands of *probanzas* (certificates) testifying to the stainless nature of their lineage in applications for positions in the church or state or for entrance into a military order, religious brotherhood, convent, guild, or the Inquisition itself. These were accompanied by innumerable dishonest testimonies and fraudulent statements about family reputations. False testimonials about the *vox publica* used as evidence of Catholic orthodoxy became common coin, and a virtual army of genealogists (*linajudos*) made a living by extortion for covering up Jewish origins or by inventing ties (for a price) between any converso named Gómez or Sandoval with some provincial noble or grandee with the same surname.[55] And, of course, many of the noble families had already incorporated conversos and falsified their genealogies, and some even had branches that commonly incorporated conversos through marriage and thereby continually accessed funds that were made accessible to the family as a whole.

There is considerable evidence that these same strategies were followed in the overseas Iberian world, where the difficulties of communication over long distances, mobility and chain migratory habits, the instability of remembrance, and the advantages of self-interest in deception or obfuscation combined to make evidence of converso family religious histories always questionable or contingent.[56] It was not that the traditional forces opposed to converso assimilation had stopped their antagonism at the Pillars of Hercules. Anti-Jewish tracts and literature reached the New World; sermons from pulpits and in autos-da-fé often demonized the Jews; and the Inquisition (with the support of the crown) created a network of tribunals, commissaries, and collaborators lay assistants (*familiares*) that drew the support of people hoping to use their association with the Holy Office as a proof of their orthodoxy and the cleanliness of their own genealogy.[57] Even the medieval Jewish stereotypes of large noses and pointed hats were on occasion employed by indigenous artists in the decoration of churches, and local versions of imagined converso blasphemies or sacrileges were reported or created from New Spain to Cuzco.[58] Nevertheless, for material considerations and reasons of state — as well as a complex combination of social attitudes and strategies of both conversos and the societies in which they lived — many conversos managed to live, and some to thrive, in the American colonies of Spain and Portugal.

Here we need to recognize the intertwining or braiding of religion, politics, and the complex chronology of the relationship between Portugal and Spain in relation to their external relations to the rest of Europe. The fact that the vast majority of conversos were identified not only as Jews but also as Portuguese was of great importance. This was so not just in their gaining access to Spain and its empire, but because as subjects of the polycentric Hapsburg Catholic monarchy they could be expected to demonstrate their loyalty personally or financially—or conversely, because they were royal subjects, they might be cajoled by offers of honor and reward or threatened by constraint and intimidation.[59] It was certainly no coincidence that the great wave of Inquisition trials in Mexico crested during the Portuguese political separation from the Hapsburg monarchy in 1640, when the distrust of the Portuguese united political and religious suspicions.[60] It is also important to remember that after that separation, the war for Portuguese independence continued for almost thirty years, not ending until 1668. During these years, competing strategies of the rival monarchies and their potential allies or enemies (England, France, Holland, Sweden, Rome, and so on), as well as Sephardi perceptions of where their interests were best served (usually they sided with the Bragança claimant to the crown), created a complex mix of national sentiment, religious affiliation, loyalty, and identity.[61]

It was not by chance, then, that Chinchilla's reference to the *barco iudaico* was written in 1650s at a moment when the separation of Portugal and Spain and the various rebellions in the Hapsburg monarchy had made Spain and its empire seem particularly vulnerable. The readmission of the Jews into England (1654), their presence in Dutch Brazil (1630–54), and the general expansion of the Sephardi trading networks—combined with various English, French, and Dutch territorial acquisitions in the Caribbean in this period—made foreign penetration of the Spanish empire a reality. Moreover, the continual smuggling, in which the "Portuguese" were active participants, threatened Seville's monopoly of the Indies trade in general and the flow of silver in particular. For those newly expanding maritime nations, Joseph Addison's often-quoted statement that the Jews had become "the instruments by which the most distant nations converse with one another and by which mankind are knit together in general correspondence, they are like the pegs and nails of a great building, which though they are but little valued in themselves, are absolutely necessary to keep the whole frame together" seemed to validate their role in mercantile expansion, a role that confirmed Spain's fears about the security of its closed system of trade.[62] However, the Sevillian exporters and *consulado* (the merchant guild linked to the key monopoly merchants in Seville) perceived that threat quite differently than the consumers in the Indies who collaborated with the contrabandists and freelance merchants.

Within this general political and chronological framework, I will examine three aspects of the place of conversos in Latin American societies and how their status and characteristics ultimately contributed to their position in the social ordering or hierarchies of those societies.

Money and Men of the Nation

At one level, wealth was at the heart of the matter in terms of how the conversos sought to avoid the restrictions, as well as why Iberian protomercantilists like the Count-Duke of Olivares in Spain in the 1620s and 1630s and the Jesuit Father António Vieira in Portugal in the following decades favored assimilation and may have even advocated at times for the readmission of Jews as a state policy.[63] The importance of commerce, and therefore the utility of the merchant class and its capital, was a theme that proconverso memorialists and the conversos themselves continuously emphasized. "Commerce is more powerful than arms," argued the converso *arbitrista* Gomes Solis, when he urged even the titled nobility to raise their sons with a sword in the right hand, but knowing of how "to count and write with the other."[64] But Gomes Solis also recognized that the nobility despised the merchant class for its success, denigrated it because its members often had converso origins, and resented it because its financial services were indispensable.[65] A converso himself, Gomes Solis left the issue of religious animosity mostly out of his analysis. For him, the opposition to commerce was principally a matter of national interest and the denigration of the merchant class made no sense, only weakening the state. Why, he asked, should Portugal —

a country whose king celebrated himself as ruler of far-flung conquests, navigation, and commerce—deprecate the merchant class that other countries found so useful? In 1643, during the first years of Portugal's struggle for independence, the Jesuit Father Antônio Vieira, who was not a converso, presented similar views and argued openly that restraining the procedures and severity of the Inquisition would result in a return of the Portuguese converso merchants who had been scattered across Europe—all of whom still thought of Portugal as their fatherland.[66] Their return from that diaspora would not only weaken Portugal's enemies, but it would also bring their skills and capital back to their homeland and secure its survival.[67] Whatever aspects of millenarian expectation Vieira shared with Jewish traditions, and whatever sympathy he expressed with the New Christians about the injustice of their treatment, his battle on their behalf was driven primarily by political and economic considerations.[68]

However, money and its association with the conversos preoccupied not only their advocates but also their opponents. Don Dinero was indeed a powerful *caballero* (gentleman), as Francisco de Quevedo, a leading anticonverso ideologue put it in the sarcastic poem he wrote in defense of an imagined aristocratic and religiously pure social order that was seemingly under attack by Jews and money.[69] That association of conversos and money was never far from the thinking of intellectuals like Quevedo or his predecessors such as the noble courtier Cristóvão de Moura, Philip II's Portuguese agent in 1580 and later viceroy of Portugal (1600–1603 and 1608–12), who opposed the assimilation of the conversos at every turn. Such ideas also figured prominently in the considerations of the Inquisition, which was a principal ally of the nobility in its opposition to the conversos—not only because of its concerns with orthodoxy but also because of its ability to confiscate the possessions and assets of the accused. The Inquisition sought to balance orthodoxy and its interests, showing leniency and acceptance by assimilating conversos like Heitor Mendes de Brito (a wealthy leader of the community, a merchant in the India trade, and a generous supporter of the crown and the Inquisition), but also defending its interests at crucial political junctures.[70] It used the considerable propagandistic powers inherent in its staging of autos-da-fé and in the manipulation and promotion of incidents of sacrilege and associated "miracles" to intensify popular sentiments against any concessions to the conversos, any relaxation of their exclusion, and any change in its own procedures and policies of confiscation.[71]

On both sides of the argument, money as much as theology determined policy and attitudes toward the conversos and the enforcement of limpieza de sangre statutes.[72] We can see this clearly in the negotiations over the general pardon of conversos granted for a princely sum by Philip III in 1605, its retraction a few years later, and its discussion again in the 1620s.[73] The pardon had emptied the Inquisition jails of conversos accused of Judaizing and allowed them to travel and conduct international commerce, and it even sought to stop the Inquisition from confiscating the properties of those accused of heresy. While the pardon was essentially a form of extortion imposed by Philip III and his advisors to resolve the state's financial problems and line the pockets of the Duke of Lerma and other advisors at court, the enemies of these policies saw them as further evidence of the power of Jewish bribes and subversion.[74]

The concessions given to the New Christians by Philip III had made the Inquisition particularly defensive. Thus, when the Count-Duke of Olivares came to power in 1621 as the principal minister (*valido*) of Philip IV, the Inquisition moved quickly to gain his support and forestall his reformist plans to seek converso funding and financial resources to meet the challenges of government. The three Portuguese tribunals and a papal representative in Portugal each wrote to Olivares complaining about the perfidy of the Jews, the way in which their heresy had spread, and the need to rip this religion out by the roots. The inquisitors emphasized the valuable role of the tribunals in controlling the threat, and they flattered Olivares by telling him that divine intervention had put him in office. His help to the Inquisition, they said, was indispensable, and they prayed to God for his health as guardian of the public welfare.[75] However, such flattery and urgings did not deter Olivares from turning to Portuguese New Christian bankers to finance the government, assume large state contracts, and help him break the crown's dependency on Genoese financiers. Olivares responded to the critics of his dependence on the conversos with a direct attack on the purity of blood regulations, calling them "unjust and impious, against divine law, natural law, and the law of nations." He added, "In no other government or state in the world do such laws exist."[76] However, Olivares's position on the purity laws and his desire to reintegrate the conversos was short-lived.[77] After his fall from power in 1642, the forces that had opposed him on this issue dominated state policy, and there was a turn away from *raison d'etat* and *politique* (politically practical) approaches to issues involving the conversos.

Such financial considerations were no less present in the American colonies. A case in point is the so-called great complicity campaign by the Inquisition against the Portuguese conversos in Lima in 1635–39. A hundred people were arrested during the campaign, including some of the city's principal merchants. Some—like the wealthiest, Manuel Baptista Pérez—were prosecuted, their assets confiscated, and their role in the viceroyalty's economy virtually eliminated. None of conversos arrested were members of the Lima *consulado*, but at least fifteen of their competitors in the *consulado* were *familiares* of the Inquisition. Clearly, the Inquisition had been mobilized to eliminate competitors. Moreover, whatever religious concerns and commercial rivalry had motivated the tribunal, it had its own financial interests in this campaign.[78] All three of the Spanish American tribunals were experiencing fiscal difficulties. They depended on royal funding, but since 1625 the financially strained crown had been threatening to terminate that support, and in 1633 it finally did so. The tribunals were anxious to become financially independent. The path to this independence lay in their confiscation of the assets of the accused. The silver alone seized in 1635 from conversos equaled one-third of the total value of all the American silver received by Spain in that year.[79] The Marquis de Mancera, viceroy of Peru, later complained that the million pesos that the Lima Inquisition had sequestered in the great complicity campaign had simply disappeared, but in reality they had been invested in interest-bearing loans (*censos*) to support the tribunal's operations.[80]

The potential benefit from the arrests of the Portuguese New Christians was not lost on other tribunals. The Mexico City tribunal was so corrupt that in 1658 the Inquisition conducted an inquiry that brought 175 charges against its own inquisitors.[81] The Inquisition of Cartagena, learning of the arrests in Lima and itself in serious financial straits, promised that if it was allowed to arrest certain individuals, it too could discover a conspiracy of Jews — and that by doing so, like the tribunals of Lima and Mexico, it would "leave behind its misery."[82]

The clear financial motivations of Inquisition tribunals have led some historians to completely deny the religious motives of the Inquisition or doubt the reality of converso crypto-Judaism and see the prosecutions as purely a product of material interests.[83] In fact, the existence of a religious motive did not exclude the reality of material considerations. The Inquisition tribunals did prosecute the poor and the humble conversos, from whom they could gain little, but the wealthy *hombres de la nación* were always preferred targets. For the same reason, they were also a major concern of the political advisors, who hoped to profit from their success.[84] Both their attackers and defenders tended to racialize or essentialize their commercial and financial talents or the culture that encouraged them.

How had they survived and thrived? We know a good deal about the Sephardi merchant communities in the diaspora and their role in the globalization of early modern commerce from in-depth studies of northern European or Mediterranean communities, but we know less about the strategies of those within Spain and Portugal and their empires.[85] Fortunately, we now have some answers about the Iberian Atlantic in general and about a number of specific cities.[86] Over forty years ago, David Grant Smith — then a young American scholar — in a remarkable but never published doctoral dissertation examined the merchant communities of Lisbon and Salvador, the capital city of the Portuguese colony of Brazil. His method was prosopography, a collective biography that described in much detail family arrangements, financial activities, voluntary associations, and religious activities and affiliations. In many ways, his work (with its findings and line of argument) was the precursor of the new wave of Sephardi merchant studies. Smith took the period 1620–90 and identified 364 Lisbon merchants. Of these, 78 percent were New Christians, and about 39 were essentially merchant bankers with enough capital to assume government contracts. He found that although the terms "merchant" and "New Christian" became synonymous in Portugal, Old Christians still accounted for more than 20 percent of this class in Lisbon and over half of the 179 merchants in Salvador.[87] In both ports, the commercial and social networks among the *hombres de la nación* overlapped.[88] Nevertheless, Old and New Christians shared many business connections and cooperated on a regular basis — although given the social and religious stigma attached to the blood purity laws and other forms of discrimination, they tended not to intermarry or become socially integrated. This had a number of effects, but importantly it tended to undercut the possibility that merchants as a class could consolidate their power vis-à-vis the landed nobility or other colonial elites. Instead, Old and New Christian merchants looked separately for associations with, or links to, those elites who in turn were often receptive and attracted to such alliances by dowries and other financial benefits. Some New Christian families chose to assimilate by rejecting any religious ties to Judaism, or at least pretending to do so. In fact, some of the wealthiest conversos in the Americas seem to have been sincere members of the Church. António Fernandes de Elvas, the first Portuguese New Christian to obtain the *asiento* to supply slaves to Spanish America after the union of Spain and Portugal, was connected to Sephardi merchants from Madrid to Goa, West Africa, Cartagena de Indias, and Amsterdam, but he remained a steadfast Catholic.[89] Manuel Bautista Pérez, the wealthiest man in Lima in the 1630s, denied any connection to Judaism even under torture and at the moment of his immolation. And perhaps his correspondent, the prosperous Mexico City converso merchant Simón Váez Sevilla, was also sincere in his Christianity.[90] That sincerity, however, did not protect them or outweigh the attraction of their wealth and the vulnerability of their lineage when the institutional and social pressures against conversos intensified. Sincere in their Christian faith or not, New Christians sought social standing and material advancement by acquiring properties like sugar plantations and other accoutrements of noble standing, or at least entrance into religious brotherhoods that did not enforce the blood laws. They also sought gowns (*hábitos*) in the orders of knighthood where recognition of their services to the crown would outweigh their *mala sangre* (the defect of their birth) and thus make it possible for them to achieve their social aspirations. However, shared goals and business partnerships were always personally and politically contingent.

This was the strategy of integration. We need not make religious identity the defining characteristic of the converso communities. Ties of lineage, historical experience, nationality, and common interest often seem to have been more important than religious belief in their associations, although admittedly identity and their inner life are always complex issues.[91] Accommodation to the prevailing religion in their place of residence, be it hegemonic Catholicism in the Iberian world or rabbinic Judaism in Amsterdam or Livorno, was a common practice.[92] The many cases of conversos who remained willingly in Spain, Portugal, or their colonies even after prosecution by the Inquisition; the travels of those in the diaspora to the "lands of idolatry"; and the cases of those "souls in dispute" who sought permanent readmission and reconciliation with the Church all suggest a variety of motivations—spiritual, familial, material, and emotional or affective.[93] Denounced as deceitful and duplicitous, like "ships with two rudders," or charged with lacking any belief at all, the conversos as a category were—whether by force or choice—caught between two traditions and beliefs, and their presence destabilized an existing social order based on persistent, inheritable, and essential physical and moral characteristics.[94] In a social regime defined by lineage and the transference of moral, ethical, physical, and personal qualities by blood or milk, conversos and Moriscos, no matter how sincere their Christianity, remained fish out of water and anomalies that challenged the understanding of the consistency of lineage and descent. They were the mestizos of faith, and as such they always constituted a danger. In this uncomfortable position, their existence challenged a universe of clearly marked categories and rankings, and they were precursors of the social instability created by persons of mixed race when color and phenotype replaced religion as a principal marker of social distinction.

The Utility of Acceptance

Whatever the disabilities suffered or the strategies employed by the conversos in the Americas, their situation was always framed by the legal and social practices in the places of their residence. In the context of the closed commercial economies of the Iberian empires, their mercantile skills and connections often made them not only useful but essential to local and regional economies, and that utility overrode the prohibitions on their residence and the suspicions about the sincerity of their Catholic piety.

Distance from centers of royal and ecclesiastical authorities along with utility and personal contacts probably also contributed to the degree of their acceptance.[95] Perhaps the best example of this phenomenon is the early history of Buenos Aires, where the resident Portuguese were eventually protected by a converso bishop, aided by various governors, and rescued by the Franciscans — despite the attempts of Madrid, the Lima Inquisition, and local rivals to suppress or disrupt their activities.

Buenos Aires was founded by Spain in 1536, abandoned, and reestablished in 1580. It was the outer fringe of the Spanish empire and its trade, but it served as a back door to the silver of Potosí. Dependent to some extent on commerce with Rio de Janeiro and Brazil in general, Buenos Aires attracted the Portuguese (many of them New Christians), especially after inquisitorial visitors arrived in Brazil in 1591 and 1618. Occasionally permitted to trade legally with Brazil, by 1600 merchants had developed a regular route for the clandestine commerce of slaves, textiles, and other goods in exchange for silver from Buenos Aires through Tucumán to Potosí. Royal officials, the audiencia of Charcas, and inquisitorial agents continually complained that the contrabanders were "*judíos en su ley*" (Jews in their religion).[96] Conversos obtained licenses with falsified proof of Old Christian status or arrived with no license at all, and their network grew and established itself through marriages, partnerships, and collaboration with local officials and Spanish residents. Many Portuguese became *vecinos*, while some held municipal offices. Eventually a coalition of the Portuguese and their supporters that called itself the *confederados* came to dominate local politics in opposition to the old landed original Spanish settlers (*beneméritos*).[97]

A struggle developed between the crown, which was trying to restrict illegal trade, and the contrabandists and their supporters, who profited from the commerce with Brazil and by extension with Angola, Amsterdam, and the Atlantic economy. By the purchase of treasury offices, employment as shipping inspectors, and positions in the municipal council (*cabildo*); by cooperating with governors; and even by offering positions to agents (*comisarios*) of the Inquisition, the *confederados* created a powerful consortium of seemingly unlikely allies. Even after the separation of Spain and Portugal and a decrease in Portuguese immigration to Buenos Aires, a 1678 investigation implicated the governor, his nephews, the Franciscans, and the Jesuits as collaborators in the continued immigration of persons of suspect faith.[98]

How had the conversos done it? The utility of their network and its benefits to the city and the region had created an alliance of interests so that governors who welcomed foreign trade, miners who bought contraband slaves, and Franciscans who welcomed access to building materials for the renovation of their convents could all overlook anticonverso prohibitions and prejudices.[99] Much as the residents of Santo Domingo had objected to the expulsion of the useful Moriscos in 1545, Bishop Martín de Loyola of Paraguay defended the Portuguese conversos when he told the *cabildo* in 1606 that the expulsion of the conversos would result in the "total destruction of the city." Utility and self-interest seem to have carried the day, and not until the creation of an inland customs house at Cordoba in 1621 did Spain begin to limit the Portuguese smuggling to and from Potosí.

Finally, we may ask if most of the Portuguese in the Río de La Plata were indeed New Christians, and if so, whether they were crypto-Jews. We will never know. Despite the Lima tribunal's great campaign of the 1630s and its activity thereafter, the conversos of Buenos Aires — including the wealthiest merchants like Diego de Vega; prominent figures of Portuguese converso origin like Governor Pedro de Roxas y Acevedo; and the Dominican friar Fray Francisco de Vitoria, Bishop of Tucumán — were never charged or arrested after the rebellion of Portugal and its separation from Spain in 1640, a fact that seems to attest not only to both their influence and power, but also to the perception of their importance and utility.

Strategies of survival were multiple. Some important converso families practiced endogamy to keep families pure and secrets hidden.[100] Others sought marital alliances with Old Christian lineages. Charitable donations, chapel construction, or having a son pursue an ecclesiastical career could all serve as evidence of real Christian piety or as a good disguise for feigned belief. Many converso families sought the protection and aid of powerful or well-placed collaborators. As in Spain, a creative genealogist was the converso family's best safeguard. A cleric who had spent five years in Peru reported in 1695 that membership in the military orders there had no prestige at all, since so many men of low status had received them, and for a thousand doubloons there were men who would invent genealogies as they pleased.[101] What remains a challenging question is the extent to which as this converso integration progressed there remained any sentiment of a Sephardi identity as a nation that cut across these alternative strategies and the religious and political choices that conversos made, and if that sentiment changed over time.[102]

Social Acceptance

Finally, I do not wish to leave the impression that material benefit was the only motive that protected the conversos. Along with their strategies of survival, we need to take into account the perception and attitudes of the general population. Opponents to the conversos on religious as well as economic or political grounds were never lacking. An anti-Jewish and often antisemitic literature of theological tracts and sermons filled with opprobrium and condemnation circulated widely.[103] Invective relating to and negative attitudes toward Jews became a common element in everyday speech and official correspondence, where it was common to find such essentializing phrases as "the well-known perfidy of the people of the Hebrew nation."[104] Nevertheless, the idea that the denigration and distrust of Judaism and the conversos was so widespread in the population that the Inquisition's policies and actions were simply a mirror reflecting a general attitude obfuscates the role that the Inquisition played in creating those attitudes and the fact that at particular moments it manipulated or reinforced them for its own interests or political purposes.[105] The historian Juan Ignacio Pulido Serrano has emphasized that "repression and the autos-da-fé served to pressure the government, but they also had a repercussion on Portuguese society. They deepened the social cleavage between Old and New Christians. They inflamed the problem."[106]

Despite the campaign to generalize the denigration of and institutionalize the opprobrium toward conversos, some individuals (both inside the Inquisition and the corridors of power and among the general population) remained unconvinced of the justice of discriminatory policies and even questioned the theology behind them.[107] In Spain, Portugal, and the New World there were occasional theological defenders of the conversos. They included the Franciscan Fray Francisco Gallen, who believed that the law of Moses still had its moral power and said so, to the dismay of his listeners; Pedro de Morales, in Chile, who told someone who had criticized the king of Portugal for admitting the Jews exiled from Spain that the conversos were now the best Christians; and the Jesuit Cosmé Gonçalves, in São Paulo, who in 1687 penned a defense of the New Christians, observing that while any suggestion of Jewish descent may have been the worst kind of defamation, such discrimination was theologically in error and morally unjust.[108] There also seem to have been lay attitudes of acceptance and sometimes even respect. Some observers simply admired the steadfastness of condemned Judaizers who at their executions were "like good soldiers, and never took a backward step."[109] Others — like Juan Rodriguez Afilhado, a young Algarve blacksmith living in Cádiz, who had witnessed an auto-da-fé in Evora, Portugal — questioned the justice of forced belief altogether. When one of the prisoners about to be burned was killed by stones thrown by the crowd, and someone said it was a shame because he and the others could have saved their souls by confessing their sins and dying within the Church, Afilhado objected:

> Be quiet, you know nothing about these things. How do you know they are going to hell? Each person must look after himself, and these men, and all who die in this way, die innocent and without fault.[110]

Such expressions of sympathy or questioning of the prosecution of people who still followed the law of Moses were always dangerous, and people knew it: "Con el rey y la Inquisición, chitón" (with the king and the Inquisition, keep your mouth shut) was a common expression. Nevertheless, people who questioned the policies and practices were never lacking in the metropoles or in the empire. The idea that "cada uno se puede salvar en su ley (each can be saved in his own religion)" was deeply engrained in the views of, and expressed by, both common folk and learned theologians.[111] Sometimes these tolerant attitudes were based on affection or personal contact, like those of María de Zárate in Mexico. An Old Christian married to a converso, she told the inquisitors that "God the Father was not angered by those who served God the son, and God the son was not angry at those who served God the Father."[112] Sometimes the arguments of such people were theological, but often they were simply based on experience and a sense of justice. Some people even risked defending the New Christians before the Inquisition.[113] The Goan mestizo Fernando Pereira de Castro — a widely traveled soldier who became a priest and was arrested in Brazil and sent to Lisbon — claimed that the arrests of New Christians were unjust, and in 1620 he sought to inspire the resistance of the Brazilian conversos imprisoned with him by urging them to remain steadfast and confess to nothing, because he believed that another pardon was being negotiated.[114]

But despite such questioning of the discriminatory policies, the tradition of rejection and the habit of condemnation weighed heavily on society and everyday discourse. We can hear the tension and confusion this created in the words of Juan Gómez, a blasphemous Galician traveling salesman (*trajinante*) arrested in the Indian town of Xochicuautla near Pachuca, Mexico. When he had failed to sell his load of clothing, he complained that God had given him little despite the fact that he was the son of Spaniards and a good Christian, and thus, he was better than God—who, after all, was a Jew.[115] Such language was *mal sonante* (bad sounding—that is, offensive to pious ears), but that was not what brought Gómez to the attention of the authorities. He had gotten into trouble and been arrested not for speaking against the Jews, but for speaking in their favor. He had said that as a solder in Oran he had been honestly treated by them, they were punctual and responsible in their dealings, and they never failed to provide for the poor—and Muslims were the same. For his blasphemies and defense of the Jews, the corregidor of Pachuca ordered Gómez's Indian assistants to arrest and mistreat him, calling him, "Jew, Hebrew, Portuguese, and Samaritan." Gómez responded by saying that he would prefer to be a Jew than an Indian. The corregidor put him in the stocks, sold his goods and personal belongings, and gagged him as a blasphemer.[116] The case was brought to the Inquisition. Gómez remained imprisoned for seventeen months, but he was eventually released and had his goods restored to him because the Inquisitors treated this Old Christian leniently, saying that his remarks about Indians were just hyperbole; his comment about being better than God had not questioned God's divinity; and his words about Jews and Muslims had not praised their religion or beliefs, only their practices. Contradiction and confusion underlined the ambiguities of theology and practice.

While it is easy enough to cite examples of repression and discrimination throughout the Iberian empires, it is also possible to find considerable evidence of a quotidian disregard for the cleavages between Old and New Christians.[117] The daily life of the conversos indicates that they continuously had contacts with all levels of society. Here, let me turn to some evidence from Portuguese Brazil. Religious identity meant a great deal, but not everything, and not to everybody. Despite a growing body of exclusions and legal restrictions, contacts, daily interactions, and marriages between New and Old Christians were common enough. The first generations of settlement had weakened the boundaries of difference for people like Isabel Fernandes, who described herself as a mameluca with the *raça* (race) of New Christian, the daughter of a white Old Christian man who was honorable enough to be of the governing class of the town and of his mameluca wife, herself the daughter of a New Christian and an Indian woman (*negra brasila*). This case and others like it seem to imply that marriage to partners with the stain of so-called impure blood was not inconceivable, and that for some it seems to have not even been a consideration. When Diogo Carneiro, a sugar cane farmer, told the inquisitors that he was an Old Christian and that he had no idea if his wife was an Old or New Christian, he may have been lying either fully or in part, but he was probably implying an indifference to those distinctions that ran contrary to the increasing liabilities being imposed by various institutions and supported by certain social sectors.[118] Evidence of interaction between Old and New Christians is extensive.

How the Conversos Became White

It would seem that in multiracial Brazil and other areas of the Iberian New World colonies, the perceived defects or the disadvantages suffered by conversos were to some extent mitigated or modified by their identification as white Europeans, and that as such, they shared Old Christians' attitudes about slavery, race, and class.[119] Although some racial theorists tried to define Jews as physically or phenotypically distinct, they had little success. Even as conversos maintained their own corporative identity, they employed the current tropes and vocabularies of distinction, sometimes even echoing the arguments of the limpieza de sangre regulations to set themselves apart from other collectivities.[120] In a similar way, the Inquisition in particular and the Church more generally employed its anti-Jewish categories and rhetoric in sermons and used autos-da-fé to reinforce its authority and message among Old Christians in Iberia as well as among the castas, the population of mixed origins, the enslaved, and the indigenous populations of the Americas. Conversos' minority status did influence their relationship with servants and slaves, because it made conversos vulnerable to denunciation, but sometimes it also made them attractive as potential allies or models of resistance. A mulatto slave who had seen the determined courage of the converso Tomás Treviño de Sobremonte before his execution in the Mexico City auto-da-fé of 1649 had been impressed. When in his cups, the slave would announce to the world: "I'm no Christian, I'm Treviño!"[121] On the other hand, slaves, free people of color, and indigenous people like the chronicler Guaman Poma de Ayala sometimes adopted the prevailing Christian prejudices toward Jews and conversos as a demonstration of their own integration into colonial society and a marker of their own respectability. Despite scattered evidence of slaves who converted to Judaism or manumissions granted, there is little evidence that conversos (or Jews in places like Surinam or Jamaica) treated their slaves or conceived of them any differently than did their Old Christian neighbors. Moreover, despite the considerable evidence of social and sexual contact with the indigenous peoples and mixed-race populations — a contact that was, of course, generalized among the European settlers as a whole — conversos shared others' negative attitudes and stereotypes and were ready to hurl the epithet of *perro mestizo* (mestizo dog) when affronted or challenged in some way.[122] As the historian Jonathan Schorsch has put it, these racial attitudes served as an "antidote to their own exclusion, a tincture to ensure their own whiteness."[123]

By the mid-eighteenth century, as the phenotypical hierarchy of the *sistema de castas* was taking its final form in the Americas, the converso trading network had pulled away from the colonial trades and become less important as new ideas of state mercantilism flourished in Spain under the Bourbons, in Portugal from 1755 to 1777 under the Marques de Pombal (Sebastião de Carvalho e Melo), and throughout Western Europe in general. By this time, too, after a spate of further prosecutions in the 1720s in an attempt by a weakening institution to retain its authority, the Inquisition's focus has shifted from the imaginary threats of Judaism to new dangers among the growing number of libertines, rationalists, atheists, and other disturbers of the public order.[124] But the conversos remained. They had been, as Jonathan Israel called them, "victims and agents of empire."[125] Families and lineages that had survived the persecutorial storms of the seventeenth century were still present. Assimilation was gradual, but communal memories were fading.[126] In Livorno, Venice, or Amsterdam, and maybe in Brazil, there was still a sense of the nation. However, in Spanish America, the inquisitorial campaigns of the mid-seventeenth century had disrupted the networks that had bound the conversos together and weakened their ties with Jewish communities as well.[127] In many places, there was no longer an identifiable social community of conversos: money and time had made their survival possible, while false genealogies had covered the tracks of past generations. In a few places — Tras os Montes, perhaps New Mexico, and northeastern Brazil — a Marrano identity lingered and some practices, habits, and traditions remained. But as Nathan Wachtel has poetically written, over time "forgetfulness did its work."[128]

Nevertheless, the ancient suspicion of the conversos and fear of the Jews was still present at the turn of the century. In 1800, when the Jews of Curaçao sought to flee from a French invasion of that island to the coast of Venezuela, where they had often done business, the governor of Venezuela — perhaps aware that in the 1750s Curaçao Jews had even donated funds and materials for the construction of a church in Coro — favored their move. However, the audiencia of Venezuela refused their petition, still fearing the "infection that they could introduce into the religious and political order."[129]

A decade later — in 1812, in the midst of revolutionary upheaval — Father Miguel de Hidalgo, the hero of Mexican independence, was captured by royalist forces and, as a priest, turned over for trial by ecclesiastical authorities. The fact that among the charges against this revolutionary Catholic cleric was that of being a *judai-zante* revealed that like moro, the terms "Jew" and "converso" had also taken on metaphorical meanings as the existential "other" — the enemy of Catholic Spain and Portugal and of the established order. By that time, however, conversos' contested place in society and the challenge of their hybridity to the social order had already become less of a concern than that of the far greater plebian mass of people of mixed ethnic origins, or what one viceroy of New Spain called the "monster of many species that are the inferior castes."[130]

{ 3 }

Mestizos

"A Monster of . . . Many Species"

The monarchs of both Spain and Portugal had justified their imperial ambitions by the dream of a universal Church that would include all the peoples of the world. By the mid-sixteenth century, these empires now included many peoples who were culturally and phenotypically different, and because of their dissimilarities from Spanish or Portuguese cultural norms and practices were often considered lesser — barbaric, savage, or lacking in reason. In the Americas, exclusionary policies of immigration, missionary campaigns of conversion, and the extirpation of Native American and African religious practices and beliefs all sought to maintain the religious unity of these empires. But even after conversion, the non-European inhabitants — the Native Americans and Africans brought as slaves and their progeny — were still often treated with a distain that seem to repudiate the goals of Christian unity. Juan Plata, a cleric in a convent in the city of Puebla, New Spain, who was accused in 1593 of being an *alumbrado* (someone who practiced a mystical Christian heresy), lifted his voice to denounce the social divisions and hostilities that he witnessed daily as a negation of the dream of a universal Christian monarchy and of his hope that Mexico would become a "New Jerusalem." His jeremiad was a warning in apocalyptic terms:

> After the East and West Indies and Guinea were discovered, the nations have become mixed, and they have not conformed or united with each other as [the prophet] Daniel had called for, as can be seen because they call each other "Indian dog,"

"mulatto dog," "mestizo dog," and so they remain in discord among themselves, and we await that which must come.[1]

It was that cultural and biological "mixture" of peoples, or mestizaje, and the divisions and animosities it created that preoccupied Plata, but he was not alone.

Belief and Blood

Sexual and cultural contact and the creation of new categories of peoples in the Americas, as well as a new social order, drove the shift from distinctions based on religion to a those seemingly based on color or phenotype — or what many have argued should be called "race." Over time, racial taxonomies appeared, but the process of mestizaje was never simply a biological one. Social and historical circumstances always set the parameters of the categories of peoples and their changing definitions over time. Who and what was a mestizo, Spaniard, Indian, or pardo and what these categories implied were never fixed in time or place but were unstable designations. That fluidity eventually became a matter of both considerable confusion and increasing concern in the eighteenth century, as the boundaries of religious limpieza de sangre were augmented, transformed, and to some extent replaced by the new terminology of what came to be known in Spanish America as the *sociedad de castas*, a social hierarchy seemingly based on color and descent. Religious purity and the maintenance of phenotypical boundaries may not seem at first glance to be necessarily related, but in a society of orders or estates in which social categories such as knights and commoners or religious differences between Muslims, Jews, and Christians were viewed to be intrinsic and unchanging, individuals or groups that crossed those boundaries were viewed as dangerous and disruptive to the harmony of established order. The experience of Spain and Portugal provided a model. Despite enthusiastic acceptance of the early converts from Judaism in the fifteenth century and subsequent theological disagreement about limitations on their integration into Christian society, converts easily fell into the category of boundary crossers. In effect, a converso or Morisco was perceived as a hybrid and hence was unsettling to a social and juridical system based on fixed categories. Pluralism and indeterminate or "fuzzy" categories of belief challenged the idea of religious or ethnic purity in Spain and Portugal, just as mestizos presented a parallel challenge to the supposed hierarchical divisions of the castas.[2]

The castas' labels of racial taxonomy were not in themselves necessarily meaningful markers of identity—that is, ways in which people defined themselves or perceived their collective interests. Ethnic and color categories that were either applied to people by the state or local indigenous and Hispanic elites or employed for self-identification resulted from a variety of practical considerations, such as responsibility for taxes or military service, access to resources, required labor service, and desire for social mobility. They did not necessarily reflect identities. The designations and labels affixed to people were regionally and temporally variable, and historically specific. In fact, much colonial legislation was an unsuccessful attempt to impose some stability on the taxonomy, maintain order in society, and force a convergence between identities and what became the racial categories used in civil and ecclesiastical records. The casta system developed over time, but it always presented an establishment view of society that gave order to the privileges, concessions, and exclusions of traditional rule.[3] The people that it defined and labeled did not necessarily accept its terms but could not totally ignore them.

The process of conquest and European colonization created a myriad of new human categories and purported affiliations, of which sexual or reproductive miscegenation (the "mixing of blood") was only one of many types of cultural and physical contacts. African or Native American wet nurses suckled children born to Spanish mothers, Europeans sometimes "went native," Indian chieftains sought Spanish coats of arms, Indian commoners often dressed like Spaniards or mestizos to avoid paying tribute, and mestizos could claim to be Indians and avoid the jurisdiction of the Inquisition. In short, there were cultural *passeurs* of many kinds. The process of conquest was probably the most transformative force in creating new categories. Spaniards had defined and labeled indigenous peoples by their hostility (*caribes*) or their amity as allies (*guatiao*) or by their political organization, labeling and to some extent transforming them into tribes or kingdoms. Among indigenous societies, the processes of fission, migration, fusion, and recombination—all of which had preceded the Europeans' arrival—probably intensified thereafter. All sorts of new statuses and definitions were created. The Caribbean conquest alone produced caciques (chieftains), *naborías* (dependents who were virtually but not really slaves), and *allegados* (Indians no longer living in their original villages). Similar processes were repeated elsewhere, sometimes using the Caribbean vocabulary but often applying other regional terminologies. Whole new colonial categories like Indian, Creole, and mestizo emerged, and even a term like "Spaniard"—while lexically unchanged—acquired a different semantic significance as it came to mean anyone accepted as a member of the conquering class who possessed certain cultural characteristics.[4]

The Iberian empires had not insisted on religious and cultural homogeneity all at once. Prior to 1540, the Portuguese in Goa had permitted the residence of non-Catholics and had not restricted marriages with them. In the Caribbean, there were even some Spanish attempts to promote intermarriages, and Spain eventually created and maintained the concept of the coexistence of two separate spheres: the republic of the Spaniards and the republic of the Indians, each of which was to have its own hierarchies and differing legal responsibilities and laws.

During the first decades after 1492 in the Spanish American conquests, however, there was a relative absence of references to the children resulting from Spanish-Indian sexual relations—that is, mestizos. This was surely not because they did not exist. All the early chroniclers make abundantly clear that there was no lack of sexual contact, and in 1501 the crown ordered Christians who had taken the wives and daughters of Indians to return them.[5] The rapes, concubinage, and formalized unions surely produced a generation of children of mixed origins, but there are remarkably few references to them in the surviving documents. That absence was a matter not of reproduction, but of definition.

Legislation and reports of the first decades of contact had spoken in terms of contact between Christians and Indians, but the term "mestizo" appears in the documentation as early as the 1520s. However, "mestizo" was not like other descriptive terms determined by appearance (such as *blanco* or *negro*), perhaps suggesting the influence of astrology, food, the humors of the body, or climate on an individual's origins, color, or physical form. Instead, it was a term suggesting a person's casta or breed, a result of blood and lineage defined by degrees of purity. In effect, the term "mestizo" was a negation of fixed social, ethnic, or racial categories like Spaniard or Indian. It was a term emptied of its phenotypical significance that over time became a racial designation. "Casta" originally was a term that implied lineage, as we might speak in English about the breed of a thoroughbred horse, so the idea of a mixed-race casta was an inherent contradiction and, as such, a challenge to the system as a whole. Over time the term came to be associated with degradation and a taxonomic confusion that called for an imposed order. Like the concept of limpieza de sangre, the colonial casta categories sought to create and maintain bounded social groupings, like orders or estates, but the groupings were continuously subverted by a dynamic process of social class formation in which people who were of mixed origin or involved in ethnic "passing" played an increasingly important role.[6]

To be sure, mestizo was an invented category, but so too of course were Indian, Creole, and even Spaniard. Two interwoven processes were at work. The first was ethnogenesis: the creation of new peoples and new kinds of peoples, with mestizaje being one of a number of ways in which this took place.[7] The second was a process of social definition and labeling according to the Iberian juridical corporative hierarchies that harked back to a medieval society based on estates or orders, but that in the American colonial world added differentiations based on occupation, color, origins, rank, and status — characteristics that were often subsumed in the term *calidad* (quality). How the combination of these characteristics was perceived was not a product of biology or race alone, but rather a socially determined act.[8] As the historian Verena Stolcke aptly observed, "mestizos are not born, they are created."[9]

Mestizos: Changing Status and Changing Contexts

The existence and relative status of mestizos had a history. The early conquest and settlement of the Caribbean provides an example, but one that was repeated with regional variations across the Americas. At first clerics and administrators ideologically deplored sexual license and violence during the conquest and at times urged formal unions between Spanish men with Indian women to avoid concubinage and other moral lapses. Spaniards also wed Native American women to obtain economic and social advantages. Such marriages were projected in the Laws of Burgos (1512) and expressly permitted by a royal order in 1514. In his instructions to the first Jeronymite missionaries on Española, Cardinal Francisco Ximenes de Cisneros promoted marriages between Spaniards and the daughters of Indian caciques so that in a generation all the chieftainships would be held by Spaniards.[10] That not only revealed the cardinal's political goals but also disclosed an assumption that the children of such unions would be accepted as Spaniards.[11] As colonization progressed, Spanish authorities, under pressure from missionaries, increasingly criticized unrestrained sexual exploitation and concubinage and — as the Portuguese were to do in their Indian Ocean colonies — encouraged settlement by married men (casados), even if those unions were with Indian women.[12] Later in Mexico and Peru there were many unions with the women of the preconquest indigenous ruling class that produced children who, especially if legitimate, passed easily into Spanish society and sometimes claimed noble status based not only on the exploits of their fathers, but also on the lineage of their mothers. These unions were the result of both European and indigenous strategies to seek advantages, and the eminence or class of brides and grooms was as important as their ethnicities.[13] Their children, especially their daughters, usually found a privileged path in either Iberian or Indian society. Gender mattered, and by the 1550s throughout the Indies, as the number of mestizos grew, the preference for women of mixed origin rather than Indian women as marriage partners became clear, although unions with an Inca noble woman or daughter of a cacique could still bring economic and status benefits.[14]

The earliest generation of mestizos (first in the Caribbean and then elsewhere) produced by some legal and many illegal unions were not so much a new category of people as a "new kind of people" not contained within the usual social definitions of caste or lineage and thus in an ambivalent position in terms of status.[15] Their mixed cultural background often made them valuable to the colonizing society. Throughout the empires, they often used their bicultural position to advantage—especially in the early stages of settlement when their numbers were small and their talents in short supply, even though their status and lineage remained undefined. However, their cultural position was not entirely dependent on the dominant Hispanic colonial regime. The relationship of mestizos to their maternal family, clan, or kinship units and their dependency on their mother's lineage or rank as well as on their father's patronage, status, and resources all determined their position. As long as there was an indigenous society as a referent—such as Taino, Inca, Nahua, Chibcha, and Tupinambá—mestizos had some choice in their interests, identity, and attachments. In that sense, the early Caribbean was something of an anomaly. There, especially in the Greater Antilles, the precipitous collapse of the indigenous population essentially left the mestizos within a generation or two without a function as cultural intermediaries and with an existence only in relation to Hispanic society or with the growing number of Africans brought in to meet the demands of labor. Thus, the mestizos' options of identity or of definition were limited. Mestizos could become Spaniards or a neoteric indigenous population (*gente de la tierra*), but they could not (for long) become Indians. That, as we will see, was not the case elsewhere in the empires.

Mestizos could play key roles as intermediaries between Hispanic and indigenous societies under certain conditions. They were readily accepted into Hispanic society if they were legitimate and

1. SANTIAGO MATAMOROS

Santiago (St. James) the Moor-slayer, who supposedly appeared in a 9th-century battle against the Muslim invasion of the Iberian peninsula, became the patron saint of Spain in the 17th century. He represented a militant Catholicism, and was a spiritual symbol particularly favored by the conquistadores *for obvious reasons.*

Unknown Cuzco School artist, Cuzco, Peru, circa 1745–1755
Reproduced courtesy of the New Orleans Museum of Art

2. SANTIAGO MATAINDIOS

*The transformation of Santiago into a popular saint in the Spanish colonies underlined
the continuities between the reconquest of Spain and the conquest in America as well as the
perceived equivalencies between the* moros *and the native peoples of America. Curiously,
Santiago as a victorious warrior also became a popular saint among Indians as well.*
Artist unknown, first half of the 19th century
Iglesia de Pujiura, Cusco, Peru
Courtesy of the Archbishop of Cusco, Peru

3. JUEGO DE CANAS

*A popular enacted equestrian combat in Christian Spain and its empire in which
competing sides dressed as Christians and Muslims engaged in noble combat. The
event depicted here was observed in Toledo, Spain, when Kling Carlos I passed
through with his court after the conquest of Tunis in 1535.*
Jan Cornelisz Vermeyen, 1538
Private collection

4. DESECRATION OF THE CRUCIFIX

The episode of the Cristo de Paciencia *in 1629 in which a group of Portuguese*
conversos *supposedly whipped a crucifix became an important incident in the
Inquisition's campaign to maintain exclusionary policies. In this painting by Francisco
Camilo, the Jews portrayed in this sacrilege are undistinguished in their attire or
appearance, and thus dangerous because they are not easily identifiable.*

Francisco Camilo (1615–1673)
Courtesy of the Museo del Prado, Madrid

8.
De Eſpañol, y Torna atras; Tente en el ayre.

5. DE ESPAÑOL E ÍNDIA, NACE MESTIZO

Casta paintings represented the theoretical categories of persons of mixed race resulting
from sexual contact between people of different racial categories. Although many sets of
these images were produced, especially in Mexico, it remains unclear who was the intended
audience and market, or if the 16 or so categories of race usually included in the sets had
any real social utility outside of the paintings.
Miguel Cabrera (1695–1768), circa 1763
Private collection

even more so if they were women, since European women were still in short supply. Their usefulness as go-betweens often depended on their linguistic abilities. In 1578, for example, of the six interpreters employed by the audiencia of Mexico, five were mestizos.[16] But their bicultural position and command of languages and knowledge of both cultures also made them potentially dangerous and therefore distrusted. The viceroyalty of Peru, where there were mestizo rebellions in Cuzco (1567) and Quito (1583), provides many references to these fears, but similar comments could be found across the Spanish Indies and in Portuguese Brazil.[17] The Count of Neiva (viceroy of Peru in 1561–64) realized that many of the first generation of mestizos were the children of conquistadors and Inca noble women, but he believed that they were naturally inclined to evil (*mala inclinación*).[18] This perception became generalized. A royal order sent to Peru in 1568 called mestizos "bad intentioned" and ordered that they should be prohibited from carrying arms, since "some are better *arcabuceros* [gunners, or soldiers skilled in the use of the harquebus] than the Spaniards."[19] Their liminal status and origins made them dangerous, since as sons of conquistadors, they were anxious to receive the rewards due their fathers, but at the same time, royal officials feared that they would join with their mothers' families to restore the Inca kingdom.[20] The Jesuit José de Acosta warned that mestizos and native peoples were "all of one caste and relatives, and they understand each other because they were raised together."[21] Their potential to grow in numbers and their tendency to disrupt the order of colonial society made them a constant threat, both military and moral. Viceroy Francisco de Toledo had warned in 1570 that there were many of them, and if they joined the Indians in rebellion, the danger was great since they were Hispanized and "skilled in the use of horses and arms."[22] A rector of the Jesuit college of Cuzco believed that mestizos who joined the Indians in their drunkenness and witchcraft could not be trusted. As he put it, they rarely heard mass or knew about the law of God, and they certainly did not follow it even if they did.[23] Eventually the Jesuits and other religious orders prohibited or restricted mestizos' admission, and the Church in general limited mestizo vocations, often pointing to their illegitimate birth as the principal reason for their exclusion from the clergy.[24]

The word "mestizo" had appeared in the Caribbean as early as the 1520s, but it was rarely used—which is surprisingly similar to the case in Peru, Ecuador, and Paraguay, where less pejorative terms like *genízaro* or *montanés* (mountaineer) were also preferred at first.[25] In Puerto Rico there were probably more mestizos than Spaniards by the seventeenth century. Nevertheless, in his comments about the island's population, the bishop presiding over the synod of San Juan in 1645 made no mention of the mestizos. What seems to be at stake here is not the definition of mestizo but that of Spaniard. Mestizos, especially if born from a legitimate union and living according to colonial norms, were being accepted as Spaniards—a term no longer being applied to a person's place of origin alone but having been expanded to indicate status and level of acceptance based on cultural attributes and probably to some extent on appearance or phenotype.

We get a clue to why mestizos were being accepted in a statement that was part of the 1514 assignment of Indian laborers on Española. Apparently, some Spaniards had previously appropriated the children of mixed unions as laborers. The representatives of the king prohibited this, and their precise language is revealing:

> It is said that if some sons and daughters of Christians are registered in the division of laborers (*repartimiento*), it being said that they are children of women, natives of the island, and that they have been assigned to one person or another, that assignment (*encomienda*) is voided, and that the children of Christians be free of all subjugation and servitude, and that their parents or relatives do with them, whatever they desire.[26]

In these first decades of contact the Indian-white offspring were defined as "children of Christians" rather than as mestizos or some other category based on phenotype or ethnicity. Genealogy had overridden nurture, and in a sense, Spanish blood had trumped milk for this first generation. The fact that they were Christians by birth (*cristianos por natura*) and not converts defined them. There may be a hint here, at the outset of empire, that being born of a Christian parent was a defining characteristic and a clear extension of a system of social discrimination based on religion as the basis of limpieza de sangre that had developed in Iberia. It would seem that white Spanish (assumed to be Old Christian) blood was strong enough to overcome the deficiencies of other, usually darker, nations. And this concept would gain importance in the late eighteenth century as the *sistema de castas*, with its emphasis on color, developed more fully.

The term "mestizo" and perhaps the perception of it began to change slowly. A proposal of 1533 to populate Española by bringing together colonists from Spain with Negroes and mestizos showed that the category existed, and judging by its equivalency with persons of African descent, it already had pejorative associations. At a time when some mestizos had joined the Taino resistance to Spanish control of Española, Francisco de Barrionuevo wrote to King Carlos I that there were many mestizos and that they were "naturally bellicose, mendacious, and friends to every evil." He suggested that they be sent to Spain when very young and kept there until their temperament could be assured, because otherwise they could cause a rebellion of "blacks and natives."[27] Of course, expulsion or removal was a strategy that had already been used with the Jews and Muslims and was later to be applied to the Moriscos, but unlike the Moriscos (who were also ostensibly Christians), the policy applied to mestizos was only to be temporary—apparently because their loyalty to the Church was not in question.

In the Caribbean the mestizos disappeared into other categories, and as the demography of the islands changed and the importation of African slaves significantly increased, the composition of the population altered—and so did the perception of mestizaje and the status of persons of mixed origin. Father Abbad y Lasierra, a visitor to Puerto Rico in the late eighteenth century, stated that sexual relations between mestizos and other nations or categories such as *zambos* (persons of African and Native American parentage), mulattoes, and blacks were so frequent and intertwined that everyone on that island had become a pardo, and even the whites were not really white. Mestizo in the Caribbean came to mean not just a mixture of Spaniards and Indians but any mixed origins, and the term was often employed as a self-identifier as a way to avoid being a mulatto, a descriptor that carried a lower status. In fact, to escape the stigma of any of the categories of mixture, free people in the islands began to refer to themselves simply as criollos (creoles) or native born, a term that elsewhere in Spanish America came to mean a white person born in America. This was a regional response to the disadvantages posed by racial mixture, a way to lighten the burdens of genealogy in a society built on the myth of fixed social categories with inherent moral, religious, and cultural characteristics.

Mestizos were not only missing in the Caribbean, but they were also disappearing in other places.[28] An early Portuguese observer in Brazil complained that the *mestiços* (Portuguese for mestizo) often shed their red skins like snakes and put on the airs of gentlemen.[29] In the Spanish colonies the absorption of mestizos into the social world of Indians or into the Spanish population has been well documented in New Granada, Peru, and Ecuador. In frontier areas like Chile, Paraguay, the Brazilian Amazonian region, and northern New Spain, they continued to play an important if still ambivalent role throughout much of the colonial era. But in Peru, Central Mexico, and coastal Brazil, the heavily populated hearts of the empires, the status of the majority of mestizos began to decline as the colonial regimes took shape. The first generations of mestizos — born as they were of rape, casual, or consensual unions — and those lacking any distinction because of their mother's rank or the recognition or support of their fathers tended to become part of Indian society or to drift to the geographical and social margins of the colonial world. They were a concern. A collection of laws for Spanish America made at the end of the seventeenth century listed four issued between 1533 and 1569 dealing with vagabondage and specifically mentioning that mestizos were uncontrolled and shiftless (*anden perdidos*), and that they should be taught some trade or placed in homes where they would learn good habits.[30] Local administrators in the Spanish Indies from Peru to Guatemala also expressed similar concerns.[31] A 1565 law (*cédula*) in Guatemala noted that the children of Spaniards and Indian women had been abandoned and should be removed from Indian communities and taken to live in Spanish cities.[32] A tentative 1558 project to create mestizo towns parallel to the resettlement of Indians in towns (*reducciones*) was never carried out, but if it had been, the term "mestizo" might have rapidly become a separate ethnicity and even an identity.[33] Instead, the mestizos' position in society remained liminal, contradictory, and ambiguous. Those who did succeed in Hispanic society often assumed the attitudes of the conquerors — or at least that was the complaint of the Native American intelligentsia and leadership. Those elites resented mestizo competition for chieftainships or positions in municipal government, and chroniclers like Guaman Poma in Peru or Domingo Chimalpahin of Chalco in New Spain condemned the mestizos who rejected their Indian origins and acted like the conquerors. Chimalpahin claimed that "they do not want to acknowledge that part of the blood they have is ours, but rather imagine themselves fully Spaniards and mistreat us and deceive us the same way the Spaniards do. . . . We are all descended from Adam and Eve, although our bodies are divided into three kinds."[34]

However, in Hispanic society illegitimacy and mestizaje became closely associated, and the legitimate children of the conquistadors had no sympathy for their mestizo siblings. "Of the bastards my pen falls silent," wrote Baltasar Dorantes de Carranza in 1604. Since they were not favored by divine or civil law, nothing was owed them, and it would be a mistake to deprive legitimate heirs by giving anything to the "people of this race."[35] Juan de Solórzano Pereira, a judge and great legal scholar, reflected around 1639 on the changing attitude toward the mestizos and mulattoes and argued that those born of legitimate unions should be fully accepted, but that the majority were illegitimate because few honorable Spaniards would marry black or Indian women — and thus the offspring were born with a tendency toward "vicious customs."[36]

Hispanic society, especially in the population centers, began to exclude mestizos from any positions of authority, such as memberships on town councils, holders of *encomiendas*, positions of military command, and memberships in the more prestigious artisan guilds.[37] Like Indians, mestizos were barred from clerical careers, although some exceptions were made since Rome could find no theological objections to their ordination, and because in 1588 the Peruvian mestizos successfully petitioned the king to retract limits on their clerical vocations.[38] A few mestizos were upwardly mobile and able, despite legislation, to assume positions as caciques in Indian communities (often in spite of the objections of the state-recognized indigenous nobility) or to succeed in Hispanic society. However, the vast majority of them were increasingly pushed toward plebian occupations in the countryside and the cities. Their distinct status as the children of Spaniards began to disappear. Often separate parish registers of births or marriages for mestizos were abandoned, and like the annual tribute paid by Indians, a tax was imposed on them and mulattoes — although given their mobility, it apparently yielded very little revenue. In Brazil — where the process of settlement was slower and where in some areas like São Paulo, people of mixed origin probably constituted half the Portuguese population — the process of *mestiço* exclusion began somewhat later. In Natal, for example, in 1723 the town council tried to prevent *mestiços* and mulattoes from serving as aldermen because there were now enough whites to perform that function, and the mixed-race aldermen were untrustworthy and inferior people who had shown "their natural inclination toward perturbation and disruption of the republic."[39] At about the same time, the governor of the gold mining area of Minas Gerais complained that while "the mulattoes of all Brazil are pernicious since they are restive and rebellious, those of Minas are worse because they are rich." He warned that they would soon outnumber the whites. His solution was to import white couples as colonists and prohibit mulattoes from inheriting their fathers' property as a way of limiting mulattoes' presumption and presence.[40]

Burdens of Lineage

In Spanish America, those mestizos who were linguistically and culturally Hispanized and who might once have been incorporated into local Hispanic society and joined the ranks of the American-born whites or Creoles were by the close of the sixteenth century suffering from the discriminations and prejudice developing against all the castas. Creole competition with the peninsular-born Europeans in commerce or for offices, control of religious orders, and ecclesiastical benefices made Creoles the targets of attacks on their competence and character that lowered the status of the Creoles. The ability of some mestizos to enter Creole ranks had been an advantage to the mestizos, but while their indeterminate status and the blurring of categories had facilitated their social mobility, their liminality was a double-edged sword because in the long run it had lowered the status of the Creoles as well. As a governor of Paraguay noted in the 1590s, "in the Creoles one can put little trust, and in the mestizos, none at all."[41] While the purity of creoles was being questioned because of their associations with mestizos, more and more Indian people sought to avoid forced labor and tribute payments by leaving their natal communities and claiming to be mestizos. They dressed in shirts and trousers, wore shoes, spoke Spanish, carried swords, and had a hybrid lifestyle.[42] Caciques and royal officials complained about the loss of revenues and the absence of laborers, but neither they nor the constantly updated sumptuary legislation could keep Indians from seeking to escape their status by culturally becoming mestizos — and by doing so, they reinforced the narrative that categories of persons with any claims to honor had been diluted and the system of social hierarchy was in disarray.[43]

As the position of the descendants of European-Indian unions was changing, so was the social context in the Iberian colonies. A relatively small number of African slaves had arrived in the Caribbean in the first decades of the sixteenth century, but their numbers began to swell in the 1550s as the native populations declined as a result of warfare, disease, and social disruption and dislocation.

The development of mining, the growth of Hispanic urban centers, and commercial agriculture all created a demand for these enslaved laborers, which by 1590 was being satisfied by Portuguese contractors. By about 1640 as many as half a million African slaves had been introduced to the Spanish colonies, along with more than a quarter of a million to the urban centers and the growing sugar plantation economy of Portuguese Brazil.[44] One result of this demographic infusion was a whole new set of sexual contacts between Africans, Europeans, and Native Americans, complicating the social order and creating a new taxonomy of combinations. It amounted to the Africanization of mestizaje.[45]

Attitudes toward sub-Saharan Africans were ambiguous. Non-Muslim Africans did not bear the stigma of the traditional enmity felt toward Islam or that of deicide ascribed to Jews and their descendants. In fact, some free people of color had also legally emigrated to the Indies from Spain by claiming that they were Old Christians without religious disability. Nevertheless, the long history of African slavery in the Mediterranean world had created the widely held belief that Africans and their mulatto offspring were servile, uncivilized, lacking in honor or moral rectitude, and given to criminal behavior.[46] As Viceroy Martín Enriquez of New Spain warned in 1574, although there were many mestizos who had bad habits and questionable lives, at least they were the children of Spaniards and after five years or so, left the influence of their indigenous mothers and joined their fathers' people. However, mulattoes continued to be raised by their black mothers, and from neither them nor their fathers did they learn good habits, living instead in liberty, not cultivating the soil or learning a trade, and taking advantage of mestizos and Indians. The viceroy believed that if God and the king did not address the problem, the mulattoes would be the "perdition of this country," but notably his opinion was mostly based on their upbringing, not on their blood — in other words, their deficiency was in their nurture, not their nature.[47]

The increasing number of persons of African origins or of mixed parentage including African origins negatively influenced the status of all persons of mixed origins and the process of mixing in general. As the numbers of what came to be called castas grew and the imaginary lines separating the categories of people in the colonies broke down, the social standing of all Americans was affected. People who seemed to live outside or on the margins of the theoretical boundaries of the republic of the Spaniards or the republic of the Indians—the two supposedly parallel social hierarchies into which the society of Spanish America had been theoretically divided—destabilized the social order. Spanish administrators viewed Indians who left their natural lords or became Hispanized or urbanized, mestizos, mulattoes, and freed slaves as potential disrupters of public order, lazy, drunk, lascivious, vagabonds naturally inclined to criminality, a plague in the Spanish cities, and corrupters of Indian communities.[48] We can see this attitude clearly in a warning around 1654 from Bartolomé de Góngora in his guide for magistrates of Indian towns in New Spain. According to him, "bad mestizos, blacks, and mulattoes are a casta without a king, but free [unrestrained], very free . . . and more or less the three types are all the same."[49] While Góngora admitted that there might be exceptions, and even a few blacks as good as any white person, he thought that they were rare.[50] He wrote of one exception that proved the rule. A prominent churchman in Mexico City stopped his coach when he saw a well-dressed, elderly, white-haired mulatto. The priest called him over and said:

In what I have read there is no mention of a mulatto saint nor that mulattoes could even be one. Go with God, for I canonize you, because a mulatto that seems honorable, and has lived to have so much white hair, and has not been either hung or knifed must be a saint.[51]

Such attitudes would have been shared by the most governmental and lettered elites.[52]

Under any circumstances, conversos and Moriscos, real or imagined, would have been a minuscule minority in the Iberian Americas and would clearly remain so. The growing population of Creoles and people of mixed origin was another matter altogether. The realization of that demographic reality took place more or less as the concept of limpieza de sangre (already present in the colonial world as a marker of religious and social status) was redeployed and increasingly applied to people of mixed origin or to categories like free blacks (*negros libres*) whose members were—despite a few exceptions—considered to be without honor or purity and often associated with criminality.

Spanish administrators believed that by association and infection, Creoles of Spanish parentage were tainted by this multiethnic contact. Of course, such prejudices against the Creoles could not be based only on biological genealogy. Thus, the old arguments, some originating with Aristotle, about the effects of food and climate; Hippocratic and Galenic ideas about the imbalance of the bodily humors; and belief in the importance of birthplace and astrology were all employed to suggest the deficiencies of the American born.[53] So too were child-rearing practices, as the letter of Viceroy Enríquez suggested. Creoles as white and the children of Spanish parents might be genetically Europeans, but by the seventeenth century various observers—such as a Spanish inquisitor in Mexico, the Portuguese Jesuit Antonio Vieira, and Guaman Poma de Ayala, an indigenous Peruvian chronicler—believed that Creoles' capacities were diminished, or noted that because Creoles were suckled by Indian or black wet nurses, they had inherited those women's characteristics and impurities.[54] This was an opinion that undercut lineage's role as the principal determinant of status and that reinforced the idea of inferiority of nonwhites.[55] Concerns about the dangerous and debilitating effects of living in America could even penetrate the psyche and raise the anxiety level of peninsular-born Spaniards residing in the Indies, as we learn from the dreams of Diego Martínez de Arce, a merchant from Burgos living in Mexico City who in 1699 reported himself to the Inquisition. His oneiric notebooks revealed that he was concerned that his skin was getting darker and that he was attracted to the mulatto women who surrounded him on the streets, even though he was critical of men who had relations with them.[56]

Such insecurities and the negative views of American stars, climate, soils, food, and peoples in the critical writings of peninsular natural historians and their competitors led to an Indianization of the Creoles — a campaign to lower their status vis-à-vis their peninsular opponents. Those opponents argued that the American born were incapable for a variety of reasons: having deficiencies of blood, since many Creoles were biologically mestizos or were really Indians culturally passing as mestizos; living under the wrong stars, even if born of European parents; having humors that had become unbalanced by the poor foods of America; or, worst of all, having been fed the milk of people who were deficient in terms of religious background or moral and intellectual capacities.[57]

While the Creoles had at times sought to use their close association with Indians or people of mixed origin to argue that they were the best prepared to govern the colonies, the attempt to lower their status and blur the distinctions between them and the Indian, African, and mixed-race populations made them particularly sensitive to those distinctions and anxious to reinforce the separation between themselves and the castas. That sensitivity led to American elites' continuous fixation on or obsession about acquiring the status, markers, and accoutrements of European nobility. These included titles, coats of arms, *mayorazgos* (entailed estates), memberships in the military orders of knighthood and elite confraternities, municipal positions, judicial offices, and positions as *familiares* of the Inquisition. All of these distinctions required limpeza de sangre examination or testimonials, and all of them could be employed to establish claims to a "clean" lineage that was the gateway to noble status.[58] It is around these issues of nobility, religious purity, status, and class that the ties between limpieza de sangre and what emerged in America as an ordering by phenotype — the *sociedad de castas* — came together in the eighteenth century.

Honor, Nobility, and Blood

The Iberian societies transferred to the Americas were based on the corporative medieval juridical model of three orders or estates — clergy (*oradores*), nobles (*defensores*), and commoners (*labradores*), each of which had defined privileges, functions, and responsibilities to the body politic.[59] There were many gradations and subranks in these estates, and differences in income, profession, or functions created those divisions that would later be called classes.[60] The core of this juridical structure was the division between the mass of commoners and the nobility—whose members were, because of their function to defend society by arms, exempted from taxes; privileged before the law; entitled to hold positions of authority; and assumed to inherently possess all the honorable characteristics such as bravery, fidelity, and religious purity that distinguished them from the masses. Although these orders or estates were conceived of as corporative and relatively closed units, by service (usually military, administrative, or financial) to the ruler, it was possible to rise into the ranks of the nobility, and flaws in background, occupation, or lineage could be overlooked. The ideal existence of the nobility—living on one's rents without recourse to manual labor or shop keeping and maintaining an aristocratic lifestyle supported by retainers, servants, peasants, or slaves—permeated society and operated as a goal that many people hoped to attain. Titles of nobility in Spanish America were relatively few, but many persons could at least hope to achieve the rank of hidalgo and the privileges, exemptions, and honors that went with it.[61]

The concept of religious fidelity or purity had developed in relationship to this juridical vision of society and with the drive for religious unity that had emerged in medieval Iberia. At its origins in the mid-fifteenth century, the restrictions based on limpieza de sangre defined by a Christian ancestry never tainted by a blood or marital relation with Jews, Muslims, or heretics had been created specifically to discriminate against formerly Jewish converts.[62] While these regulations had never become general royal laws or Church policies, they were broadly adopted by cathedral chapters, other religious institutions, guilds, universities, and military orders.[63] However, we should recognize that despite their anticonverso origin, these restrictions also applied to any other category of people who, because of their status or character, could also be assumed to lack honor. Thus, persons of plebian origins and anyone of illegitimate birth or descended from a lineage with a vile occupation were also considered to be of defective blood. By the late sixteenth century, it was common to see in institutional regulations calling for purity of blood language that excluded anyone of illegitimate birth; a mechanic occupation; or a lineage that included Moors, Jews, converted persons, mulattoes, or Negros—the last two categories included because the first implied illegitimacy and both implied servile occupation or slavery. Noticeable here is the fact that what the restrictions assessed was not only fidelity to the Church but the inherited dishonorable characteristics of *mala sangre* that would inevitably lead to disloyalty, betrayal, and apostasy. We should also note that this expansion of restrictions beyond religion to categories like black and mulatto that we call racial definitions took place as the conquest and settlement of the Indies was achieved. Thist raises the possibility that instead of predetermining the racial components of the social system of the Americas, limpieza de sangre restrictions were strengthened and augmented by that overseas experience—thus inverting, or at least complicating, the assumed genealogy between racial ideology and empire. In addition, if indeed race is a concept that is socially constructed, then it is possible to see how in the New World colonies, any association with individuals of mixed origins—especially those of African descent, most of whom were assumed to have the disadvantages of illegitimacy, manual labor, slavery, or plebian status—contributed to the creation of a racially based discourse of inherited negative character traits.

Finally, as Jean-Frédéric Schaub has reminded us, politics was usually involved in the creation and manipulation of racial and other social categories, and this can be seen both in the creation and application of limpieza de sangre statutes in Spain and in the formation and attempted imposition of social divisions and hierarchies in the Iberian colonial societies.[64] Noble status provides a good example of political manipulation of social status. In the conquest of the Indies in the sixteenth century the promise of nobility had been dangled before many Spaniards to induce them to serve, but kings were reluctant to create a new class of nobles with potential demands and interests in opposition to those of the crown. In a similar fashion, although the native chiefs had been viewed by Spanish monarchs as necessary allies and intermediaries with the indigenous populations during the conquest, and were thus awarded the accoutrements and privileges of nobility, their status was always precarious and subject to political considerations. At various moments of crisis—such as during the debate over the *encomienda* in the 1560s or following the Tupac Amaru rebellions of the 1780s, when the indigenous nobility of Peru were stripped of the the right to bear arms, ride horses, and make any use of the symbols of Inca lordship—the colonial regime reminded the indigenous nobility that their status was fragile and contingent on political considerations.[65] They may have been nobles, but they were still Indians.

The purity laws from their beginning had met with stiff objections, on both theological and practical grounds. Creating divisions within the Christian community seemed to contradict St. Paul's exhortation to remove the differences between Greeks and Jews in the early Church. In defense of conversos, some theologians asked how the lineage of Christ and his mother could seriously be held to be dishonorable, while others argued that whatever Jewish honor had been obscured by deicide could be restored by baptism. Many reasoned that a Christian theology of exclusion was flawed, and furthermore that the practical result would upset the existing order of society. Even members of the Inquisition argued in 1626 that so many noble families over the centuries had married conversos that to now exclude their descendants would only rob the country of its brightest and most distinguished members, as well as elevating and inflating the pretensions of Old Christians commoners who often were lacking in talents and accomplishments.[66] The whole system of testimony about and proofs of limpieza had become so marked by forgery, graft, and corruption and its use to attack rivals and settle scores that it had weakened the moral state of the country. In any case, the purity restrictions that were imposed on all members of a tainted lineage ad infinitum were unfair and contrary to civil law. Despite such objections, however, the limpieza de sangre restrictions continued and were tacitly supported by the crown and introduced into the New World.[67]

In the New World colonies, of course, the restrictions were applied in theory to conversos and Moriscos (with the exceptions and evasions I have mentioned above), but in the Americas there was another problem. Native people, Africans, and their descendants had also become New Christians. Were they too to be excluded? The lawyers, missionaries, humanists, and theologians took up the issue. There were regional differences. In some places like Yucatán, where idolatry seemed to make a comeback, it took a century to settle the debate. The winning imperial argument was that of Solórzano Pereira, who argued that Indians might be New Christians, but unlike the Jews and Muslims, they had previously lived only under natural law — not another real religion — so they should be treated differently.[68] Moreover, by the seventeenth century, most Indian families had been Christians for at least three generations, so the ad infinitum stain also no longer applied to them. In fact, they were entitled to call themselves Old Christians and enjoy the privileges attached to that status.[69] Moreover, the Spanish crown recognized the preconquest existence and validity of indigenous nobilities that were also free of semitic impurities.[70] The native lords and their descendants quickly learned how to use their claims to nobility and thus to blood purity to reinforce their status and advance their interests.[71] When Carlos II decreed at the end of the seventeenth century that Indians were entitled to claim both purity of blood and if qualified, nobility as well, official recognition basically concluded the debate, although attitudes in America did not necessarily follow suit.[72]

Somewhat similar recognition of non-European social hierarchies was also made in the case of non-Islamic Africans — for example, in the Christianized Kongo kingdom. Color or ethnicity by itself did not necessarily preclude blood purity or honor, although there were always individuals (including Jesuit missionaries and royal officials) who held Africans and blacks in general in low esteem, whatever their claims to nobility.[73]

Such negative attitudes surely increased over time, as contacts with Africa increasingly turned toward the slave trade. And since any association with slavery implied a genealogical stain, almost anyone with an African in the family tree who wished to establish his credentials as pure thus required royal dispensation. Nevertheless, these exceptions (like *composiciones* [state contracts] and other methods of dispensation) and complications demonstrate that despite obvious similarities with later forms and functions of modern racism, the Iberian social hierarchy was based on a distinct set of principles that drew on medieval precedents, assumptions, and experiences using not only phenotype, ethnicity, and color but also religion, lineage, legitimacy, occupation and culture.

The historian María Elena Martínez has noted that the ruling of Carlos II at the end of the seventeenth century recognizing the religious purity of Native Americans should be contextualized within the demographic recovery of the indigenous population of the Americas, the presence of many African and Afro-American persons as a result of the slave trade, and the growing presence of large populations of mixed origins. All of this caused the population with European origins to become more protective of its status and increasingly insistent on its definition according to religious purity and by phenotype or blood. Cultural elements like cuisine, dress, habits, and language still had a role in defining status, but ultimately lineage had become the dominant feature in at least the official definition of social position. Still, an inconsistency or contradiction remained, because although genealogical descent was supposedly a fixed or permanent characteristic, status and color or casta definitions were mutable and depended on context, perceptions, regional variations, and many other factors.[74]

There are two elements here that I believe need further attention. By the late sixteenth century, limpieza de sangre had become as much about illegitimacy, non-noble origins, and ignoble or "mechanic" occupations as it was about religion. Hidalgo status had always been scarce in the Iberian American colonies, as a reward often promised but seldom granted. Less than 2 percent of the men who had participated in the conquest were of hidalgo rank, and except for viceroys, almost none of Castile's titled nobility were involved. In the whole sixteenth century only two *títulos de Castilla* were awarded in Spanish America: one to Hernán Cortés (Marques del Valle de Oaxaca) and the other to Francisco Pizarro (Marques de la Conquista). The first three decades of the next century saw only three titles created in Peru, one of which was awarded to an Inca noblewoman. And for the whole century, even when the crown needed money, and was willing to "negotiate" rewards, only 31 were created in Peru, while in Spain over 380 such grants were made.[75] Grants of knighthood were more common, but even with them, demand and hopes always ran far ahead of realization.[76] In Brazil, the situation was even more restrictive. Portugal never created any noble title in Brazil, and its awards in the military orders began to grow only after the wars against the Dutch in the mid-seventeenth century, when it needed to attract more men to arms.[77]

All of this indicated the reluctance of the crowns of Spain and Portugal to see the development of a colonial nobility in command of independent resources. The well-studied efforts of the crown to recover the grants of *encomienda* from the conquistadors is the best evidence of this struggle. The American elites were powerful but lacked the titles — and often the entailed estates and other privileges and symbols — of nobility. They had good reason to expect better. After all, they had won the new lands by force of arms, the traditional road to reward and hidalgo status, and Iberia had a long history of employing commoners as knights. In fact, the early orders of chivalry had been created in the fourteenth century by non-noble urban knights involved in the reconquest of Spain.[78] Frustrated individuals in Spanish America sought noble status in a variety of ways, by purchase, providing military or bureaucratic services, and membership in prestigious religious confraternities. Marriage alliances also provided opportunities for social advancement. Spanish colonists understood that marriage with high-born Inca or Nahua women was one way to acquire their properties, as well as to establish a lineal claim to their own noble status. Indigenous elites whose purity and nobility had been recognized by the Spanish crown to secure their loyalty also sought the advantages of these unions with

Spaniards to reinforce their own status. Of course, there were regional differences in these patterns, especially among peoples who had no preconquest tradition of social hierarchy. But even in Brazil, eighteenth-century genealogists later explained away the presence of Indians in the family tree of some of the leading families by claiming that the original union had been with Indian princesses.

In many regions as an elite of landowners, large-scale merchants, and miners developed, the incongruence between their power and wealth and their non-noble status increased. Their pretensions grew, "as if the noblest blood of the court in Madrid ran through their veins," said Thomas Gage, an English traveler to Chiapas, while a royal councilor observed about the early Spanish conquerors and settlers that "these people are naturally inclined to all sorts of honors."[79] A 1675 project to satisfy the demand by creating 150 new *títulos de Castilla* with prices set for each rank of nobility was discussed in Council of the Indies but then dropped.[80] In many municipalities in Castile, registers (*padrón del estado*) had been kept to list hidalgos and record the awards and distinctions of nobility, but similar registers were not in use in New Spain until 1700. Spanish immigrants, Creoles, and anyone with some claim to European origins sensitive to a lack of royal recognition and unconstrained by a lack of oversight responded by inventing their own coats of arms, claiming the honorific title of don for themselves, filling municipal offices that conveyed a certain kind of noble status (in Brazil, municipal councilors were considered *nobreza da terra* [members of a local nobility]), and by frantically seeking the status and symbols that would ensure their privileges and mark them off from the rest of the population.[81] These symbols and rewards included not just the limited number of noble titles, but also memberships in the orders of knighthood, the privilege of entail (*mayorazgo*), municipal offices, military ranks, and grants of nobility (*hidalguía*). Recognition of limpieza de sangre facilitated access to these honors, so securing a position as an assistant and informer (*familiar*) of the Inquisition itself became a goal of social climbers.[82] While few people received these Inquisition appointments, the advantages of recognition of limpieza were clear to all. Entry to universities, guilds, religious brotherhoods, many professions, civil and ecclesiastical offices, and much else supposedly required it. Thousands of people petitioned to obtain this recognition, and while many of them might have some claim to European lineage or Indian nobility, the fact that the king and his councils often made dispensations for services rendered made this goal seem achievable even to people who appeared obviously disqualified by their birth or condition.

By the second half of the eighteenth century, phenotype or race, rather than religious orthodoxy, had become the principal marker of social divisions. The old juridical divisions of the society of estates had always been somewhat unrealistic, and as they broke down in Spanish America following the conquest, there had been an Indianization of all American-born Creoles and an Africanization of mestizaje that had lowered that status — which was held by a large segment of the population.[83] In addition, the origins of anyone of American birth, and especially those of mixed parentage, were often associated with illegitimacy and mechanic occupations. The Creole elites, ever anxious to separate themselves from what since the seventeenth century had been called the plebe, now found in the Bourbon monarchy a more receptive response to their desire for noble status, and a crown willing grant noble titles for money, as well as occasionally to remove the stain of illegitimacy or African origins for an appropriate payment.[84] This also became a regular if limited practice within certain occupations like that of notary, as well as within the institutions with limpieza restrictions like the military orders — where such "dispensations were possible, despite objections by those wishing to maintain the social status quo.[85]

Throughout the Iberian Americas, but with a considerable regional variation in terminology, a complex system of classification of phenotypical types of the castas (or pardos, as the Portuguese referred to them in Brazil) had emerged. The system was based in theory on percentages of European African or Native American blood, but in reality it incorporated aspects of culture, language, and degree of conformity as well. Much debate has centered on the extent to which this system was an extension of the original ideas of limpieza (a genealogy based on religion) to an association based on lineage, color, and modern ideas of race, or if by this period the system had already been transformed into one based on class divisions. In any case, the lack of congruence between a juridical order of nobles, commoners, and clergy, combined with that of a ranking based on occupation or income, and a hierarchy of ethnic or racial casta categories created a sense of instability and insecurity. Shifting self-identifications to avoid obligations such as taxes or forced labor, or to gain advantages, contributed to this insecurity. A bureaucrat in Guanajuato who was trying to enlist "Spaniards" for militia service complained in 1796 that "the majority of the common people in New Spain are of unclean castas who mix with each other without concern for who they marry, so it is difficult to enlist only Spaniards for military service." This official had hoped that parochial registers might have clarified the issue, but he believed that those records caused other problems because of repeated carelessness in them and because, he said, at the baptisms everyone claims they are Spaniards, even "when they are not."[86]

By the eighteenth century, as people sought to better their status, this unstable typology of shifting casta categories seems to have become a general problem across the empire for those in authority. Bourbon-era censuses and other records reveal many local patterns and variations in the nomenclature of the castas and the meaning of each category, as well as in the relative demographic importance of each category. Baptismal registers were often imprecise because of clerical carelessness or parental imprecision. Marriage records from Mexico City reveal that individual shifts in casta labels were usually between categories that were phenotypically similar, with more endogamy among Spaniards at the top of the social pyramid and Indians at the base, but a seemingly boundless exogamy among the groups between them.[87] In three censuses in the period 1777–88 in Valparaiso, Chile, half of the household heads who appeared in the three listings changed their casta identification at least once, a process that underlined the fluidity of the labels.[88] The size of the mixed population varied widely between regions. A 1778 census of Buenos Aires revealed a city of about 25,000 people in which Spaniards predominated (making up 69 percent of the population), while the castas as a whole accounted for the remaining 31 percent. People of African origin (blacks and mulattoes) predominated in the castas, with Indians accounting for 8 percent of that group and mestizos—many of them women and children—for only 2 percent. These figures probably reflected not only the relatively small number of Native Americans in the city's population, but also the tendency in the city and its surrounding areas for upwardly mobile mestizos to disappear into the Spanish population.[89] However, a census of the same date of New Granada showed people of mixed origin (mestizos and pardos) making up the largest segment (44 percent) of the population, with the remainder divided among whites (33 percent), Indians (15 percent), former slaves and free people of color (3 percent) and slaves (5 percent).[90]

During the intensive period of the Bourbon reforms in Latin America after 1750, the tightening of administrative and fiscal institutions and practices and the opening of commerce began yield much higher returns to Spain, and a new wave of Spanish immigration to the colonies took place, bringing more whites of unquestionable European origin. At the same time, there was a parallel narrowing of the classificatory hierarchy in the Indies. Local governments and native elites sought to determine for tax purposes who was an Indian or a *zambo* and thus subject to tribute obligation. That search made people scramble to evade those definitions. There is some evidence that whereas previously reference to the various elements of *calidad* (such as culture, language, dress, legitimacy, and occupation) had played an important role in social labeling, increasingly reference to color or phenotype became a principal means of definition, and something much more akin to the modern form of racial distinction became operative in Latin America. We can see evidence of this in many ways and many places. During roughly a hundred years (1686–1781), petitions to the audiencia of Quito from people trying to establish their mestizo status and thus avoid tribute payments referred to how they dressed, if they wore swords, their indigenous or Spanish noble lineage, and their reputation and legitimacy.[91] A poor mestizo who dressed like an Indian argued that despite his clothes, his birth outweighed his appearance;

a greedy okcacique maintained that a man whose mother was a mestiza, but whose father was an Indian was no longer entitled to the tribute exemption of the mestizos.[92] Such considerations continued into the eighteenth century, but increasingly color and physiognomy (facial shape, sparsity of beards, body type, hair quality, and so on) entered into the petitions, testimony, and decisions. These were elements that had long played a role in determining *calidad* but that now began to predominate in definitions and the attention given to such matters. Certifications of limpieza de sangre in America by the later eighteenth century were far more attentive to somatic qualities than to religious purity.[93] These definitions of race were usually interwoven with politics. By the late eighteenth century, as the Spanish crown made accessibility to whiteness or the use of the honorific title of don available for a price, institutions in Venezuela representing the interests of Creole merchants and landowners became inveterate opponents of such policies and advocates of a color-based discrimination that protected their privileged status.[94]

Nothing appears to illustrate the complexities of the casta system better than illustrations — the so-called and now famous casta paintings — but in fact these are a deceptive source. This was a peculiarly American, and especially Mexican, genre.[95] There was nothing quite like them in Europe. Each painting displayed a man and a woman of different "racial" type and their child or children. They were usually done in sets of sixteen canvases, although a few from the eighteenth and early nineteenth centuries have all of the categories represented in panels on the same canvas. About a hundred sets are known to exist. Most were painted in New Spain, but a couple were produced in both Peru and New Granada. The earliest are from 1711; the great majority were painted between 1750 and 1780, but the theme was picked up in other genres in the nineteenth century. The artistic quality varies greatly. Some were done by well-known and much commissioned artists, while others seem to be in the tradition of folk art, in the style of *ex voto* paintings.[96] Many of the figures and scenes became stock types and images, copied and repeated from one set to the next. As an artistic corpus they are a remarkably rich kind of genre painting, and they give us a singular view of domesticity, material culture, apparel, food habits, gender relations, and child-rearing practices. The labels — "Spaniard and Indian produce mestizo," Black man and Indian woman produce *zambo*," and so on — seem to be an attempt to examine the permutations of mestizaje in the broad sense, with an implicit objective of revealing how Spanish status and whiteness can be retained or regained. See image 5 in the insert. The casta paintings have been carefully and lovingly studied, but as fascinating they are as visual images of material culture and domesticity, they raise more questions than they answer: Why were they done, for what purpose, and for whom? And did the baroque mix of interracial combinations represent functional social definitions or groupings, or are they simply an artistic demonstration of the period's fascination with taxonomies of flora, fauna, and people?

These are mysteries. The first series predates Carl Linnaeus's classic work on natural history (1735), but there seems to have been a classificatory purpose to the paintings and some relationship to the scientific gaze of the eighteenth century. A number of the sets and similar paintings of colonial types included New World fruits and plants that were labeled and identified. At least one series was commissioned by Madrid's Royal Cabinet of Natural History (Real Gabinete de Historia Natural), but the large number of sets suggests an additional noninstitutional market for exotica and natural history. We know that one set was commissioned by the Duke of Linares, who served as viceroy of Mexico in 1711–16, and that others were owned by high-level ecclesiastics. However, with very few exceptions, the paintings are curiously secular. Scenes in churches or of devotion are absent, and few religious objects are visible as personal or household items — a notable absence in a society in which Catholicism played a central role.[97] We also might ask who had the money to pay for the large outlays of canvases and paints, and who had the space to hang these on their walls? Certainly neither New Spain's elites of wealthy Creole merchants, hacienda owners, and miners nor the resident Spanish bureaucrats who had the funds to do so decorated their salons and hallways with images of lower-class castas. I believe that for the most part, these paintings did not reflect the interests, preoccupations, or fears of colonial society, or at least those of the people who could have afforded to buy or commission them.[98] The old concerns of limpieza as religious purity have no place in these paintings. There are no images of conversos in the casta sets, and the Moriscos who are included are not the descendants of converts from Islam but indicate a new colonial use of the term for light-skinned mulattoes. The sets are also ethnographically misleading or incomplete. *Chinos*—the generic term for Asians, by this period called *indios chinos*—are not present, and the word is used instead for a person of mixed black and Indian parentage. Non-Spanish Europeans (Irish, Portuguese, Genoese, Florentines, and so on) are also absent or were simply included as Spaniards because they were white.[99] Most importantly, many of the supposed categories like *salta atrás* (a child darker in color than his or her parents) or *tente en el aire* (a child whose color is no closer to white than the colors of his parents) are rarely encountered in any documentation other than the paintings themselves. The casta paintings should probably be viewed as exotica designed for export—a combination of natural history, taxonomy, and social commentary created as souvenirs or postcards of empire whose emphasis on trades and utilitarian occupations projected the value of colonies and the colonials to the metropole—rather than as a representation of the functional social categories of society.

But even if that is true, it does not negate the concern that the Iberian American societies had about the proliferation of people of mixed lineage and the implications of cross-category unions. Rather than representations of race in its present meaning or of inherent characteristics, these depictions of social types and relationships seem to be more a demonstration of *calidad*. These images often depict lower-ranking castas positively, employed in useful occupations or as loving parents or spouses, even though there are definite suggestions that certain activities or character tendencies could logically be associated with certain kinds of people. Scenes of writing, for example, always involved Spaniards, while scenes of domestic violence usually portrayed *lobos* (children of an Indian father and black mother) or mulattoes. If the casta paintings had an underlying message, it was that the stain of blackness was difficult to overcome, and there was always possibility of regression away from the category of Spaniard.

Colonial society was complicated by both patron-client relations that cut across class boundaries and a lack of convergence between its various hierarchies. The confusion these relations created opened a door to manipulation and instability. Lineage and blood still mattered, and people still sought by certificate and official recognition to claim purity of blood. With the famous Real Pragmática of 1776, the crown even tried to regulate and discourage unequal marriages across the casta boundaries by requiring parental consent, but everyone realized that it was increasingly difficult to maintain separations and exclusions based on blood. While upper-class Spaniards and many members of the indigenous population still maintained relatively high levels of endogamy, the rest of the population did not. Social interaction was common, culture was broadly shared, and daily existence drew people of different categories together as they made pragmatic choices about their personal lives, loves, desires, and daily interactions without much concern for the state's policies, a partner's family's religious origins, or the racial labels of mixture — as long as they avoided those that implied the paying of tribute or previous association with slavery. As a census taker in New Spain remarked in 1791 about the common people, "they are indifferent [to inquiries about their casta] whether they are Spaniards, *castizos* [children of a Spaniard and a mestiza, and therefore three-quarters white], or mestizos, so long as they do not degenerate into pardos or tribute-paying Indians."[100]

Similar pictorial representations of the casta divisions are (with few exceptions) lacking for other areas of Spanish America. However, there in many ways the reputation and image of people of mixed origins paralleled those of New Spain, if considerable allowances are made for regional, temporal, ethnic, and demographic variations, and if the distinctions between rural and urban life are always kept in mind. The heavy black presence portrayed in the casta paintings in New Spain might be similar to the situation in Lima or Buenos Aires, but blacks must have been far less notable in other regions. On the Chilean frontier, for example, between the Spanish settlements and the area still controlled by the independent Mapuche groups, there were some blacks and mulattoes among the many mestizos who had soldiered there and who now lived scattered among the farms and ranches. They were considered a marginal, unstable, and uneasy population. For them, the state — and presumably the restrictions of limpieza or casta — were distant concepts of little importance in their lives, and government officials tended to see them as given to immorality and banditry, basically ignoring Spanish law and living in unrestrained freedom under a kind of semilegal regime that drew on Spanish military customs and Mapuche practices.[101] On that frontier or in areas like Tucumán or New Mexico, the presence of people of African descent was much less than in the viceregal capitals or major cities, and the influence of an indigenous presence and of people of mixed heritage was much stronger.[102]

In contrast, in Portuguese Brazil the African presence was particularly strong. Portuguese institutions had adopted the restrictions of *limpeza* (cleanliness in Portuguese) more slowly than had been the case in Spanish America, but anticonverso attitudes ran deep in Portugal and its colonies. The Marques de Pombal (the reforming Portuguese minister) had abolished the distinctions between Old and New Christians in 1773 to destroy what he and his appointees called "the monster of puritanism" that had long discriminated against the New Christians.[103] However, Brazilian elites, despite the converso origins of many, continued anxiously to seek honorary recognition as agents of the Inquisition to prove their clean lineages.[104] On the issue of color and mixed-race populations, the Portuguese rulers tended to dispense with stains and award knighthoods or military offices to blacks, Indians, and persons of mixed origin to gain their loyalty and support. Still, the burdens of slavery weighed heavily on the reputation — as well as the perception of the swelling number of — free colored people or pardos, who collectively made up about a third of the colony's population by the end of the colonial era. The prejudices, stereotypes, and disadvantages associated with slavery and blackness circulated throughout the society and shaped thinking and opportunities at all levels. A supposedly all-white municipal council could question the election of a new member not only because his "mechanic" profession disqualified him, but also because nobody knew the "quality of his blood."[105] The understanding of disadvantage because of color was internalized. A black soldier could ask for a discharge after almost thirty years of service because "as a colored man he could not hope for promotion"; a mulatto woman could testify that despite her color, she was an honorable and respected person; and even troops in a pardo militia unit could complain when an African-born black—or, in another case, a man "almost black"—was placed in command of them.[106] It was difficult for anyone to live outside the parameters of the social constraints of blood or color in these societies.

Across the Iberian Americas, by the middle of the eighteenth century the concern with, and symbolism related to, blood purity and honor still preoccupied elite families, and people who wished to improve their social condition still tried to secure recognition of their qualities or a dispensation from their limitations. Of course, there is much evidence that many people lived their lives without much concern about the casta restrictions and sought to avoid the intervention or interference of the state or the Church. However, to do so entirely was difficult, and at various moments like baptism, marriage, military enlistment, tax payment, census taking, applying for a license, or becoming a member of a religious brotherhood or other voluntary association, a person's genealogy was required or recorded.[107] Innumerable modern studies based on these records have revealed the fluidity and the considerable drift between the casta categories, but the fact that people sought to change or redefine their status—usually upward—indicates that the categories were understood not to be meaningless but as having some importance and effect on status and opportunities. Moreover, people did not simply seek to ignore or evade the law and the institutions of the state; rather, they learned how to negotiate them. Despite the considerable disparities in power and influence, modern studies have revealed that indigenous communities, mistreated slaves, mulatto militiamen, disadvantaged artisans, and Native American sojourn-

ers in Spain all sought legal relief and sometimes successfully challenged the system of restrictions and disadvantages by learning how
to use legal representation, the law courts, appeals to viceregal authority, and direct petitions to the crown to defend themselves and
their interests.[108]

Plebe or People? The Autumn of Discontent

The period of reform in the eighteenth century under the new
Bourbon dynasty in Spain and the Marques of Pombal in Portugal
brought sweeping political, administrative, and economic changes
to those kingdoms and their overseas possessions. Many of these
changes were accompanied by others in social organization. Attempts to recalibrate the existing social hierarchy—with its emphasis on honor, nobility, and religious purity within the framework of juridical social hierarchy, which penalized people because
of the stains of illegitimacy, disqualifying occupations, or ethnic
background—were at times seemingly contradictory, as modernizing impulses clashed with the realities of a society in which economic and social mobility revealed the fault lines and unreality of
the established order.

Economic growth in Spain and America in the eighteenth century had allowed many people to attain some social advancement,
and that had been accompanied by their desire to acquire the symbols and status of their improved condition and increase their contacts with, and acceptance by, the existing economic and social
elites. In places like New Spain, peninsula-born and criollo elites
reacted to this pressure by seeking to keep control of civil and ecclesiastical offices protect their privileges (which were already under
attack from reformist royal policies) by underlining their difference
from the rest of society and emphasizing the allegedly inherent
distinctions in morality, capacity, and honor that separated them
from the lower classes. These tensions became clearly visible in 1778,
when the law known as the Real Pragmática that required parental
approval of "unequal" marriages was also applied to Spain's American colonies, thereby opposing the Church's former position that a

person's selection of spouse was a matter of individual volition and giving parents a way to prevent any dilution of family lineage — especially to obstruct mestizaje.[109] But such moves to reinforce the existing boundaries of ethnic and color hierarchy were contested by modernizing reforms that were designed to bring progress to Spain by ending the association of honor with the avoidance of manual labor that had long reinforced the traditional separation of nobles and commoners. A law of 1783 that made such occupations as tanner, blacksmith, tailor, and shoemaker no longer a disqualification for holding municipal offices or having hidalgo status was implemented to stimulate artisan skills and open new opportunities. In America, however, where many of these crafts were performed by the castas, the law was mostly ignored and then rescinded in 1803 because (as an official of the Council of the Indies stated in 1807, reflecting on the harm caused by the law of 1783) if the castas understood their eligibility for such honors, "disturbances and harmful consequences for the State would ensue."[110]

Philosophical changes and economic modifications could not easily sweep away the system of exclusions and privileges. As populations grew and phenotypical divisions became more complex, in the eyes of the colonial elites and many officials and administrators across the Iberian Americas, society seemed to be divided not only by ethnicity or casta but also — and more simply — by the difference between Spaniards or "whites" and those accepted as such (including native-born criollos, many mestizos, and other Europeans), all of whom were considered to be the "decent folk" or "people of reason," and the rest of society: the long-suffering but miserable Indians, supposedly always given to sloth, sin, and drunkenness; the necessary but dangerous African and Afro-American slaves; and the *turba* or *vulgo* — derogatory terms commonly used to describe the mass of inhabitants of the American colonies with their ethnic and racial hybridity, itinerancy, tendency to avoid work, and potential for crime and violence.[111] In the elite view, the *vulgo* did not really constitute the commoners or the people (the legitimate third estate of medieval society), but instead were something more troublesome and dangerous, a *populacho* or plebe that was most notable in the large cities. This plebe in general was a disorderly mass of supposedly lazy and vile people that combined the working classes of all colors as well as freed slaves, partly acculturated Indians, vagabonds, rogues, and other socially marginal people — what one Brazilian observer called an ignorant and semibarbarous "congregation of the poor."[112] These were the commoners (*vulgares*) who since the seventeenth century had been referred to by administrators and others as "pusillanimous," "ill-intentioned," "vagabond," and "lazy," a mob of castas joined by those whites whose poverty and idleness had lowered their status and diminished their honor. The Count of Revillagigedo, viceroy of New Spain, had described them in 1755 as "a monster of . . . many species."[113] This negative view — centered on the mixed origins of the plebe, its unstable or partial employment, and its poverty — had been growing since the seventeenth century among political leaders and the propertied classes. It had become generally held by colonial administrators and American elites, and it had become held more strongly as the seeming absence of useful workers became an obsession of Bourbon reformers.[114] This plebeian mass of mestizos and other castas was not only denigrated, it was feared.[115] They had been responsible for or involved in popular uprisings like those of Mexico City in 1624 and 1692 and Cochabamba in Upper Peru (Bolivia) in 1730 — and even in the Tupac Amaru Indian rebellion in 1780. In that case, people of mixed origins had joined in the Indian rebellion at various points, as they had done in Arequipa — where a crowd that attacked the customs house was composed of "young men and women, *cholos* and mestizos, lower-class people, barefoot and dressed in ponchos."[116] This fear of the plebe and its potential for social disorder naturally intensified in the aftermath of the French revolution of 1789 and the Haitian rebellion of 1791.[117]

But as the winds of economic reforms, the Enlightenment, and the political changes of the end of the century swept up the people that the Spanish called the castas and the Portuguese referred to as *mestiços* and pardos, their reaction was not only to intensify their mobility within the limitations of the existing social hierarchies. They now constituted a major segment of the American populations and in some places were the majority, and they had become increasingly restive within their societies. Many had never adopted their ascribed colonial corporate identity, others no longer thought of themselves in terms of their colonial racial labels, and still others ignored such divisions entirely. The political changes of the next decades would enable them to think of themselves no longer as simply a plebe, but as a force able to consider political alternatives in royalism or creole republicanism and to weigh the advantages of a patriarchal dependent security of monarchy against the opportunities of republican liberty and citizenship. Together in some areas with the indigenous inhabitants, they became the people. How Spain and Portugal (themselves struggling in the wake of Napoleonic invasions) or the newly forming nations of the Americas would incorporate them as citizens became the ongoing challenge of the next century.[118]

The opprobrium long heaped on the castas or plebe had provoked within it a "nationalistic antibody" that now allowed the people to see that their diversity, talents, and numbers gave them hope for the future.[119] It had mostly been local realities and the experiences, hopes, fears, and decisions of is various subpopulations that had shaped their place in society, but their actions and alternatives had always been constrained in some ways by a lack political power and by the existing ideologies of social order. While it may be true that early modern states often had little direct impact on people's everyday life, the states were still able to limit or encourage, punish or promote in ways that reflected the dominant theological, political, and social ideas. In Spain and Portugal, concepts such as nobility, lineage, bad blood, and honor were broadly shared (even within the minority populations). And while we have seen that exclusions or discriminations based on the presence or absence of those characteristics were in reality often circumvented, negotiated, or challenged, they still set parameters and limits that could not simply be ignored. A similar process took place in Spanish America and Brazil. As the Iberian societies of the Americas took shape in the shadow of the marginalizations of Moriscos and conversos, there was a tension between, on the one hand, the principles of an imagined social hierarchy based on religious purity, clear ethnic divisions, and pheno-type accompanied by a belief in inherited characteristics ascribed to particular categories of people, and, on the other hand, the reali-ties of the New World in which religious origins were often ob-scure, syncretism flourished, ethnicities were varied, identities were mutable, and social status was imprecise. That tension provided the context in which state and religious authorities attempted to guide and control people to achieve the order and stability of the idealized society. But the attempts to impose order and control also moved people collectively or individually to seek their own destinies, and to disregard when they could, negotiate when necessary, or even re-sist the social restraints placed upon them.

In Latin America, as the nineteenth century dawned and new nations—a few of them monarchies, but most of them republics—were created, the aspirations of their populations for citizenship and opportunity increased, but the ancient shadows of exclusion—limpieza de sangre, the denigration of indigeneity, the liabilities of slave origins, and the legacies and stains of casta and mestizaje—would continue to burden their lives for much of the new century, and in some places still do.

NOTES

ARCHIVAL ABBREVIATIONS IN NOTES

ACA: Archivo de Casa de Alba (Madrid)

AGI: Archivo General de Indias (Seville)

AGN: Archivo General de la Nación (Mexico City)

AGS: Archivo General de Simancas (Spain)

AHN: Archivo Historico Nacional (Madrid)

AHNQ: Archivo Historico Nacional (Quito)

AHU: Arquivo Histórico Ultramarino (Lisbon)

AMC: Arquivo Municipal de Cachoeira (Brazil)

ANTT: Arquivo Nacional da Torre do Tombo (Lisbon)

APB: Arquiivo Público da Bahia (Salvador, Brazil)

BPE: Biblioteca Pública de Évora (Evora, Portugal)

INSTITUTIONAL ABBREVIATIONS IN NOTES

CNRS: Centre National de la Recherche Scientifique

CSIC: Consejo Superior de Investigación Científica

EHESS: École des Hautes Études en Sciences Sociales

INAH: Instituto Nacional de Antropología y Historia

UNAM: Universidad Nacional Autónoma de Mexico

UNESCO: United Nations Educational, Scientific, and Cultural Organization

INTRODUCTION

1. For comparative orientations, see Anthony Pagden, *Lords of All the World: Ideologies of Empire in Spain, Britain, and France, c. 1500–1800* (New Haven, CT: Yale University Press, 1995), and Giuseppe Marcocci, *A consciência de um império: Portugal e o seu mundo (sécs. xv–xvii)* (Coimbra, Portugal: Coimbra University Press, 2012). In law, there were some concessions to local custom and practice. See Max Deardorff, "Republics, Their Customs, and the Law of the King: Convivencia and Self-Determination

in the Crown of Castile and its American Territories, 1400–1700," *Rechts-geschichte/Legal History* 26 (2018): 162–99.

2. The quoted phrase was coined by Hernando de Acuña in celebration of Charles V's Holy Roman Empire. See Charles R. Boxer, *The Church Militant and Iberian Expansion, 1440–1770* (Baltimore, MD: Johns Hopkins University Press, 1978), 77.

3. Quoted in Charles R. Boxer, "Portuguese and Spanish Projects for the Conquest of Southeast Asia," *Journal of Asian History* 3, no. 2 (1969): 136.

4. Anthony Pagden, "Afterword: From Empire to Nation," in *Imperialisms: Historical and Literary Investigations, 1500–1900*, ed. Balachandra Rajan and Elizabeth Sauer (New York: Palgrave Macmillan, 2004), 255–72. See also Ryan Dominic Crew, "An Atlantic of New Christians: The Politics of Conversion in the Canaries, Granada, and Mexico, 1470–1540" (International Seminar on the History of the Atlantic World, 1500–1825, Harvard University, unpublished working paper no. 06–03, 2006).

5. On Goa, see Ângela Barreto Xavier, "De converso a novamente convertido," *Cultura. Revista de História e Teoria das Ideias*, 22 (2006): 245–74. In theory in Spanish America there were to be two republics—one of the Indians and one of the Spaniards. In most practical terms, however, this separation was subordinated to political and economic considerations.

6. The literature on this topic is extensive, with many regional studies and vigorous theoretical debates on the relative degrees of continuity or syncretism between African and Afro-American cultures. On the debates, compare Sidney Mintz and Richard Price, *The Birth of African-American Culture: An Anthropological Perspective* (Boston: Beacon Press, 1992); Michael Gomez, *Reversing Sail: A History of the African Diaspora* (Cambridge: Cambridge University Press, 2005). For a classic study, see Gonzalo Aguirre Beltrán, *La población negra de México*, 2nd ed. (Mexico City: Fondo de Cultura Económica, 1972). For a fine representative regional monograph, see Matthew Restall, *Black Middle: Africans, Mayas, and Spaniards in Colonial Yucatan* (Stanford, CA: Stanford University Press, 2009). For a broad synthetic regional study, see Maribel Arrelucea Barrantes and Jesús Cosmalón Aguilar, *La presencia afrodescendente en el Perú* (Lima: Ministerio de Cultura, 2015). John Thornton encompasses the African diaspora in an even broader context (*Africa and Africans in the Making of the Atlantic World, 1400–1800*, 2nd ed. [Cambridge: Cambridge University Press, 1998]).

7. Adriano Prosperi, *Il seme dell'intolleranza: Ebrei, eretici, selvaggi; Granada, 1492* (Rome: Laterzza, 2011). Although Prosperi's book has not been translated into English, its argument is discussed in Jean-Frédéric Schaub, *Race Is about Politics*, trans. Lara Vergnaud (Princeton, NJ: Princeton University Press, 2019), 81–93.

8. David Nirenberg examines the origins of this genealogical thinking and its implications for the racializing of the Jewish population ("Mass Conversion and Genealogical Mentalities: Jews and Christians in Fifteenth-Century Spain," *Past and Present* 174, no. 1 [2002]: 3–41). See also Max Sebastián Hering Torres, "'Limpieza de sangre': ¿Racismo en la edad moderna? *Tiempos modernos* 9 (2003–2004): 1–16.

9. For an early attempt to trace the continuities between exclusionary policies in Spain and America, see Henry Méchoulan, *Le sang de l'autre ou l'honneur de Dieu: Indiens, juifs et morisques au siècle d'or* (Paris: Fayard, 1979).

10. Stuart B. Schwartz, *All Can Be Saved: Religious Tolerance and Salvation in the Iberian Atlantic World* (New Haven, CT: Yale University Press, 2008).

11. Over the years, I have written or coauthored a number of essays that have dealt with race, class, and *mestizaje*, a central theme of Latin American history. I will draw on them in these chapters, but in the context of this subject's relationship to systems of exclusion and discrimination. See Robert McCaa, Stuart B. Schwartz, and Arturo Grubessich, "Race and Class in Colonial Latin America: A Critique," *Comparative Studies in Society and History* 21, no. 3 (1979): 421–33; Robert McCaa and Stuart B. Schwartz, "Measuring Marriage Patterns: Percentages, Cohen's Kappa and Log-Linear Models," *Contemporary Studies in Society and History* 25, no. 4 (1983): 711–20; Stuart B. Schwartz, "Spaniards, Pardos, and the Missing Mestizos: Identities and Racial Categories in the Early Hispanic Caribbean," *New West Indian Guide* 71, nos. 1–2 (1997): 5–19, "Colonial Identities, Race, Class and Gender in the Sociedad de Castas," *Colonial Latin American Review* 4, nos. 1–2 (1995): 185–202, and "Brazilian Ethnogenesis: Mestiços, Mamelucos, and Pardos," in *Le Nouveau Monde, Mondes Nouveaux: L'expérience américaine*, ed. Serge Gruzinski and Nathan Wachtel (Paris: Éditions de l'École des Hautes Études en Science Sociale, 1996), 7–27; Stuart B. Schwartz and Frank Salomon, "New Peoples and New Kinds of Peoples: Adaptation, Readjustment, and Ethnogenesis in South American Indigenous Societies (Colonial Era)," in *Cambridge History of the Native Peoples of the Ameri-*

cas, ed. Frank Salomon and Stuart B. Schwartz, vol. 3, part 2, *South America* (New York: Cambridge University Press, 1999), 443–501.

12. I mention here only a few classics: Magnus Morner, *Race Mixture in the History of Latin America* (Boston: Little, Brown, 1967); Marvin Harris, *Patterns of Race in the Americas* (New York: Norton, 1974); Frank Tannenbaum, *Slave and Citizen: The Negro in the Americas* (New York: Vintage, 1946); Charles Boxer, *Race Relations in the Portuguese Colonial Empire, 1415–1825* (Oxford: Clarendon Press of Oxford University Press, 1963).

13. Some of the principal issues at stake are discussed in John K. Chance, "On the Mexican Mestizo," *Latin American Research Review* 14, no. 3 (1979): 153–68. A model example of this approach is John K. Chance and William B. Taylor, "Estate and Class in a Colonial City: Oaxaca in 1792," *Contemporary Studies in Society and History* 19, no. 4 (1977): 454–86.

14. See Elizabeth Kuznesof, "Ethnic and Gender Influences on 'Spanish ' Creole Society in Colonial Spanish America," *Colonial Latin American Review* 4, no. 1 (1995): 153–76; Verena Stolcke, "Invaded Women: Sex, Race, and Class in the Formation of Colonial Society," *European Journal of Development Research* 6, no. 2 (1994): 7–21.

15. The historiography is complex and extensive. I have found particularly useful and informative the following works as introductory guides: Yosef Kaplan, "La diáspora judeo-española-portuguesa en el siglo xvii: Tradición, cambio y modernización," *Manuscrits* 10 (1992): 77–89; Jaime Contreras, "Domínguez Ortiz y la historiografía sobre judeoconversos," *Manuscrits* 14 (1996): 59–80, and "Historiar a los judíos de España: Un asunto de pueblo, nación, y etnia," in *Disidencias y exilios en la España moderna*, ed. Antonio Mestre Sanchís and Enrique Giménez López (Alicante, Spain: Universidad de Alicante y Caja de Ahorros del Mediterráneo, 1997), 117–43; Mercedes García-Arenal, "Creating Conversos: Genealogy and Identity as Historiographical Problems (after a recent book by Ángel Alcalá)," *Bulletin for Spanish and Portuguese Historical Studies* 38, no. 1 (2013): 1–20; Marcos Rafael Cañas Pelayo, "Los judeoconversos portugueses de la edad moderna en la historiografía española: Un estado de la cuestión," *Revista de Historiografía* 23 (2015): 217–43.

16. Ricardo García Cárcel, La herencia del pasado: Las memorias históricas de España (Barcelona: Galaxia Gutenburg: 2011), 153–55. On Castro and the objections to his position on Jews and conversos, see Anna Menny,

"'Entre reconocimiento y rechazo': Los judíos en la obra de Américo Castro," *Iberoamericana* 38, no. 10 (2010): 143–50.

17. For a positive view of *convivencia*, see Jerrilynn D. Dodds, María Rosa Menocal, and Abigail Krasner Balbale, *The Arts of Intimacy: Christians, Jews, and Muslims in the Making of Castilian Culture* (New Haven, CT: Yale University Press, 2008). On the Inquisition and the modern state, see Irene Silverblatt, *Modern Inquisitions: Peru and the Colonial Origins of the Civilized World* (Durham, NC: Duke University Press, 2004). On Castro's essentialized view of conversos and their role in modernity, see Miriam Bodian, "Américo Castro's Conversos and the Question of Subjectivity," *Culture and History Digital Journal* 6, no. 2 (2017), http://dx.doi.org/10.3989/chdj.2017.018.

18. Benzion Netanyahu, *The Origins of the Inquisition in Fifteenth Century Spain* (New York: Random House, 1995); Christiane Stallaert, *Ni una gota de sangre impura: La España inquisitorial y la Alemania nazi cara a cara* (Barcelona: Círculo de Lectores, 2006).

19. The original is: "Y aunque la primera de hidalguía es mas honrado tenerla, pero muy más estimamos a un hombre pechero y limpio que a un hidalgo que no es limpio." For a discussion of the statement, see Jaime Contreras, *Sotos contra Riquelmes: Regidores, inquisidores y criptojudíos* (Madrid: Anaya and Mario Muchnik, 1992), 24–31. See also Méchoulan, *Le sang de l'autre*, 117–96. Using a close reading of contemporary treatises, Méchoulan explains the underlying psychosocial motivations for the discriminations based on religion and estate.

20. Jorge Cañizares-Esguerra demonstrated that astrology was believed to determine physical capacities and differences in the early modern era in a kind of precursor to scientific racism ("New World, New Stars: Patriotic Astrology and the Invention of Indian and Creole Bodies in Colonial Spanish America, 1600–1650," *American Historical Review* 104, no. 1 [1999]: 33–68). For excellent essays on premodern aspects of racial thinking, see Miriam Eliav-Feldon, Benjamin Isaac, and Joseph Ziegler, eds., *The Origins of Racism in the West* (Cambridge: Cambridge University Press, 2009). See also Geraldine Heng, "The Invention of Race in the European Middle Ages I: Race Studies, Modernity, and the Middle Ages," *Literature Compass* 8, no. 5 (2011): 315–31.

21. John Edwards, "The Beginnings of a Scientific Theory of Race? Spain,

1450–1600," in *From Iberia to Diaspora: Studies in Sephardic History and Culture*, ed. Yedida. K. Stillman and Norman A. Stillman (Leiden, the Netherlands: Brill, 1999), 179–96. The medievalists William Chester Jordan ("Why 'Race'?," *Journal of Medieval and Early Modern Studies* 31, no. 1 [2001]: 165–73) and David Nirenberg ("Was There Race before Modernity in Late Medieval Spain?," in David Nirenberg, *Neighboring Faiths* [Chicago: University of Chicago Press, 2014], 169–91) are careful in their use of the term and skeptical about the origins of the concept. A similar caution is expressed in Antonio Feros, *Speaking of Spain: The Evolution of Race and Nation in the Hispanic World* (Cambridge, MA: Harvard University Press, 2017). Jean-Frédéric Schaub provides a broad analysis of the problem, emphasizing chronological differences and political contexts in the varieties of racial thinking (*Pour une politique histoire de la race* [Paris: Seuil, 2015]).

22. Francisco Bethencourt (*Racisms: From the Crusades to the Twentieth Century* [Princeton, NJ: Princeton University Press, 2013]) and George Frederickson (*Racism: A Short History* [Princeton, NJ: Princeton University Press, 2002]) both give the Iberian experience with religious minorities and the Latin American incorporation of Native Americans and Africans an important role in the global story of racism.

23. See, for example, James Sweet, "The Iberian Roots of American Racist Thought," *William and Mary Quarterly* 54, no. 1 (1997): 143–66. For a critique of this approach, see Schaub, *Race Is about Politics*, 87.

24. José Antonio Maraval, "Trabajo y exclusión: El trabajador manual en el sistema social español de la primera modernidad," in Les problèmes de l'exclusion en Espagne (*xvie–xviie siècles*), ed. Augustín Redondo (Paris: Publications de la Sorbonne, 1983), 135–59.

25. Arlette Jouanna, *Le devoir de révolte: La noblesse française et la gestation de l'état moderne, 1559–1661* (Paris: Fayard, 1989). Spanish treatises on nobility also emphasized the Gothic or Germanic origins of Spain's nobility.

26. Antonio Domínguez Ortiz, *Las clases privilegiadas en el antiguo régimen*, 3rd ed. (Madrid: Istmo, 1985), 185.

27. José Antonio Guillén Berrendero emphasizes the contested nature of a "nobility of service" in the late sixteenth century as evidence of increasing royal power ("Los mecanismos del honor y la nobleza en Castilla y Portugal, 1556–1621" [PhD diss., Universidad Complutense de Madrid, 2009]).

28. Alexander von Humboldt, *Travels to the Equinoctial Regions of America during the years 1799–1804* (London: Henry G. Bohn, 1852), 1: 415.

29. See, for example, Barreto Xavier, "De converso a novamente convertido"; Tatiana Seijas, *Asian Slaves in Colonial Mexico: From Chinos to Indians* (Cambridge: Cambridge University Press, 2014); António Manuel Hespanha, *Filhos da terra: Identidades mestiças nos confins da expansão portuguesa* (Lisbon: Tinta-da-China, 2019); Ângela Barreto Xavier and Ines G. Zupanov, *Catholic Orientalism. Portuguese Empire, Indian Knowledge (16th–18th Centuries)* (Oxford: Oxford University Press, 2015); Patricia Souza de Faria, "A conversão das almas do Oriente. Franciscanos, poder e Catolicismo em Goa: Séculos xvi e xvii" (PhD diss., Universidad Federal Fluminense 2008).

CHAPTER 1

1. Bartolomé Arzáns de Orsua y Vela, *Historia de la villa imperial de Potosí*, ed. Lewis Hanke and Gunnar Mendoza (Providence, RI: Brown University, 1965), 1:172–74. See also "The Standard of Pizarro," *Bulletin of the Pan American Union* (January 1919): 395–99. On the transformation of Santiago into a patron of the conquest of the Indies, see Javier Domínguez Rodriguez, *De apostol matamoros a yllapa mataindios: Dogmas e ideologías medievales en el descubrimiento de América* (Salamanca, Spain: Universidad de Salamanca, 2006); Emilio Choy, "De Santiago matamoros a Santiago mata-indios: Las ideas políticas en España desde la reconquista a la conquista de América," *Revista del Museo Nacional* 27 (1958): 195–272. Ramón Mujica Pinilla uses Andean art to demonstrate the continued presence of the Moor as an enemy of the Eucharist and the equivalency of Moors and Indians ("Apuntes sobre moros y turcos en el imaginario andino virreinal," *Anuario de Historia de la Iglesia* 16 [2007]: 169–79). See also Ines Monteira Arias, "Alegorías del enemigo: La demonización del islam en el arte de la 'España' medieval y sus pervivencias en la edad moderna," in Tausiet, María (ed.). *Alegorías: Imagen y discurso en la España moderna*, ed. Maria Tausiet (Madrid: CSIC, 2014); Olivia Remie Constable, *To Live like a Moor: Christian Perceptions of Muslim Identity in Medieval and Modern Spain* (Philadelphia: University of Pennsylvania Press, 2018).

2. Chroniclers believed that Santiago had appeared thirteen times during the conquest of New Spain. See Louis Cardaillac, *Santiago apóstol, el santo*

de los dos mundos (Zapopan, Mexico: El Colegio de Jalisco-Fideicomiso Tei-xidor, 2002), 123–58.

3. While the *moros y cristianos* developed in various areas of Spain, most specialists agree that those of Andalucia provided the models adopted in the American colonies. The literature on these performances is extensive. See, for example, Milena Cáceres Valderrama, *La fiesta de moros y cristianos en el Perú* (Lima: Pontificia Universidad Católica del Peru, 2005); Demetrio E. Brisset Martin, "Fiestas hispanas de moros y cristianos. Historia y significados," *Gazeta de Antropología* 17 (2001), article 3.

4. For indigenous peoples seeking accommodation or acceptance within the colonial social and religious order, moros became an "other," useful in underlining their own status as Christians.

5. Max Harris, *Aztecs, Moors, and Christians: Festivals of Reconquest in Mexico and Spain* (Austin: University of Texas Press, 2000); Nathan Wachtel, "La vision des vaincus: La conquête dans le folklore indigene," *Annales: Économies, Sociétés, Civilisations* 22, no. 3 (1967): 554–85; Arturo Warman, *La danza de moros y cristianos* (Mexico City: INAH, 1985); Carolyn Dean, *Inka Bodies and the Body of Christ: Corpus Christi in Colonial Cuzco, Peru* (Durham, NC: Duke Univemnrsity Press, 1999), 12–15.

6. Lucette Valensi uses the reports of Venetian agents to trace Venice's shifts between admiration and aversion of the Turk (*The Birth of the Despot: Venice and the Sublime Porte* [Ithaca, NY: Cornell University Press, 1993]).

7. The first agreement with Christopher Columbus — dated April 30, 1492 — refers to "islas y tierra firme en el Mar Oceano." See Rafael Diego Fernández, *Capitulaciones colombinas (1492–1506)* (Zamora, Mexico: El Colegio de México, 1987), 124.

8. An early but still useful review of these restrictions can be found in Richard Konetzke, "Legislación sobre inmigración de extranjeros en América durante la época colonial," *Revista internacional de sociología* 3 (1945): 269–99.

9. See Woodrow Borah, *Silk Raising in Colonial Mexico* (Berkeley: University of California Press, 1942).

10. Hernán H. G. Taboada, "El moro en Las Indias," *Latinoamérica* 39, no. 2 (2004): 115–32. See also Karoline P. Cook, *Forbidden Passages: Muslims and Moriscos in Colonial Spanish America* (Philadelphia: University of Pennsylvania Press, 2016); Louis Cardaillac, "Le pròblem morisque en Amé-

rique," *Mèlange de la Casa de Velázquez* 12 (1976): 283–30. A bibliographical overview was presented in Alessandro Vanoli, "Between Absence and Presence: New Paths in the Historiography of Islam in the New World," *Journal of Medieval Iberian Studies* 2, no. 1 (2010): 77–91, but this should be updated by the abovementioned book of Cook as well as Hernán H. G. Taboada, *Extrañas presencias en Nuestra América* (Mexico City: UNAM, 2017).

11. The original is: "libros de molde de historias profanas como las de Amadis" (AGI, letter of audiencia judges Cerrato and Grajeda to Carlos I, April 23, 1545, Santo Domingo 49, *ramo x*iv, n. 95).

12. AGI, letter of audiencia judges Cerrato and Grajeda to Carlos I. The document has been published in Genaro Rodríguez Morel, *Cartas de la real audiencia de Santo Domingo (1530–1546)* (Santo Domingo, Dominican Republic: Archivo General de la Nación, 2007), 431–41. The crown suspended the order until further consultation. See AGI, letter of Licenciado Hurtado to Carlos I, June 30, 1551, Santo Domingo 49, ramo 21, n. 134, published in Genaro Rodríguez Morel, *Cartas de la real audiencia de Santo Domingo (1547–1575)*, Archivo General de la Nación, vol. cxlix (Santo Domingo, Dominican Republic: Archivo General de la Nación, 2011), 134. There has been a growing recognition of attitudes that were more favorable to Moriscos in Spain. See Trevor J. Dadson, *Los moriscos de Villarubia de los Ojos (siglos xv-xviii)* (Madrid: Iberoamericana Vervuert, 2007); Barbara Fuchs, *Exotic Nation: Maurophilia and the Construction of Early Modern Spain* (Philadelphia: University of Pennsylvania Press, 2009).

13. The Jesuit Pedro de Guzmán lamented that while the "expulsion of our times [the Moriscos in 1609] and that of our grandparents [the moros after the Alpujarras rebellion?] were deserved because of their infidelity: nevertheless, these were the people who worked and cultivated the land, and the people who remained refuse to do this work" (*Bienes del honesto trabajo y daños de la ociosidad en ocho discursos* [Madrid: Emprenta Real, 1614], 230). It should be noted, however, that prior to the expulsion, anti-Morisco xenophobia went to the extremes of suggesting castration and forms of genocide. See Jean Vilar, "De quelques barbares conseils (l'imaginaire de la solution finale au Siecle d'Or)," in *La violence en Espagne et en Amérique*, ed. Jean-Paul Duviols and Anne Molinie-Betrand (Paris: Université de Paris–Sorbonne, 1998), 255–69.

14. The historiography on the topic is extensive. See, for example, José

María Perceval, *Todos son uno: Arquetipos, xenophobia y racismo: La imagen del morisco en la monarquía española durante los siglos xvi y xvii* (Almería, Spain: Instituto de Estudios Almerienses, 1997); Carlos Garriga, "Enemigos domésticos: La expulsion católica de los moriscos (1609-1614)," *Quaderni Fiorentini per la storia del pensiero giuridico moderno* 38 (2009): 225-87; James B. Tueller, *Good and Faithful Christians: Moriscos and Catholicism in Early Modern Spain* (New Orleans, LA: University Press of the South 2002); David Coleman, *Creating Christian Granada: Society and Religious Culture in an Old World Frontier City* (Ithaca, NY: Cornell University Press, 2003); Benjamin Ehlers, *Between Christians and Moriscos: Juan de Ribera and Religious Reform in Valencia, 1568-1614* (Baltimore, MD: Johns Hopkins University Press, 2006); Pedro de Valencia, *Tratado acerca de los moriscos de España* (Málaga, Spain: Editorial Algazara 1997).

15. Mercedes García-Arenal, "Moriscos e indios para un estudio comparativo de métodos de conquista y evangelización," *Chronica Nova* 20 (1992): 153-75. Prosecutions of people for following Islamic practices or customs in the Inquisition tribunals of Lima, Mexico City, and Cartagena accounted for less than 1 percent of the total number of trials, and even though accusations of Morisco origins can be found in prosecutions for other sins such as blasphemy, bigamy, or heretical propositions, the total number remains small. See Antonio Garrido Aranda, *Moriscos e Indios: Precendentes hispánicos de la evangelización de México*, 2nd ed. (Mexico City: UNAM, 2013), 123-46; Taboada, "El Moro en las Indias." On the West African jihads that produced large numbers of captives sold into the Atlantic slave trade, see Paul Lovejoy, *Jihād in West Africa during the Age of Revolutions* (Athens: Ohio University Press, 2016).

16. Cook, *Forbidden Passages*, 53-79.

17. Leyla Bartet, "Tensiones en los orígenes del Perú colonial: Españolas y moriscas en el siglo xvi," Centro Virtual Cervantes [http://cvc.cervantes .es/literatura/mujer_independencias/barteto1.htm#np3]. See also Nelson Manrique, *Vinieron los sarracenos: El universo mental de la conquista* (Lima: Desco, 1993), 542-72.

18. AGI, Justicia, 403, n. 2. There were other cases of enslaved Moriscas in Peru and Chile, including the wife of an *encomendero* who bore a slave brand on her face. See Jean-Paul Zúñiga, *Espagnols d'Outre-Mer* (Paris: EHESS, 2002), 44-45.

19. Perceval, *Todos son uno*. Ambiguity has also characterized the historiography about the Moriscos. See Bernard Vincent, *El río morisco* (Valencia, Spain: Universitat de Valencia, 2006), 131–44.

20. For an anti-Morisco sermon preached in Mexico, see Robert Ricard, "Les morisques et leur expulsion vus du Mexique," *Bulletin Hispanique* 33, no. 3 (1931): 252–54.

21. For a demonstration of how charges of Muslim or Morisco origins were also used in Spain against Native Americans or Asians in lawsuits to justify their enslavement, see Nancy E. van Deusen, "Seeing Indios in Sixteenth-Century Castile," *William and Mary Quarterly*, 3rd ser., 69, no. 2 (2012): 205–34, and (in a more detailed presentation) *Global Indians: The Indigenous Struggle for Justice in Sixteenth-Century Spain* (Durham, NC: Duke University Press, 2015).

22. AHN, Relación de causa 1651-2, Inquisición, Tribunal de Cataluña, libro 734, ff. 193v. Quoted in Xavier Torres Sans, "Frailes y campesinos en la guerra de separación de Cataluña (1640–1660)," *Hispania* 75, no. 249 (2015): 77.

23. AGI, Justicia, *legajo* 980, folios (fs.) 60–62; Taboada, "El Moro en las Indias," 120. On Juan Suárez de Peralta, the son of one of the companions of Hernán Cortés, see Enrique González González, "Nostalgia de la encomienda: Releer el tratado del Descubrimiento de Juan Suárez de Peralta (1589)," *Historia Mexicana* 59, no. 2 (2009): 533–603.

24. Luce López Baralt and Josué Caamaño, "Un morisco puertorriqueño, médico y alcalde de San Juan de Puerto Rico en pleitos con Juan Ponce de León," *La Torre* 12, nos. 44–45 (2007): 335–64; Karoline P. Cook, "'*Moro de linaje y nación*': Religious Identity, Race and Status in Sixteenth-Century New Granada," in *Race and Blood in the Iberian World*, ed. Max Hering Torres, María Elena Martínez, and David Nirenberg (Berlin: Lit Verlag, 2012), 81–98. The classic overview of the Moriscos is still Antonio Domínguez Ortiz and Bernard Vincent, *Historia de los moriscos: Vida y tragedia de una minoría* (Madrid: Alianza Editorial, 2003). For an excellent guide to the literature on both conversos and Moriscos, see James Amelang, *Historias paralelas: Judeoconversos y moriscos en la España moderna* (Madrid: Akal, 2011).

25. Javier Irigoyen-García, *Moors Dressed as Moors: Clothing, Social Distinction, and Ethnicity in Early Modern Iberia* (Toronto: University of Toronto Press, 2017), 99–124.

26. AHN, case of Pedro Moreno, Inquisición, legajo 2022.

27. For an excellent summary of the question of Morisco circumcision, see Bernard Vincent, "Los moriscos y la circuncisión," in Bernard Vincent, *Minorías y marginados en la España del siglo xvi* (Granada, Spain: Diputación Provincial de Granada, 1987), 83–99. Apparently the frequency of the practice among Moriscos varied across Granada, Aragon, and Castile. On the use of circumcision to identify converts to Islam, see the 1622 case of Diego Díaz presented in Richard Kagan and Abigail Dyer, eds., *Inquisitorial Inquiries*, 2nd. ed. (Baltimore, MD: Johns Hopkins University Press, 2011), 147–79.

28. Nabangongo was a region dependent on the Kongo kingdom.

29. AHN, case of Pedro Moreno, Inquisición, legajo 2022.

30. Karoline P. Cook, "Muslims and Chichimeca in New Spain: The Debates over Just War and Slavery," *Anuario de Estudios Americanos* 70, no. 1 (2013): 17.

31. AGI, Lima 51, *libro* 3, fs. 96–97. See also Stuart B. Schwartz, "Panic in the Indies: The Portuguese Threat to the Spanish Empire, 1640–50," *Colonial Latin American Review*, 2, nos. 1–2 (1993): 165–187.

32. Mercedes García-Arenal, *Ahmad al-Mansur: The Beginnings of Modern Morocco* (Oxford: OneWorld, 2009), 79–96.

33. See María Antonia Garcés, *Cervantes in Algiers: A Captive's Tale* (Nashville, TN: Vanderbilt University Press, 2002). See also Willard King, "Cervantes, el cautiverio y los renegados," *Nueva revista de filogía hispánica* 40, no. 1 (1992): 279–91. On the ransoming of captives, see Ellen G. Friedman, *Spanish Captives in North Africa in the Early Modern Age* (Madison: University of Wisconsin Press, 1975). José Antonio Martínez Torres concentrates on the French efforts to ransom captives (*Prisioneros de los infieles: Vida y rescate de los cautivos cristianos en el Mediterráneo musulmán* [Barcelona: Bellaterra, 2004]).

34. Andrew C. Hess, "Moriscos: An Ottoman Fifth Column in Sixteenth-Century Spain," *American Historical Review* 74, no. 1 (1968): 1–25. See also Bernard Vincent, "El peligro morisco," in Vincent, *El río morisco*, 65–74.

35. Oran is particularly interesting since as a Spanish outpost in North Africa with both a Muslim and Jewish population. After 1492 it remained a site where Spanish policy toward these religions was not based on exclusion. See Jean-Frédéric Schaub, *Les juifs du roi d'Espagne: Oran 1509–1669*

(Paris: Hachette Litterératures, 1999); Gregorio Sanchez Doncel, *Presencia de España en Oran (1509–1792)* (Toledo, Spain: Estudio Teológico de San Ildefonso, 1991); Beatriz. Alonso Acero, *Oran-Mazalquivir, 1589–1639: Una sociedad española en la frontera de Berbería* (Madrid: CSIC, 2000).

36. Important in this regard are the works of Ahmed Boucharb, "Les conséquences socio-culterelles de la conquête ibérique du littoral marocain," in *Relaciones da la península Ibérica con el Magreb: siglos XIII-XVI—Actas del coloquio* (Madrid: CSIC, 1988), 487–537, and *Os pseudo-mouriscos de Portugal no século xvi* (Lisbon: Hugin, 2004) (based on "Les Crypto-Musulmans d'origine marocaine et la société portugaise au XVIe siècle" [PhD diss., Université de Montpellier, 3 vols., 1987]). See also Ahmed Boucharb, "Les métiers des morisques du Portugal pendent le XVIe siècle," in *Métiers, vie religieuse et problematiques d'histoire morisque*, ed Abdeljelil Temimi (Zaghouan, Tunisia: Publications du Centre d'Études et de Recherches Ottomanes et Morisques de Documentation et d'Information, 1990), 51–60. Also important are Rogério de Oliveira Ribas, "Filhos de Mafoma: Mouriscos, crypto-islamismo e Inquisição no Portugal quihentista," 2 vols. (PhD diss., Universidade de Lisboa, 2004) and Isabel M. R. Mendes Drumond Braga, *Mouriscos e cristãos no Portugal quinhentista* (Lisbon: Hugin, 1999). For a bibliographical overview of the topic in Portugal and a discussion of the discrimination suffered by Moriscos, see Isabel M. R. Mendes Drumond Braga, "Marcas de infâmia: Sangue mouro e dificuldade de acesso ao 'Estado de Meio,'" in *Minorias étnico-religiosas na península ibérica*, ed. Maria Filomena Lopes de Barros and José Hinojosa Montalvo (Lisbon: Colibri, 2008), 411–30.

37. Mercedes Garcia-Arenal, "Moriscos e indios: Para un estudio comparado de métodos de conquista y evangelización," *Chronica Nova* 20 (1992): 153–75. See also Antonio Garrido Aranda, *Moriscos e Indios: Precendentes hispánicos de la evangelización de México*, 2nd ed. (Mexico City: UNAM, 2013). Ignacio de las Casas, a Morisco Jesuit, inverted the process and suggested that the missionary methods used in the Indies could be applied to the conversion of the Moriscos in Spain. See Youssef El Alaoui, *Jésuites, morisques, et indiens: Étude comparative des méthodes d'evangélisation de la Compagnie de Jésus d'après les traités de José de Acosta (1588) et d'Ignacio de las Casas (1605–07)* (Paris: Honoré Champion, 2006).

38. Hernán H. G. Taboada, La sombra de Islam en la conquista de América (Mexico City: Fondo de Cultura Económica, 2004).

39. Juan Suárez de Peralta, *Tratado del descubrimiento de las Indias y su conquista*, ed. Giorgio Persinotto (Madrid: Alianza, 1990), 51.

40. AGI, Justicia, legajo 980, fs. 60–62v.

41. See Álvaro Huerga, *Ataques de los caribes a Puerto Rico en el siglo xvi* (San Juan, Puerto Rico: Academia Puertorriqueña de Historia, 2006), 252, 258, and 263.

42. AGI, Santo Domingo, legajo 50, ramo 9, n. 26, published in Genaro Rodríguez Morel, *Cartas de la real audiencia de Santo Domingo (1547–1575)*, *Archivo General de la Nación, vol. cxlix* (Santo Domingo: Dominican Republic: Archivo General de la Nación, 2011), 303.

43. Cook, "Muslims and Chichimeca," 29–31.

44. AGI, "Sobre la utilidad de desterrar a los indios esclavizados capturados en guerra," Patronato, 229, ramo 3.

45. Using Mediterranean analogies intentionally as a way of getting imperial support for ransoming is suggested by Daniel Villar and Juan Francisco Jiménez ("Un argel disimulado: Aucan y poder entre los corsarios de Mamil Mapu [segunda mitad del siglo xviii]," September 2, 2005, https://journals.openedition.org/nuevomundo/656). The authors suggest that just as the chronicler Diego de Rosales compared the wars on the Chilean frontier to the wars in Flanders, reports from the Argentine frontier in the eighteenth century compared the area to Algiers to gain the attention of bureaucrats in Spain. See also Harris, *Aztecs, Moors, and Christians*; Wachtel, "La vision des vaincus"; Warman, *La danza de moros y cristianos*; Dean, *Inka Bodies and the Body of Christ*.

46. José Toribio Medina, *Historia de la tribunal del Santo Oficio de la Inquisición de Chile* (Santiago, Chile: Ercilla, 1890), 2:271. Another famous case is the probably apocryphal story of Emir Cigala, a Muslim who was born in Constantinople of a Greek mother and made a fortune at Potosí under the pseudonym of Captain Gregorio Zapata. He then returned to Algiers, where in 1598 he freed from captivity a friend from his time in the Andes because "although of a different faith, he was thankful to the true God, to his neighbors, and to the Cerro [of Potosí]" (Bartolomé Arzáns de Orsua y Vela, *Relatos de la villa imperial de Potosí: Antología*, ed. Leonardo García Pabón [La Paz, Bolivia: Plural, 2000], 68).

47. Antonio Garrido Aranda, "El morisco y la Inquisición novohispana (actitudes antiislámicas en la sociedad colonial)," in *Andalucía y América en*

el siglo xvi, ed. Bibiano Torres Ramírez and José Hernández Palomo (Seville, Spain: CSIC, 1983), 1:501–33.

48. AHN, Relación de causa, Cartagena de Indias, 1711 Inquisición, legajo 5349/5.

49. Bartolomé Bennassar and Lucille Bennassar, *Les Chrétiens d'Allah: L'histoire extraordinaire des renégats (XVIe–XVIIe siècles)* (Paris: Perrin, 1989). See also Anita González-Raymond, *La croix et le croissant: Les inquisiteurs des îles face à Islam, 1550–1700* (Paris: CNRS, 1992); Isabel M. R. Mendes Drumond Braga, *Entre a cristanidade e o islão (séculos xv–xvii), cautivos e renegados nas franjas de duas sociedades em confronto* (Ceuta, Morroco: Instituto de Estudios Ceutíes, 1998). The Italian historiography is well developed. See Lucetta Scaraffia, *Rinnegati: Per una storia dell'identità occidentale*, 2nd ed. (Rome: Laterza, 2003); Marco Lenci, *Corsari: Guerra, schiavi, rinnegati nel Mediterraneo* (Rome: Carocci, 2006); Salvatore Bono, "Conversioni all'islam e riconciliazioni in Levante nella prima metà del Seicento," in *I turchi, il Mediterraneo, e l'Europa*, ed. Giovanni Motta, 7th ed. (Milan, Italy: Franco Angeli, 2008), 325–39. I have previously discussed this theme in relation to attitudes of tolerance or religious relativism. See Stuart B. Schwartz, *All Can Be Saved: Religious Tolerance and Salvation in the Iberian Atlantic World* (New Haven, CT: Yale University Press, 2008), 71–74.

50. Diego de Haedo, *Topographia e historia general de Argel* (Valladolid, Spain: Diego Fernández de Cordova y Oviedo, 1612), 9. Interesting questions have been raised about the authorship of this text and the extent to which it was based on the writings of Antonio de Sosa, a former captive, that were edited by Haedo. See Garcés, *Cervantes in Algiers*, 34–49.

51. An interesting exception to this is Tobias Graf, *The Sultan's Renegades: Christian-European Converts to Islam and the Making of the Ottoman Elite* (Oxford: Oxford University Press, 2017). For a number of studies on the theological and ethical issues of conversions to and from Islam, see Mercedes García-Arenal, ed., *Islamic Conversions: Religious Identities in Mediterranean Islam* (Paris: Maisonneuve et Larose, 2002).

52. Lucia Rostagno, *Mi faccio turco: Esperienze e immagini dell'Islam nell'Italia Moderna* (Rome: Oriente Moderno, 1983). On the interpenetration of Islamic and Christian cultural spheres around the Mediterranean and the appeal of Islam, see Giovanni Ricci, *Ossessione turca. In una retrovia Cristiana dell'Europa moderna* (Rome: Il Mulino, 2002). For an excellent

historiographical overview, see Francesca Trivellato, "Renaissance Italy and the Muslim Mediterranean in Recent Historical Work," *Journal of Modern History* 82 (March 2010): 127–55.

53. Diogo de Couto, *Da Asia: Década sétima* (Lisbon: Régia Oficina Tipográfica, 1782–83), cited in Maria Augusta Lima Cruz, "Exiles and Renegades in Early Sixteenth-Century Portuguese India," *Indian Economic and Social History Review* 23, no. 3 (1986): 250–62. See also Dejanirah Couto, "Quelques observations sur les renégats portugais en Asie au xvie siècle," *Mare Liberum* 16 (1998): 57–85, and "L'itinéraire d'un marginal: La deuxième vie de Diogo de Mesquita," *Arquivo do Centro Cultural Calouste Gulbenkian* 39 (2000): 9–356. A good discussion is found in Sanjay Subrahmanyam, *The Portuguese Empire in Asia, 1500–1700*, 2nd. ed. (Oxford: Wiley-Blackwell, 2012), 262–69.

54. David L. Graizbord, *Souls in Dispute: Converso Identities in Iberia and the Jewish Diaspora, 1580–1700* (Philadelphia: University of Pennsylvania Press, 2004); Isabel M. R. Mendes Drumond Braga, *Entre duas maneiras de adorar a deus: Os reduzidos em Portugal no século xvii* (Lisbon: Colibri, 2010), and "Uma estranha diaspora rumo a Portugal: Judeus e cristãos novos reduzidos à fé católica no século xvii," *Sefarad* 62, no. 2 (2002): 259–74. Natalio Ohanna considers the complexity of the conversion process and the common absence of theological considerations in the decision of Christian captives to convert ("Remedio para renegados: Jerónimo Gracián y la disuasión de las conversiones al islamismo," *Lusiania Sacra* 27 [January–June, 2013]: 81–98).

55. In the Treaty of Santa Fe, Ferdinand and Isabel had guaranteed the safety of Christian converts to Islam and the safe passage of those *tornadizos* who wished to leave, but like other aspects of the treaty, these promises were not kept. There is some philological dispute about the use of the terms *tornadizo* and *elche* and whether they are interchangeable. See Mercedes Abad Merino, "'Aqui hay necesscidad de persona capaz en muchas lenguas': El oficio de intérprete en las últimas fronteras de Castilla," *Tonos: Revista Electrónica de Estudios Fililógicos*, 10 (2005), www.tonosdigital.com. On the policies of Ferdinand and Isabel toward Muslims who came under their rule, see Mark D. Meyerson, *The Muslims of Valencia in the Age of Ferdinand and Isabel* (Berkeley: University of California Press, 1991).

56. AHN, Inquisición, libro 1028., f.639v-640.

57. AHN, charges against Sebastián Herrera, Inquisición, libro 1027 Lima, 1579-80, fs. 93-97v.

58. AHN, Inquisición, libro 1023, fs. 302-5. I have previously presented this story in some detail (see Schwartz, *All Can Be Saved*, pp. 87-88). For more details, see Beatriz Alonso Acero, "Heterodoxia e Inquisición en las sociedades hispanas de Berbería, siglos xvi-xvii," *Hispania Sacra* 55, no. 112 (2003): 481-99, especially 492-93.

59. For a brief overview, see Stuart B. Schwartz, "The Greek Gunners and the Spanish Conquest," in *Grecia en España, España en Grecia*, ed. Anthony N. Zahareas and Yangos Andreadis (Madrid: Ediciones Clásicas, 1999), 337-42. On Greeks and renegades in Peru, see Jean-Pierre Tardieu, *L'Inquisition de Lima et les hérétiques étrangers (xvie-xviie siècles)* (Lima: L'Harmattan, 1995), 141-49.

60. Molly Greene, *A Shared World: Christians and Muslims in the Early Modern Mediterranean* (Princeton, NJ: Princeton University Press, 2000). See also Anastassia Papadia-Lala, "I Greci fra Venezia e i turchi nell'arco della lunga durata," in *I turchi, il Mediterraneo e l'Europa*, ed. Giovanni Motta, 7th ed. (Milan, Italy: Franco Angeli, 2008), 185-96.

61. The Council of Castile, considering the admission of Spartan families from Morea into Castile, made clear its objections on the basis of religion and on the pernicious effects of introducing different customs and languages. See Fernando Bouza Álvarez, "De otomanos, chinos y moriscos: Nuevas poblaciones de espartanos en tiempos de Carlos II," in *Negociar la obediencia*, ed. Jean-Paul Zúñiga (Granada, Spain: Editorial Comares, 2013), 103-12.

62. AHN, Inquisición, libro, 1029, 259-60. Another fascinating case is that of Alejandre Testanegra, a Greek who fled to Venice, came with the fleets from Seville to New Spain, traveled to the Philippines and China, served in the viceroy's guard, and was eventually tried in 1580 by the Inquisition on suspicion of being circumcised. See Aranda, "El morisco y la Inquisición novohispana," 1:501-34.

63. In many ways the experience in the Spanish and Portuguese enclaves in North Africa, where Europeans were a minority amid a much larger indigenous population, presents a closer analogy to the situation in the Ameri-

cas than do the conditions in sixteenth-century Iberia. For an excellent overview, see Beatriz Alonso Acero, *España y el norte de África en los siglos xvi y xvii* (Madrid: Sintesis, 2017).

64. There are extensive literatures about captives and captivity narratives in all the American colonial experiences. The difficulty that women and their children had in returning to their original societies is often a central theme. See, for example, John Demos, *The Unredeemed Captive: A Family Story from Early America* (New York: Knopf, 1994). On Spanish America, Susan Migden Socolow's "Spanish Captives in Indian Societies: Cultural Contact along the Argentine Frontier," *Hispanic American Historical Review* 72, no. 1 (1992): 73–99, is based on depositions by former captives. See also Yéssica González, "Indias blancas tierra adentro: El cautiverio feminino en la frontera de la Araucanía, siglos xviii y xix," *Anuario colombiano de historia social y de la cultura* 43, no. 2 (2016): 185–214.

65. Rolena Adorno, *The Polemics of Possession in Spanish American Narrative* (New Haven, CT: Yale University Press, 2007), 220–45.

66. The other classic American captivity tale is that of Alvar Nuñez Cabeza de Vaca. It is treated in the context of Mediterranean captivity in Natalio Ohanna, *Cautiverio y convivencia en la edad de Cervantes* (Alcalá de Henares, Spain: Centro de Estudios Cervantinos, 2011), 155–202.

67. Fray Pedro de Aguado recounted a similar story from the conquest of Venezuela about Francisco Martin, a soldier lost from an early expedition who had been found by the Indians, married a chieftain's daughter, and become a military leader. After three years, he was rescued by Captain Juan de San Martín, but he so missed his wife and children that he returned to them (*Historia de Venezuela* (Madrid: Jaime Ratés, 1918), 1: 96–97 and 104.

68. Gonzalo Fernández de Oviedo y Valdés, *Historia general y natural de las Indias, Islas y Tierra Firme del Mar Océano*, ed. José Amador de los Ríos (Madrid: Real Academia de la Historia, 1881–85), 4:232–33. There was also a Morisco slave who joined the Arawaks in Venezuela, became a military leader, and led a large group against the Spanish settlement on Margarita Island in 1544. For this and other examples, see Stuart B. Schwartz and Frank Salomon, "New Peoples and New Kinds of Peoples: Adaptation, Readjustment, and Ethnogenesis in South American Indigenous Societies (Colonial Era)," in *Cambridge History of the Native Peoples of the Americas*,

ed. Frank Salomon and Stuart B. Schwartz, 34, part 2, *South America* (New York: Cambridge University Press, 1999), 471–77.

69. The classic study is Albert A. Sicroff, *Los estatutos de limpieza de sangre: Controversias en los siglos xvi y xvii* (Madrid: Taurus, 1985). See also Juan Hernández Franco, *Sangre limpia, sangre española: El debate sobre los estatutos de limpieza (siglos xvi y xvii)* (Madrid: Cátedra, 2011). On the application of purity statutes in the Spanish colonies, see María Elena Martínez, *Genealogical Fictions: Limpieza de Sangre, Religion, and Gender in Colonial Mexico* (Stanford, CA: Stanford University Press, 2008); Jennifer M. Spear, *Race, Sex and Social Order in Early New Orleans* (Baltimore, MD: Johns Hopkins University Press, 2009). It is also important to remember that the issue of lineage and blood was not only considered in religious and racial terms but was also an essential concept related to the maintenance of noble privilege and social differentiation. See David García Hernán and Miguel F. Gómez Vozmediano, eds., *La cultura de la sangre en el siglo de oro* (Madrid: Silex, 2017). The development of Spanish racial thought is carried into the nineteenth century in Antonio Feros, *Speaking of Spain: The Evolution of Race and Nation in the Hispanic World* (Cambridge, MA: Harvard University Press, 2017).

70. José Toribio Medina, *Historia de la Inquisición de Lima* (Santiago, Chile: Gutenberg, 1887), 2: 6. For a wide-ranging discussion of Hispanic captives among various Indian peoples on the imperial frontiers in the eighteenth century, see David J. Weber, *Bárbaros: Spaniards and Their Savages in the Age of Enlightenment* (New Haven, CT: Yale University Press, 2005), 221–34.

71. Ana María Lorandi, *Spanish King of the Incas: The Epic Life of Pedro Bohorques* (Pittsburgh, PA: University of Pittsburgh Press, 2005).

72. Domingos Abreu e Brito, *Um inquérito a vida administrativa e económica de Angola e Brasil*, ed. Alfredo de Albuquerque Felner (Coimbra, Portugal: Universidade de Coimbra Imprensa, 1931), 9. Similar opinions about the military prowess of mestizos abounded in Spanish America. See, for example, Thierry Saignes, "Entre 'Bárbaros y cristianos' el desafío mestizo en la frontera chiriguano," *Anuario de Estudios Historicos-Sociales* 4 (1989), 13–39; Gabriel Guarda Geywitz, "Los cautivos en la Guerra de Arauco," *Boletín de la Academia Chilena de la Historia* 54, no. 98 (1987): 93–157.

73. For a discussion and examples of these cultural crossovers in the Spanish Indies, see Angel Rosenblatt, *La población indígena y el mestizaje en América* (Buenos Aires: Editorial Nova, 1954), 2:34 and 76. For similar situations in French Canada, see Phillipe Jacquin, *Les indiens blancs: Français et indiens en Amérique du Nord (xvie–xviie siècles)* (Paris: Payot, 1987).

74. On the Santidade movement, see Ronaldo Vainfas, *A heresia dos índios: Catolicismo e rebeldia no Brasil colonial* (São Paulo, Brazil: Companhia das Letras, 1995); Alida Metcalf, *Go-Betweens and the Colonization of Brazil* (Austin: University of Texas Press, 2005).

75. Ignacio Chuecas Saldías, *Dueños de la frontera: Terratenientes y sociedad colonial en la periferia chilena: Isla de Laja, 1670–1845* (Santiago, Chile: Biblioteca Nacional de Chile y Centro de Investigaciones Diego Barros Arana, 2019).

76. On Spanish orientalism, see James Monroe, *Islam and the Arabs in Spanish Scholarship: Sixteenth Century to the Present* (Leiden, the Netherlands: Brill, 1970); Jacinto Bosch Vilá, "El orientalismo español: Panorama histórico: Perspectivas actuales," lecture given November 13, 1966, at the Centro Regional de Orientalistas, University of Salamanca, Salamanca, Spain. See also Hernán H. G. Taboada, "Latin American Orientalism: From Margin to Margin," in *Paradoxical Citizenship: Essays on Edward Said*, ed. Silvia Nagy-Zekmi (Lanham, MD: Lexington Books, 2008), 121–28; Silvia Nagy-Zekmi, *Moros en la costa: Orientalismo en Latinoamerica* (Madrid: Iberoamericana Vervuert, 2008).

77. Weber, *Bárbaros*, 227.

78. The original is: "Es el llamado de la frontera, es la frontera vivida como añoranza de lo otro y como un nuevo destino." Carlos Mayo and Amalia Latrubesse, *Terratenientes, soldados, y cautivos: La frontera 1763–1815*, 2nd. ed. (Buenos Aires: Biblos, 1998), 97. The literature nf these frontiers in Chile and Argentina is highly developed, and excellent work on renegados has been done by a number of scholars. See, for example, Daniel Villar and Juan Francisco Jiménez, "El continuo trato con infieles: Los renegados de la región pampeana centro-oriental durante el último tercio del siglo xviii, *Memoria Americana* 13 (2005), 151–79; Leonardo León, "Que la dicha herida se la dio sin que interviniese traición alguna . . . : El ordenamiento del espacio fronterizo mapuche, 1726–1760," *Revista de Historia Social y de las Mentalidades* 5 (Winter, 2001), 129–65; Sara Ortelli, "Marginalismo y relaciones

interétnicas: Blancos e indios en la frontera rioplatense en el siglo xix," *Revista Complutense de Historia de América* 26 (2000): 181–98.

79. Daniel Villar and Juan Francisco Jiménez, "Un argel disimulado: Aucan y poder entre los corsarios de Mamil Mapu (segunda mitad del siglo xviii)," September 2, 2005, https://journals.openedition.org/nuevomundo /656).

80. Jerónimo de Quiroga, *Memorias de los sucesos de la Guerra de Chile*, comp. Sérgio Fernández Larrain (Santiago, Chile: Andrés Bello, 1979), 9. On Quiroga, see Fernando Casanueva, "Jerónimo de Quiroga, militar y cronista: Visión de una sociedad colonial señorial: Chile en el siglo xvi," *Alp: Cuadernos Angers—La Plata* 2, no. 2 (1998), http://www.memoria.fahce .unlp.edu.ar/art_revistas/pr.2621/pr.2621.pdf.

81. The original is: "los más iníicuos y bárbaros que hay en estas provincias. Hoy hay muchos mas blancos que nosotros, y casi todos son caballeros de armas contrarias; son genízaros o mestizos que basta para ponderación." Quoted in Osvaldo Silva Galdames, "El mestizaje en el reino de Chile," *Senri Ethnological Studies* 33 (1992): 124.

82. Cited in Carlos Mayo and Amalia Latrubesse, *Terratenientes, soldados, y cautivos: La frontera 1763–1815*, 2nd ed. (Buenos Aires: Biblos, 1998), 94. Such comparisons preceded the traces of an Argentine orientalism that viewed the pampa as a desert and the lifestyle of the gaucho as comparable to that of Berbers or Arabs. These traces can be seen in the classics by Domingo Faustino Sarmiento (*Facundo: Civilización y barbarie* [Santiago, Chile: Imprenta del Progreso, 1845]) and José Hernández (*El Gaucho Martín Fierro* (Buenos Aires: Imprenta de La Pampa, 1872]). See Isabel de Sena, "Beduinos en la pampa: El espejo oriental de Sarmiento," in *Moros en la costa: Orientalismo en Latinoamerica*, ed. Silvia Nagy-Zikmi (Madrid: Iberoamericana Vervuert, 2008), 69–90.

83. On Moorish garb as a symbol of elite status and manly virtues, see Irigoyen-García, *Moors Dressed as Moors*. See also the discussion in Joanne Rappaport, *The Disappearing Mestizo: Configuring Difference in the Colonial New Kingdom of Granada* (Durham, NC: Duke University Press, 2014), 166–69. The presence of Moorish traditions in Portuguese and Brazilian popular culture and folklore is examined by Luís da Câmara Cascudo (*Mouros, franceses e judeus* [São Paulo, Brazil: Perspectiva, 1984], 1–40).

84. For overviews, see Sylviane Diouf, *Servants of Allah: African Mus-*

lims Enslaved in the Americas (New York: New York University Press, 1998); Michael Gomez, *Black Crescent: The Experience and Legacy of African Muslims in the Americas* (Cambridge: Cambridge University Press, 2008). I have previously outlined these African events in relationship to the Brazilian slave revolts. See Stuart B. Schwartz, *Sugar Plantations in the Formation of Brazilian Society: Bahia (1550–1835)* (Cambridge: Cambridge University Press, 1985), 474–76.

85. Lovejoy, *Jihād*. See also Paul E. Lovejoy, "Jihad na África Ocidental durante a 'Era das Revoluções,'" *Topoi* 15, no. 28 (2014): 22–67, and the response by João José Reis, "Reposta a Paulo Lovejoy," *Topoi* 16, no. 30 (2015): 374–89.

86. Rio de Janeiro, another major slaving port in Brazil, also received slaves from the Bight of Benin (which the Portuguese called the Costa da Mina), although the vast majority of Africans who were delivered to Rio de Janeiro came from Angola. See Mariza de Carvalho Soares, ed., *Rotas atlânticas da diaspora africana; Da Baía do Benim ao Rio de Janeiro* (Niterói, Brazil: Editora da Universidade Federal Fluminense, 2007); Juliana Barreto Farias, Carlos Eugênio Libano Soares, and Flávio dos Santos Gomes, eds., *No labirinto das nações: Africanos e identidades no Rio de Janeiro, século xix* (Rio de Janeiro, Brazil: Arquivo Nacional, 2003).

87. Reis uses the slave trade data base to provide an estimate of the volume of the slave trade that came out of the ports on what the Portuguese called the Mina coast ("Resposta a Paul Lovejoy"). Determining the percentage of Muslims in these figures is difficult, but ethnic origins provide at least some guide.

88. For the most substantial account of the largest Brazilian revolt, see João José Reis, *Slave Rebellion in Brazil: The Muslim Uprising of 1835*, 2nd ed. (Baltimore, MD: Johns Hopkins University Press, 2003). On Cuba, see Manuel Barcia, *West African Warfare in Bahia and Cuba: Soldier Slaves in the Atlantic World, 1807–1844* (Oxford; Oxford University Press, 2014), 1–21.

89. The maintenance of Islamic traditions and the levels of syncretism and knowledge of the Koran among Muslim slaves and freedmen in the Americas are matters of debate. It should be noted that in the 1860s, a French book dealer in Rio de Janeiro annually sold about a hundred very expensive copies of the Koran in Arabic to slaves and freed people, many of whom were migrants from Bahia. He also sold Arabic grammars to help his customers learn

to read the texts. See Alberto Costa e Silva, "Buying and Selling Korans in Nineteenth-Century Rio de Janeiro," *Slavery and Abolition* 22, no. 1 (2001): 72–83. For a life history of a Muslim in Brazil in this period, see João José Reis, Flávio dos Santos Gomes, and Beatriz Gallotti Mamigonian, *O alufá Rufino: Tráfico, escravidão e liberdade no Atlântico negro* (São Paulo, Brazil: Companhia das Letras, 2010).

CHAPTER 2

1. David Nirenberg, *Communities of Violence: Persecution of Minorities in the Middle Ages* (Princeton, NJ: Princeton University Press, 1996). For a useful summary on sexual separation, see Jonathan Ray, *The Sephardic Frontier: The Reconquista and the Jewish Community in Medieval Iberia* (Ithaca, NY: Cornell University Press, 2006), 145–76.

2. Such legislation appears in the Siete partidas and in the Cortes of Soria (in 1380). See the discussion in Antonio Domínguez Ortiz, *La clase social de los conversos en Castilla en la edad moderna* (Madrid: Instituto Balmes de Sociología y CSIC, 1955), 8–9.

3. References to *raza* (race) in testimony concerning "limpieza de sangre," became common in the overseas areas — and, but by the late sixteenth century, in Spain and Portugal as well. "He is an Old Christian, without race of Jew, Muslim, or Mulatto," was a common phrase in these documents. See, for example, Consulta Council of Portugal, AGS, Secretaria/Portugal 1468, fs. 163–66, 292v. (1626).

4. The strange dialogic relationship that made Judaism's persistence necessary as the opposite of Christianity and proof of its truths following the mass forced conversions of 1391 is explored in David Nirenberg, "Spanish 'Judaism' and 'Christianity' in an Age of Mass Conversion," in *Rethinking European Jewish History*, ed. Jeremy Cohen and Moshe Rosman (Portland, OR: Littman Library of Jewish Civilization, 2009), 149–72.

5. This point is made clearly in Jean Pierre Dedieu, "¿Pecado original o pecado social? Reflexiones en torno a la constitución y la definición del grupo judeo-converso en Castilla," *Manuscrits* 10 (1992): 61–76.

6. Paulino Rodríguez Barral, *La imagen del judío en la España medieval: El conflicto entre cristianismo y judaísmo en las artes visuales góticas* (Barcelona: Universitat de Barcelona, 2009). See also Sara Lipton, "The Jew's Face: Vision, Knowledge, and Identity in Medieval Anti-Jewish Caricature," in

Late Medieval Jewish Identities: Iberia and Beyond, ed. Carmen Caballero-Navas and Esperanza Alfonso (New York: Palgrave, 2010), 259–85.

7. Dedieu, "¿Pecado original o pecado social?," 64. See also Rodríguez Barral, *La imagen del judío en la España medieval*.

8. For an analysis of the visual and literary representations of moros and Moriscos, see Borja Franco-Llopis and Francisco J. Moreno Díaz del Campo, *Pintando al conversos: La imagen del morisco en la península ibérica (1492–1614)* (Madrid: Cátedra, 2019. Also useful is Olivia Remie Constable, *To Live like a Moor: Christian Perceptions of Muslim Identity in Medieval and Modern Spain* (Philadelphia: University of Pennsylvania Press, 2018), 15–62. On the use of art as a tool for the conversion and control of Muslims and Jews, see Borja Franco-Llopis, "Art of Conversion? The Visual Policies of Jesuits, Dominicans, and Mercedarians in Valencia," in *Polemical Encounters: Christians, Jews, and Muslims in Iberia and Beyond*, ed. Mercedes García Arenal and Gerald Wiegers (University Park: Penn State University Press, 2019), 179–202; Borja Franco Llopis, "Nuevas tendencias historiográficas en torno al análisis del uso del arte en los procesos de asimilación de la minoria morisca: Propuestas de estudio," *eHumanista/Conversos* 1 (2013): 63–75; Felipe Pereda, *Las imágenes de la discordias: Política y poética de la imagen sagrada en la España del 400* (Madrid: Marcial Pons, 2009), and "Through a Glass Darkly: Paths to Salvation in Spanish Painting at the Outset of the Inquisition," in Judaism and Christian Art, ed. Herbert Kessler and David Nirenberg (Philadelphia: University of Pennsylvania Press, 2011), 263–90.

9. Nirenberg focuses on the problems of identification following conversion ("Mass Conversion and Genealogical Mentalities: Jews and Christians in Fifteenth-Century Spain," *Past and Present* 174, no. 1 [2002]: 10–17). I will not address here the fascinating and much debated question about converso "inner life" that has generated an extensive and impressive historiography centered on the questions of their beliefs; whether or not they were crypto-Jews, and if they were, what the characteristics of marranism (their form of nonrabbinic Judaism) were; how the necessity of religious dissimulation and duplicity influenced their actions and *mentalité*; and if they were precursors of a skepticism or philosophical rationalism associated with modernity.

10. Yosef Hayim Yerushalmi, *From Spanish Court to Italian Ghetto: Isaac*

Cardoso: A Study in Seventeenth-Century Marranism and Jewish Apologetics (New York: Columbia University Press), 12–18.

11. Anne Fanshawe, *Memoirs of Lady Fanshawe* (London: Henry Colburn, 1829), 117.

12. The anthropologist Victor Turner's theory of liminality as a kind of social alienation during a transition between social categories has sometimes been used to explain the position of Iberian converts, but I find it more helpful in understanding the converts' sense of inferiority and detachment than in analyzing its effects on the structures and process of discrimination. See "Liminality and Communitas," in Victor Turner, *The Ritual Process: Structure and Anti-Structure* (New York: Transaction Press, 1969), 94–130.

13. Dedieu emphasizes the changing and complex nature of the limpieza statutes and their application, as well as the manner in which descent, wealth, occupation, family, and residence entered into the definition of individuals as Old or New Christians ("¿Pecado original o pecado social?"). See also Kevin Ingram, *Converso Non-Conformism in Early Modern Spain: Bad Blood and Faith from Alonso de Cartagena to Diego Velázquez* (London: Palgrave, 2018).

14. Gerard Wiegers, "Fuzzy Categories and Religious Polemics: The Daily Life of Christians and Muslims in the Medieval and Early Modern Mediterranean World," *Common Knowledge* 19, no. 3 (2013): 474–88. Christina H. Lee emphasizes the threat that the lack of recognizable difference produced in Hispanic society (*The Anxiety of Sameness in Spain* [Manchester, UK: Manchester University Press, 2016]).

15. Claude B. Stuczynski, "From 'Potential' to 'Fuzzy' Jews to 'Non-Jewish Jews'/'Jewish Non-Jews': Conversos Living in Iberia and Early Modern Jewry," in *Connecting Histories: The Jews and Their Others in Early Modern Europe*, ed. Frances Bregoli and David B. Ruderman (Philadelphia: University of Pennslyvania Press, 2019), 197–204. The quotation appears on page 197 in a discussion of the critique of the separation of Portuguese society made by the exiled Portuguese converso António Nunes Ribeiro Sanches in 1735.

16. Estimates of the numbers of Jews who migrated to Portugal, which at the time had a total population of about one million and a Jewish population of about 30,000, have varied from 30,000 to 200,000. See Maria José

Pimenta Ferro Tavares, *Los judios en Portugal* (Madrid: Mapfre Editorial, 1992), 131–39. For a useful review of the historiography of the estimates, see Santiago López Rodríguez, "Persecución y expulsión de los judíos: Fuentes históricas y literarias en la península Ibérica," *Vegueta: Anuario de la Facultad de Geografía e Historia*, 17 (2017): 175–97.

17. Bruno Feitler and Claude Stuczynski provide an excellent introduction to the subject ("A Portuguese Jewish Exception? A Historiographical Introduction," in *Portuguese Jews, New Christians, and "New Jews": A Tribute to Robert Bachmann*, ed. Claude Stuczynski and Bruno Feitler [Leiden, the Netherlands: Brill, 2018], 1–30). For a useful summary, see Miriam Bodian, "The Formation of the Portuguese Jewish Diaspora," in *The Jews in the Caribbean*, ed. Jane S. Gerber (Oxford: Oxford University Press 2014), 17–28.

18. For an extensive review essay that raises some of the central questions about the Sephardi trading networks, see Jonathan Schorsch, "Sephardic Business: Early Modern Atlantic Style," *Jewish Quarterly Review* 100, no. 5 (2010): 483–503.

19. James C. Boyajiyan argues that the Goa tribunal's main target was the New Christians, a policy motivated not only by fear that active Jewish communities in India and the Middle East would influence New Christians to revert to Judaism, but also because their extensive trade network posed a direct threat to the royal monopoly of Asian commerce and the privileged role of *fidalgos* in its administration ("Goa Inquisition: New Light on First 100 Years [1561–1660]," *Purabhilekh-Puratatva* 4, no. 1 [1986]: 1–40). A decree of 1585 expelled all New Christians from the Estado da India, but the number of New Christians was so great and the reach of Portugal across the Indian Ocean so limited that the law was ineffective. See James Boyajian, *Portuguese Trade in Asia under the Hapsburgs, 1580–1640* (Baltimore, MD: Johns Hopkins University Press, 1993), 30–31, 88–89, and 201.

20. Ângela Barreto Xavier, "Conversion and the Push to Conformity in the Portuguese Empire" (unpublished paper). Between 1560 and 1623 the Goa Inquisition tried 3,444 people, of whom 1,484 (43 percent) were accused of Hindu or other non-monotheistic religious practices, generally referred to as *gentilismo*. See Luiza Tonon da Silva, "Os réus do Índico: Olhares sobre processados pela Inquisição de Goa (1560–1620)," paper presented at XXIX Simpósio de História Nacional, Brasília, 2017, www. snh2017. Anpuh .org.

21. For example, a new Christian convicted of stabbing a dying woman to keep her from denouncing him to the Inquisition asked for and received the punishment of exile (*degredo*) to Brazil in 1546. See António da Silva Rego, ed., *As Gavetas do Torre do Tombo* (Lisbon: Centro de Estudos HJistóricos Ultamarinos, 1960–77), 1:46. A law of June 30, 1567, that prohibited New Christians from emigrating to any overseas possession on pain of forfeiture of all property and five years of exile to Brazil was corrected the following year because of its obvious contradiction. The Portuguese inquisition tribunals exiled 311 prisoners accused of Judaism to Brazil — or 52 percent of all prisoners sent to that colony. See Geraldo Pieroni, "Outcasts from the Kingdom: The Inquisition and the Banishment of New Christians to Brazil," in *The Jews and the Expansion of Europe to the West, 1450–1800*, ed. Paolo Bernardini and Norman Fiering (New York: Berghahn Books, 2001), 242–53. On Portuguese penal exiles in general, see Timothy Coates, *Convicts and Orphans* (Stanford, CA: Stanford University Press, 2001), 78–85.

22. Elias Lipner, *Os judaizantes nas capitanias de cima* (Rio de Janeiro, Brazil: Brasiliense, 1969).

23. Cited by José Antônio Gonsalves de Mello, *Gente da Nação: Cristãos novos e judeus em Pernambuco, 1542–1654*, 2nd ed (Recife, Brazil: Fundação Joaquim Nabuco, 1990), 201–55.

24. The positive material expectations about Brazil are evident in the promotional text of Ambrósio Fernandes Brandão, a New Christian sugar planter. See Ambrósio Fernandes Brandão, *Dialogues on the Great Things of Brazil*, ed. Frederick Arthur H. Hall, William F. Harrisonm, and Dorothy Winters Welker (Albuquerque: University of New Mexico Press, 1986).

25. The original is: "são parvos os que ca moram em não viver no Brasil onde estiveram a sua vontade." Quoted by Anita Novinsky, "A Inquisição na Bahia: Um relatório de 1632," *Revista de História* (São Paulo, Brazil) 74 (1968): 422.

26. For the relevant documentation, see Stuart B. Schwartz, "When Brazil Was Jewish: New Sources on the Fall of Bahia, 1624, in the Context of Portugal's Political and Social Conditions in the Seventeenth Century," in *Pour l'histoire du Brésil: Mélanges offerts à Katia de Queirós Mattoso*, ed. François Crouzet and Denis Rolland (Paris: L'Harmattan, 2000), 245–60.

27. José Justino Andrade e Silva, *Colleção chronologica da legislação portuguesa (1603–1700)* (Lisbon: F.X. de Souza, 1854–59), 3:50. See the discussion

in Bruno Feitler, *Inquisition, juifs et nouveaux-chrétiens au Brésil* (Leuven, Belgium Leuven University Press, 2003), 64–66. Feitler attributes the failure to establish a permanent tribunal in Brazil to institutional competition, bureaucratic rivalries, and costs. He also points out that the Hapsburg kings appointed bishops in Bahia with inquisitorial experience to make up for the absence of a tribunal ("Usos políticos del Santo Oficio português en el Atlántico [Brasil y África Occidental]: El período filipino," *Hispania Sacra* 59, no. 119 [2007]: 269–91). New Christian influence on governing officials in Salvador is reported in Novinsky, "A Inquisição na Bahia," 417–20.

28. Quoted in Consuelo Varela and Juan Gil, *Cristóbal Colón: Textos y documentos completos* (Madrid: Alianza, 1982), 424–25.

29. Enrique Soria Mesa, "El origen judeoconverso de la nobleza indiana," in *Familias en el Viejo y el Nuevo Mundo*, ed. Ofelia Rey Castelao and Pablo. Cowen (Buenos Aires: Universidad Nacional de la Plata, 2017), 155–85. For Chilean examples, see Günter Bohm, "Crypto-Jews and New Christians in Colonial Peru and Chile," in *The Jews and the Expansion of Europe to the West, 1450–1800*, ed. Paolo Bernardini and Norman Fiering (New York: Berghan Books, 2001), 203–12.

30. Juan Gil, "El paso de los conversos a Indias," in *Los Conversos y la Inquisición*, ed. Juan Gil (Seville, Spain: Fundación El Monte), 57–95. For the estimate for New Spain, see Eva Alexandra Uchmany, "The Participation of the New Christians and Crypto-Jews in the Conquest, Colonization, and Trade of Spanish America, 1521–1660," in *The Jews and the Expansion of Europe to the West, 1450–1800*, ed. Paolo Bernardini and Norman Fiering (New York: Berghan Books, 2001), pp. 186–202. For an excellent overview, see Nathan Wachtel, "Une Amérique souterraine: Réseaux et solidarités marranes," Nathan Wachtel, *Entre Moïse et Jésus: Études marranes (XVe–XXIe siècle)* (Paris: CNRS, 2013), 165–202.

31. Between 1500 and 1650 only 389 Portuguese obtained licenses of naturalization in the Spanish American Indies, but the Portuguese residents probably numbered about 15,000–17,000, or 5–6 percent of the European settler population in the Spanish Indies. See Daviken Studnicki-Gizbert, "Invasion by Migration: Merchants and Migrants in the Portuguese Community of the Spanish Atlantic, 1590–1640" (unpublished paper).

32. In 1630, Cartagena had 184 resident foreigners, of whom 154 (84 per-

cent) were Portuguese. In the early seventeenth century, Venezuela had 125 foreign residents, of whom 115 were Portuguese. In cosmopolitan Potosí, the 74 Portuguese accounted for over 50 percent of the 144 foreigners. See Enriqueta Vila Vilar, "Estranjeros en Cartagena (1593–1630)," *Jahrbuch für geschichte von staat, wirtschaft, und gesellschaft lateinamerikas* 16, no. 1 (1979): 147–84.

33. Studnicki-Gizbert, "Invasion by Migration"; Vilar, "Extranjeros en Cartegena"; Jonathan I. Israel, "The Portuguese in Seventeenth-Century Mexico," *Jahrbuch für geschichte von staat, wirtschaft, und gesellschaft lateinamerikas* 11 (1974): 12–32.

34. Quoted in Fernando de Montesinos, *Auto de Fe celebrado en Lima el 23 de enero de 1639* (Lima: Pedro de Cabrera, 1639), 59.

35. These were men like Marcos de Baena, who farmed and rented lands to other conversos and whose son Simón was fluent in Otomí and well liked by the indigenous peoples of the town. Modern DNA studies reveal that about 6 percent of modern Otomí men from Ixquimilpan carry the J haplogroup, which is characteristically more common among Sephardic populations. Jonathan Graham, "Environmental, Social, and Political Change in the Otomí Heartland: A Hydraulic History of the Ixmiquilpan Valle (Hidalgo State, Mexico)," (PhD diss., Yale University, 2018). Graham cites Inês Nogueiro, João C. Teixeira, et. al. "Portuguese Crypto-Jews: The Genetic Heritage of a Complex History," *Frontiers in Genetics* 6 (2015): 1–12. For another study of Portuguese settled in a marginal area of New Spain, see Woodrow Borah, "The Portuguese of Tulancingo and the Special Donativo of 1642–1643," *Jahrbuch für geshichte von staat, wirtschaft und gessellschaft lateinamerikas* 4, no. 1 (1967): 386–98.

36. The idea that Jews and Indians were related and shared certain rites and rituals appears not only in a number of Inquisition trials and in various Spanish chronicles, like the 1589 one of the Jesuit José de Acosta, but also famously in a text from 1650 by Rabbi Menasseh ben Israel. See Henry Méchoulan and Gérard Nahon, eds., *Menassah ben Israel: The Hope of Israel* (Oxford: Oxford University Press, 1987). On potential aid to rivals, Spanish claims that Salvador, Bahia, was taken by the Dutch in 1624 due to New Christian collaboration preceded the arrival of official reports and characterized many Spanish accounts of the events, but not those of most Portuguese

authors. See Stuart B. Schwartz, "Voyage of the Vassals: Royal Power, Noble Obligations, and Merchant Capital before the Portuguese Restoration of Independence, 1624–40," *American Historical Review* 96, no. 3 (1991): 735–62.

37. After 1640 the viceroy of Peru was concerned that the Portuguese *bandeirantes* (backwoodsmen) who were capturing Indians in Paraguay might be teaching their captives the use of firearms and so cause "great confusion" in the region. See AGI, Viceroy Marquis of Mancera to Council of the Indies, June 8, 1641, Lima, 50.

38. AGI, Lima, 51, libro 3 *despachos* (July 20, 1642). I have discussed this previously. See Stuart B. Schwartz, "Panic in the Indies: The Portuguese Threat to the Spanish Empire," in *Rebelión y resistencia en el mundo hispánico del siglo xvii*, ed. Werner Thomas and Bart De Groof (Leuven, Belgium: Leuven University Press, 1992), 205–26. See also Irene Silverblatt, "New Christians and New World Fears in Seventeenth-Century Peru," *Comparative Studies in Society and History* 42, no. 3 (2000): 524–46. For a discussion of fear related to the ability of Portuguese New Christians in Lima to speak African languages, see ibid., 535–36.

39. BPE, memorial de Fray Antonio de Chinchilla, CVIII/2–12.

40. Ana Hutz, *Homens da nação e de negócios: Redes comerciais no mundo ibérico, 1580–1640* (São Paulo, Brazil: Intermeios, 2017); Jonathan Schorsch, "New Christian Slave Traders: A Literature Review and Research Agenda," in *The Sephardic Atlantic: Colonial Histories and Post-Colonial Perspectives*, ed. Sina Rauschenbach and Jonathan Schorsch (London: Palgrave, 2019), 23–55.

41. The historiography on the *asientos* of the slave trade to Cartagena is well developed. See, for example, Enriqueta Vila Vilar, *Hispanoamérica y el comercio de esclavos: Los asientos portugueses* (Seville, Spain: Escuela de Estudios Hispanoamericanos, 1977); David Wheat, *Atlantic Africa and the Spanish Caribbean, 1570–1640* (Chapel Hill: University of North Carolina Press, 2016).

42. For classic studies, see Alice Canabrava, *O comércio português no Rio da Prata (1580–1640)* (Belo Horizonte, Brazil: Itatiaia, 1984); Zacarías Moutukias, *Contrabando y control colonial em el siglo xvii: Buenos Aires, el Atlántico y el espacio peruano* (Buenos Aires: Consejo Empresarial de América Latina, 1988).

43. The bishops of Buenos Aires, Tucumán, and Córdoba were given in-

quisitorial responsibilities. See Jonathan I. Israel, "Buenos Aires, Tucumán, and the River Plate Route: Portuguese Conversos and the 'Commercial Subversion' of the Spanish Indies (1580–1640)," in Jonathan I. Israel, *Diasporas within a Diaspora: Jews, Crypto-Jews and the World Maritime Empires (1540–1740)* (Leiden, the Netherlands: Brill, 2002), 125–50.

44. David Sorkin, "Merchant Colonies: Resettlement in Italy, France, Holland, and England, 1550–1700," in *Reappraisals and New Studies of the Modern Jewish Experience*, ed. Brian M. Smollett and Christian Weise (Leiden, the Netherlands: Brill, 2015), 123–44.

45. Sorkin, "Merchant Colonies," 125.

46. Jaime Contreras Contreras, "Cristianos de España, Judíos de Amsterdam: Emigración, família y negocios," *Estudis* 20 (1994): 122. Jonathan I. Israel provides a synoptic narrative of the Jewish return to Western and Central Europe (*European Jewry in the Age of Mercantilism, 1550–1700* [Oxford: Clarendon Press of Oxford University Press, 1985], 35–69).

47. Juan Ignacio Pulido Serrano, "Political Aspects of the Converso Problem: On the Portuguese Restauração of 1640," in *The Conversos and Moriscos in Late Medieval Spain and Beyond*, ed. Kevin Ingram (Leiden, the Netherlands: Brill, 2012), 219–46.

48. In New Spain over one-third of all the prosecutions for Judaizing took place in the period 1642–49, and the persecutions then were far more numerous than in previous or subsequent periods. A similar pattern holds true for Lima (1635–41) and Cartagena (1636–38). See Alfonso W. Quiroz, "The Expropriation of Portuguese New Christians in Spanish America, 1635–1649," *Ibero-Amerikanisches Archiv* 11, no. 4 (1985): 407–65.

49. The historiography is extensive. For recent work, see, for example, Irene Silverblatt, *Modern Inquisitions: Peru and the Colonial Origins of the Civilized World* (Durham, NC: Duke University Press, 2004); Ana E. Schaposchnik, *The Lima Inquisition: The Plight of the Crypto-Jews in Seventeenth-Century Peru* (Madison: University of Wisconsin Press, 2015). See especially Nathan Wachtel, *La foi du souvenir: Labyrinthes marranes* (Paris: Seuil, 2001), *La logique des büchers* (Paris: Seuil, 2009), and *Entre Moïse et Jésus*.

50. For an exemplary case, see Claude B. Stuczynski, "Entre la etnia conversa, la burguesia mercantile y la nobleza: Heitor Mendes de Brito 'O Rico': Nuevos documentos, nuevas interpretaciones," in *La monarquía hispánica y las minorías: Élites y negociación política en la España de los Austrias*, ed. Fran-

cisco Javier Moreno Díaz del Campo and Ana Isabel López Salazar (Madrid: Sílex, 2019), 277–312.

51. Natalia Muchnik seeks to answer these questions in Spain ("Religion et mobilité sociale: L'ascension des marranes dans l'Espagne inquisitoriale [xvie–xviie siècles], *Genèses* 66, no. 1 [2007]: 90–107). She emphasizes spatial mobility, communal connections, and economic resources and connections. Jonathan Elukin examines relations across the Middle Ages in Europe and also suggests long periods of relatively benign normality (*Living Together, Living Apart: Rethinking Jewish-Christian Relations in the Middle Ages* [Princeton, NJ: Princeton University Press, 2007]).

52. Notable in this line of interpretation are Linda Martz, *A Network of Converso Families in Early Modern Toledo: Assimilating a Minority* (Ann Arbor: University of Michigan Press, 2003) and Enrique Soria Mesa, *La realidad tras el espejo: Ascenso social y limpieza de sangre en la España de Felipe II, Cátedra Felipe II* (Valladolid, Spain: Universidad de Valladolid, 2016). For a discussion of converso intellectuals' employment of humanism and nobility of merit and intellect as the keys to social qualification, see Ingram, *Converso Non-Conformity*, 225–42.

53. The term "cardiologist" is from Nicolás Broens, *Monarquía y capital mercantile: Felipe IV y las redes comerciales portuguesas (1627–1635)* (Madrid: Universidad Autónoma de Madrid, 1989), 70. A classic example of reformist policy recommendations, or what Spaniards called *arbitrismo*, is the pro-converso policies that are the subject of Israel S. Revah, "Le plaidoyer en faveur des 'nouveaux chrétiens' portugais du Licencié Martín González de Cellorigo (Madrid, 1619)," *Revue des Études Juives*, 4th ser., 2 (1963): 280–398. See also Claude B. Stuczynski, "Harmonizing Identities: The Problem of the Integration of the Portuguese Conversos in Early Modern Iberian Corporate Polities," *Jewish History* 25 (2011): 229–57; Antonio Irigoyen López, "Religión católica y estatutos de limpieza de sangre: A propósito de un memorial al Conde-Duque de Olivares," *Sefarad* 70, no. 1 (2010): 141–70.

54. Fernanda Olival, "Rigor e interesses: Os estatutos de limpeza de sangue em Portugal," *Cadernos de estudos sefarditas* 4 (2004): 151–82.

55. Ruth Pike, *Linajudos and Conversos in Seville: Greed and Prejudice in Sixteenth- and Seventeenth-Century Spain* (New York: Peter Lang, 2000).

56. For a model study of these American genealogical manipulations, see Evaldo Cabral de Mello, *O nome e o sangue: Uma fraude genealógica no*

Pernambuco colonial (São Paulo, Brazil: Companhia das Letras, 1989). Jean-Paul Zúñiga emphasizes that in Chile and Peru, Spanish colonizers and office seekers practicing genealogical deception were more outspoken in claiming noble lineage then in avoiding the stigma of converso origins (*Espagnols d'Outre-Mer* [Paris: EHESS, 2002], 130–47).

57. For example, on Brazil, see James Wadsworth, *Agents of Orthodoxy: Honor, Status, and the Inquisition in Colonial Pernambuco, Brazil* (Lanham, MD: Rowman and Littlefield, 2007); Aldair Carlos Rodrigues, *Limpios de sangue: Familiares do Santo Ofício: Inquisição e sociedade em Minas Gerais* (São Paulo, Brazil: Alameda, 2011); Daniela Calainho, *Agentes da fé: Familiares da Inquisição portuguesa no Brasil colonial* (Bauru, Brazil: Editora da Universidade da Sagrada Coração, 2006).

58. François Soyer, "The Passion of Christ in the Church of San Cristóbal de Rapaz: An example of Medieval Anti-Jewish Iconography in Colonial Peru," *eHumanitas/Conversos* 5 (2017): 392–416. Soyer presents the image of the flagellation of a crucifix by conversos in the Tambo de Montero in Cuzco, an incident that supposedly took place in the seventeenth century but that seems to be a story inspired by the famous 1632 case of the Cristo de Paciencia in Madrid. Noticeably, in the Peruvian canvas once again the conversos are indistinguishable from other Spaniards in their physical appearance and clothing.

59. For example, after the rebellion of Portugal in 1640, Portuguese residents in Seville were required to make a "donation" to help restore Portugal to its rightful king. Under the direction of the Council of the Indies, funds were collected from 105 individuals. See AGI, "Los portugueses vecinos y establecidos en Sevilla con el motibo del lebantimiento del Reino de Portugal ofrecieron servir al Rey," Contracción, legajo 4882.

60. Richard Greenleaf, "The Great Visitas of the Mexican Holy Office, 1645–1669," *Americas* 44, no. 4 (1988): 399–420; Stanley M. Hordes, "The Inquisition as Economic and Political Agent: The Campaign of the Mexican Holy Office against the Crypto-Jews in the Mid-Seventeenth Century," *Americas* 39, no. 1 (1982): 23–38.

61. Israel provides considerable evidence that the Jewish community of Amsterdam, their New Christian contacts in Portugal, and Dutch commerce as a whole profited considerably during the Portuguese restoration ("Spain and the Dutch Sephardim, 1609–1661," *Studia Rosenthaliana* 12,

nos. 1–2 [1978]: 1–6). See also Jonathan I. Israel, "The Sephardi Diaspora and the Struggle for Portuguese Independence from Spain (1640–1668)," in Jonathan I. Israel, *Diasporas within a Diaspora: Jews, Crypto-Jews and the World Maritime Empires (1540–1740)* (Leiden, the Netherlands: Brill, 2002), 313–54.

62. Joseph Addison, *Spectator*, September 27, 1712.

63. The theme of Jews and money has long preoccupied Spanish historians' considerations of the conversos. See, for example, Julio Caro Baroja, *Los judíos en la España moderna y contemporánea*, 2nd ed. (Madrid: Istmo, 1978), 2:13–115.

64. Duarte Gomes Solis, *Discursos sobre los comercios de las Indias* (Lisbon: n.p., 1622). For discussions of Gómez Solis, see Studnicki-Gizbert, *A Nation on the Ocean Sea*, 129–35; Nathan Wachtel, "La théorie mercantiliste 'marrane' de Duarte Gomes Solis," in Nathan Wachtel, *Des archives aux terrains* (Paris: EHESS, 2014), 437–64.

65. When Philip II of Spain assumed the Portuguese crown at the Cortes of Thomar in 1581, the Portuguese nobility demanded complete exclusion of "the men of the nation" from all offices but also sought to limit the ability of *letrados* to gain access to honors or state employment (Fernando Bouza Álvarez, "Portugal en la monarquía hispánica [1580–1640] Felipe II, Las Cortes de Thomar y la genesis del Portugal Católico," [PhD diss., Universidad Complutense, 1986], 1:476–80).

66. Francisco de Sousa Coutinho, the Portuguese ambassador to the Dutch Republic wrote from Amsterdam in 1644, "As much Jews as they are, the Portuguese here have an affection for Portugal that makes them prefer to serve Your Majesty more than the Flemings" (Virginia Rau, "A embaixada de Tristão de Mendonça Furtado e os arquivos notariais holandeses," *Anais da Academia Portuguesa da História*, 2nd ser., 8 [1958]: 102). Father António Vieira also argued that "men of the nation" would be helpful to Portugal's struggle for independence. See Stuart B. Schwartz, "The Contexts of Vieira's Toleration of Jews and New Christians," *Luso-Brazilian Review* 40, no. 1 (2003): 33–44. It is interesting to note that the converso merchants Lope Ramires in Amsterdam and his brother Jacob Curiel (Duarte Nunes da Costa) in Hamburg both served as agents for the Bragança throne during the Portuguese restoration. Despite the fact that both were practicing Jews, they were granted titles as gentlemen knights of the Royal House

(*cavalheiro fidalgo da Casa Real*) as a reward for their services. Ramires was later dropped for pro-Castilian sentiments, but the Curiel family held fidalgo titles as Bragança agents until 1795. See Rau, "A embaixada," 120.

67. José Calvert de Magalhães, *História do pensamiento económico em Portugal* (Coimbra, Portugal: Coimbra University Press, 1967), 247–49.

68. João Lúcio de Azevedo, *História de António Vieira*, 3rd ed. (Lisbon: Clássica Editora, 1992), 1:53–159, is often cited on Vieira's economic plans and the New Christians despite the author's jaundiced opinions about the conversos. For more balanced works, see Richard Graham, *Antônio Vieira and the Economic Rehabilitation of Portugal* (São Paulo, Brazil: Arquivo do Estado, 1978); Leonor Freire Costa, *O transporte no Atlântico e a Companhia Geral do Comércio do Brasil, 1580–1663*, 2 vols. (Lisbon: Comissão Nacional para as Comemorações dos Descobrimentos Portugueses, 2002).

69. "Poderoso caballero es don Dinero" (the sarcastic poem) is available in Francisco de Quevedo, *An Anthology of Quevedo's Poetry*, ed. R. M. Price (Manchester, UK: Manchester University Press, 1969), 60–62. From Quevedo's remarkable pen came a number of antisemitic works. See especially Francisco de Quevedo, *Execración contra los judíos*, ed. Fernando Cabo Aseguinolaza and Santiago Fernández Mosquera (Barcelona: Crítica, 1996), which circulated in manuscript, and *La hora de todos*, a play about an international Jewish conspiracy—a precursor to the *Protocols of the Elders of Zion*. See Francisco de Quevedo, *La hora de todos y la fortuna con seso*, ed. Lía Schwartz (Madrid: Castalia, 2009).

70. Stuczynski, "Entre la etnia conversa"; Olival, "Rigor e interesses."

71. I refer here to specific incidents of sacrilege or so-called blood libel, such as the Niño de La Guardia (in Toledo in 1491), the *crucifijo de la paciencia* (Madrid, 1632), and the sacrilege of Odivelas (Lisbon, 1671). See also Juan Ignacio Pulido Serrano, *Injurias a Cristo: Religión, política y antijudaísmo en el siglo xvii* (Alcalá, Spain: Universidad de Alcalá de Henares, 2002); Jorge Martins, *O senhor roubado: A Inquisição e a questão Judaica* (Lisbon: Europress, 2002).

72. Dedieu, "¿Pecado original o pecado social?," 70–72.

73. For a useful overview of these issues, see António Borges Coelho, "Política, dinheiro e fé: Cristãos-novos e judeus portugueses no tempo dos Filipes," in his *Política, Dinheiro e Fé* (Lisbon: Editorial Caminho, 2001), 109–50.

74. Noticeably, the opponents of the pardon in Portugal were just as willing to offer a monetary service to the king to block the New Christians' request for a pardon. A similar situation had arisen in 1595–99, when Portuguese New Christians had offered the crown an interest-free loan but had been blocked by the Inquisition—which succeeded in getting the governor of Portugal to offer the funds instead. In 1605, some of the New Christians opposed the pardon and argued that they were not "a separate republic, but lived as part of the mystic body with the Old Christians of the kingdom" (ANTT, Conselho Geral Santo Oficio, *livro* 314, f. 51, quoted in Juan Ignacio Pulido Serrano, "Las negociaciones con los cristianos nuevos en tiempos de Felipe III a la luz de algunos documentos inéditos [1598–1607]," *Sefarad* 66, no. 2 [2006]: 368). See also Juan Ignacio Pulido Serrano, *Os judeus na Inquisição nos tempos dos Filipes* (Lisbon: Campo da Comunicação, 2007), 79–88; Ana Isabel López-Salazar Cordes, *Inquisición portuguesa y monarquía hispánica en tiempos del perdón general de 1605* (Lisbon: Colibri, 2010). For a general discussion of corruption at the court of Philip III under his favorite, the Duke of Lerma, see Antonio Feros, *Kingship and Favoritism in the Spain of Philip III, 1598–1621* (Cambridge: Cambridge University Press, 2000).

75. ACA, Inquisitors of Coimbra to Olivares, June 1623, *caja* 118, f. 62, and Inquisitors of Lisboa to Olivares, May 6, 1624, f.103. The inquisitors reported on a recent autoda-fé in which António Homem, a professor of canon law at the University of Coimbra, was burned for being the senior rabbi (*rabino maior*), a claim that supposedly demonstrated not only the extent to which Judaism had penetrated Portuguese society but also why the work of the Inquisition was so important and merited Olivares's help. A similar effort from the tribunal of Evora noted that "all depends on the holy zeal of the King, and on that which Your Excellency has for the public good" (ACA, July 19, 1624, caja 118, f. 112).

76. Quoted in John H. Elliott, *The Count Duke of Olivares: The Stateman in an Age of Decline* (New Haven, CT: Yale University Press, 1986), 10–11 and 118. See also Irigoyen López, "Religión católica."

77. Olivares's enemies often accused him of philo-judaism, but that charge has been revealed to have been greatly exaggerated by his personal desire to avoid converso family contacts. Nevertheless, his policies—especially the granting of freedom of movement to conversos, which allowed them to travel and move their assets—was a major concession. See Mauricio Ebben,

"El triángulo imposible: La corona española, el Santo Ofício y los banqueros portugueses, 1627–1655," *Hispania* 53, no. 2, no. 184 (1993): 541–56; Shai Cohen, "El retorno de los judeoconversos portugueses en época del conde duque de Olivares," *Hipogrifo* 1, special supplement (2018): 191–215.

78. Harry Cross, "Commerce and Orthodoxy: A Spanish Response to Portuguese Commercial Penetration in the Viceroyalty of Peru, 1580–1640," *Americas* 35, no. 2 (1978): 151–67.

79. Gonçalo de Reparaz, *Os portugueses no vice-reinado do Peru (séculos xvi e xvii)* (Lisbon: Instituto de Alta Cultura, 1976), 25–27.

80. Quiroz, "The Expropriation of Portuguese New Christians," 421–28; Maurice Birckel, "Recherches sur le trésorerie inquisitoriale de Lima," *Mélanges de la Casa de Velázquez* 5 (1969): 223–307, and "Recherches sur le trésorerie inquisitoriale de Lima- II," *Mélanges de la Casa de Velázquez* 6 (1970): 309–57. See also Schaposchnik, *The Lima Inquisition*, 47–49. On the financial status and politicization of the Mexican tribunal, see Eva Alexandra Uchmany, "Simón Váez Sevilla," *Estudios de historia novohispana* 9 (1985): 67–93.

81. Hordes, "The Inquisition as Economic and Political Agent," 32–35.

82. AHN, Inquisition of Cartagena to the Supreme Council of the Inquisition (October, 1635), Inquisición, legajo 1012. I have provided an extended translation of the request and some details on this case previously. See Schwartz, "Panic in the Indies," 205–26.

83. A case in point is António José Saraiva, *Inquisição e cristãos novos*, 5th ed. (Lisbon: Estampa, 1985). First published in 1969, Saraiva's work questioned the reality of any Inquisitorial charges of crypto-Judaism, but it was seriously challenged by the French scholar Israel S. Révah. Their debate is published as an appendix to the 1985 edition cited here.

84. Juan Ignacio Pulido Serrano places the campaign of the three American inquisitions in a broad Atlantic context as an attack on converso control of transatlantic commerce, but he sees its origins in the heated anticonverso atmosphere of the 1630s in Lisbon and Madrid ("Converso Complicities in the Atlantic Monarchy: Political and Social Conflicts behind the Inquisitorial Persecutions," in *The Conversos and Moriscos in Late Medieval Spain and Beyond*, ed. Kevin Ingram and Juan Ignacio Pulido Serrano [Amsterdam: Brill, 2015], 3:117–28).

85. For example, see Miriam Bodian, *Hebrews of the Portuguese Nation:*

Conversos and Community in Early Modern Amsterdam (Bloomington: Indiana University Press, 1997); Yosef Kaplan, *Judíos nuevos en Amsterdam* (Barcelona: Gedisa, 1996); Francesca Trivellato, *The Familiarity of Strangers: The Sephardic Diaspora, Livorno, and Cross-Cultural Trade in the Early Modern Period* (New Haven, CT: Yale University Press, 2009). The classic study—Louisa Schell Hoberman, *Mexico's Merchant Elite, 1590–1660* (Durham, NC: Duke University Press, 1991)—gives limited attention to ethnic/religious dimensions.

86. On the Iberian diaspora in general, see Daviken Studnicki-Gizbert, *A Nation upon the Ocean Sea: Portugal's Atlantic Diaspora and the Crisis of the Spanish Empire, 1492–1640* (Oxford: Oxford University Press, 2007). For an extensive local study, see Gleydi Sullón Barreto, *Extranjeros integrados: Portugueses en la Lima virreinal, 1570–1680* (Madrid: CSIC, 2016).

87. David Grant Smith, "The Portuguese Mercantile Class of Portugal and Brazil in the Seventeenth Century: A Socioeconomic Study of the Merchants of Lisbon and Bahia, 1620–1690" (PhD diss., University of Texas, 1975). See also James Boyajian, "The New Christians Reconsidered: Evidence from Lisbon's Portuguese Bankers, 1497–1647," *Studia Rosenthaliana* 13, no. 2 (1979):, 129–56; Studnicki-Gizbert, *A Nation upon the Ocean Sea*; Cátia Antunes, "On Cosmopolitanism and Cross-Culturalism: An Enquiry into the Business Practices and Multiple Identities of the Portuguese Merchants of Amsterdam," in *Cosmopolitanism in the Portuguese-Speaking World*, ed. Francisco Bethencourt (Leiden, the Netherlands: Brill, 2018), 23–39.

88. See Leonor Freire Costa, "Merchant Groups in the 17th Century Brazilian Sugar Trade: Reappraising Old Topics with New Research Insights," *eJournal of Portuguese History* 2, no. 1 (2004): 1–11. The theoretical aspects of the change from communal or ethnic commercial networks to anonymous markets and exchanges among the Sephardi is explored in Francesca Trivellato, "Sephardic Merchants in the Early Modern Atlantic and Beyond," in *Atlantic Diasporas: Jews, Conversos, and Crypto-Jews in the Age of Mercantilism*, ed. Richard L. Kagan and Philip D. Morgan (Baltimore, MD: Johns Hopkins University Press, 2008), 99–120.

89. On Fernandes de Elvas, see Hutz, *Homens da nação e de negócios*.

90. Silverblatt, "New Christians and New World Fears," 536–39; Studnicki-Gizbert, *A Nation upon the Ocean Sea*, 174; Schaposchnik, *The Lima Inquisition*, 174–75. Questions remain about the veracity of the

charges against Simón Váez Sevilla. See Eva Alexandra Uchmany, "Simón Váez Sevilla," *Estudios de Historia Novo Hispana* 9 (1985): 67–93.

91. Thomas F. Glick, "On Converso and Marrano Identity," in *Crisis and Creativity in the Sephardic World, 1391–1648*, ed. Benjamin R. Gampel (New York: Columbia University Press, 1997), 59–76. Studnicki-Gizbert (*A Nation upon the Ocean Sea*) and Israel (*Diasporas within a Diaspora*) emphasize the non-religious aspects of the Sephardi networks. Schorsch complains that this "econocentric" approach may miss the influence of religious life and custom on their integration as a community, and he points out the more balanced approach of Trivellato (*The Familiarity of Strangers*) and the cultural richness achieved in Kaplan's studies on Sephardi communities, particularly that of Amsterdam (see *Judíos nuevos en Amsterdam*).See Schorsch, "Sephardic Business," 498–99.

92. Bernardo López Belinchon, *Honra, libertad y hacienda (Hombres de negocios y judíos sefardíes)* (Madrid: Universidad de Alcalá, 2001), 417–21.

93. Yosef Kaplan, "The Travels of Portuguese Jews from Amsterdam to the 'Lands of Idolatry,'" in *Jews and Conversos: Studies in Society and the Inquisition*, ed. Yosef Kaplan (Jerusalem: Magnes Press, 1985), 197–224; David L. Graizbord, *Souls in Dispute: Converso Identities in Iberia and the Jewish Diaspora, 1500–1700* (Philadelphia: University of Pennsylvania Press, 2004).

94. "Ships with two rudders" became a common negative description of the conversos. See Brian Pullan, "'A Ship with Two Rudders': 'Righetto Marrano' and the Inquisition in Venice," *Historical Journal* 20, no. 1 (1977): 25–53.

95. Stanley M. Hordes, "Between Toleration and Persecution: The Relationship of the Inquisition and Crypto-Jews on the Northern Frontier," in *Religion in New Spain*, ed. Susan Schroeder and Stafford Poole (Albuquerque: University of New Mexico Press, 2007), 218–37.

96. See also Licensiado Gutierrez de Ulloa to Phillip II (March 12, 1597); Real Cédula (royal decree) of Philip III, 1602; Francisco de Trexo to the Lima Inquisition (April 11, 1622); and Francisco de Trexo to the Lima Inquisition (April 22, 1619), all reprinted in Mario J. Saban, *Judíos conversos* (Buenos Aires: Editorial Distal, 1993), 2:55–56, 65–66, and 151–54.

97. In *Contrabando y sociedad en el Río de la Plata colonial* (Buenos Aires: Editorial Dunken, 2006), Macarena Perusset incorporated the findings of

the earlier classics of Zacarias Moutoukías (*Contrabando y control colonial en el siglo XVII: Buenos Aires, el Atlántico, y el espacio peruano* [Buenos Aires: Centro Editor de América Latina, 1988]) and Eduardo Saguier ("The Social Impact of a Middleman Minority in a Divided Host Society: The Case of the Portuguese in Early Seventeenth-Century Buenos Aires," *Hispanic American Historical Review* 65, no. 3 [1985]: 467–91).

98. Andrés Millé, *Crónica de la orden franciscana en la conquista del Perú, Paraguay y el Tucumán y su convento del antigua Buenos Aires* (Buenos Aires: Emece Editorial, 1961), 219–20. The Franciscans gave sanctuary to some conversos fleeing civil justice.

99. In 1595, the Portuguese contractor Pedro Gomes Reinel received a royal contract to legally supply to Spanish America 4,250 slaves a year, or 38,250 slaves over the nine years of the contract.

100. Studnicki-Gizbert suggests that bringing conversos into observance of the law of Moses in lands in which the Inquisition operated was an "invitation into a world of secrecy, that only unconditional trust could sustain" — that is, another way of reinforcing the confidence that buttressed business relations (*A Nation upon the Ocean Sea*, 72–73).

101. This is cited in João Manuel Vaz Monteiro de Figueiroa Rego, "'A honra alheia por um fio': Os estatutos de limpeza de sangue no espaço de expressão Ibérica (sécs. xvi-xviii)" (PhD diss., Universidade do Minho 2009), 315. See also Soria Mesa, "El origen judeoconverso."

102. Claude B. Stuczynski, "Toward a Repolitization of the Converso Phenomenon in Portugal and Beyond," *Journal of Levantine Studies* 6 (2016): 5–12.

103. See Bruno Feitler, *The Imaginary Synagogue: Anti-Jewish Literature in the Portuguese Early Modern World (16th–18th Centuries)* (Leiden, the Netherlands: Brill, 2015); David Nirenberg, *Anti-Judaism: The Western Tradition* (New York: Norton, 2013).

104. AGS, *Carta régia* to the Archbishop Viceroy of Portugal (July 30, 1614), Secretaria provincial/Portugal 1511, f. 131v.-132. Typical of this invective is this anonymous advice to Felipe IV: "This kingdom is infected with heresies, principally by perfidious Judaism that like a lightning bolt burns all, the cause of all the ills that we suffer; making it necessary to put a brake on those people suspect in this matter so that they recognize that with Your

Majesty they will never find any favor, but always punishment" (Hispanic Society of America, New York, manuscript 2/13).

105. José Pedro Paiva and Giuseppe Marcocci take this position (*História da Inquisição portuguesa [1536–1821]* [Lisbon: Esfera dos Livros, 2013]).

106. Pulido Serrano, *Os judeus*, 153.

107. Irigoyen López, "Religión católica." See the classic article by Henry Kamen, "Uma crisis de conciencia en la edad de oro en España: Inquisición contra 'limpieza de sangre,'" *Bulletin Hispanique* 88, nos. 3–4 (1986): 321–56. See also Helen Rawlings, "Augustín Salucio's Rehabilitation of the Converso and the Revisionist Debate over Racial and Religious Discrimination in Early Seventeenth-Century Spain," *Bulletin of Spanish Studies* 94, no. 10 (2017): 1649–67.

108. AHN, Inquisición Toledo, legajo 2105/28; José Toribio Medina, *Historia del tribunal del Santo Oficio de la Inquisición en Chile* (Santiago, Chile: Ercilla, 1890), 1:291–92; Arlindo Rupert, *A Igreja no Brasil* (Santa Maria, Brazil: Palotti, 1981), 1:260.

109. AHN, case of Fernando de Ludena, Inquisición de Murcia, legajo 2022, Relación de causa, 1596, n. 25.

110. AHN, Relación de causa, Sevilla, 1638, Inquisición. 2075/37, fs. 6v-7.

111. I have written about this issue more fully elsewhere. See Stuart B. Schwartz, *All Can Be Saved: Religious Tolerance and Salvation in the Iberian Atlantic World* (New Haven, CT: Yale University Press, 2008), 59–60. The idea of divine justice for all who respected natural law also existed in the Sephardic community in the diaspora and can be seen in the discussions of Juan del Prado and Orobio de Castro and in the writings of Rabbi Menasseh ben Israel. See Henry Méchoulan, "Menasseh ben Israel and the World of the Non-Jew," in *Menasseh ben Israel and His World*, ed. Yosef Kaplan, Henry Méchoulan, and Richard H. Popkin (Leiden, the Netherlands: Brill, 1989), 83–97. On the Iberian influence on Jewish skepticism and religious doubt, see the somewhat divergent essays by Yosef Kaplan ("'From Christianity to Judaism' Revisited: Some Critical Remarks More than Thirty Years after Its Publication," in *Menasseh ben Israel and His World*, 15–30) and Natalia Muchnik ("Orobio contra Prado: A Trans-European Controversy," 31–56, in *Isaac Orobio: The Jewish Argument with Dogma and Doubt*, ed. Carson Wilke [Berlin: Walter de Gruyter, 2018], 31–56).

112. AGN, trial of María de Zarate, Inquisición de México, vol. 500. The trial text has been published in Boleslao Lewin, *La inquisición en México: Racismo inquisitorial (El singular caso de María de Zarate)* (Puebla, Mexico: J. M. Cajica, Jr., 1971), where her statement appears on page 61. The case is also presented in detail in Wachtel, *La foi du souvenir,* 161–228.

113. The various forms of criticism of the Inquisition have been studied by Yllan de Mattos (*A Inquisição contestada: Críticos e críticas ao Santo Oficio português [1605–1681]* [Rio de Janeiro, Brazil: Mauad, 2014]).

114. Schwartz, *All Can Be Saved,* 215–18.

115. AGN, trial of Juan Gómez (1656), Inquisición, vol. 506, *exp[idiente]* 8, fs. 395–481. The claim was not uncommon. For example, Bartolomé Vizcaino, from Baeza, claimed that he was better than God, since God was from Judea and a Jew while he was an Old Christian and a gentleman. See AHN, Relación de causa, Seville, 1604–5, Inquisición legajo 2075. There are shades here of the old apocryphal story of the Castilian and the Portuguese who disputed which was the oldest Christian. The Portuguese claimed priority, saying that he was a relative of Christ, and the Castilian replied with distain, "So then you are a Jew!" No, said the haughty Portuguese, the relationship is on the divinity side (*que o parentesco é por parte da divinidade*). See Miguel Herrero García, *Ideas de los españoles del siglo xvii,* 2nd ed. (Madrid: Gredos, 1966), 230.

116. AGN, trial of Juan Gómez, Inquisición, vol. 506, *expediente* 8, fs. 395–481 [1656]. See also the summary of this case in AHN, Inquisición, libro 1065, fs. 320v.–324v.

117. For a parallel discussion involving quotidian contact with Moriscos, see Trevor J. Dadson, "El día a día de la convivencia entre cristianos viejos y nuevos en la Mancha," in *Identidades y fronteras culturales en el mundo ibérico en la edad moderna,* ed. José Luís Beltrán, Bernat Hernández, and Doris Moreno, 2nd ed. (Barcelona: Bellaterra, 2016), 107–20.

118. João Capistrano de Abreu, ed., *Primeira visitação do Santo Officio às partes do Brasil pelo licenciado Heitor Furtado de Mendoça, Confissões da Bahia, 1591–92* (Rio de Janeiro, Brazil: Briguiet, 1935), 108. For similar conditions with a minority population in Spain, see Dadson, "El día a día de la convivencia," 109.

119. Jonathan Schorsch, *Jews and Blacks in the Early Modern World* (Cambridge: Cambridge University Press, 2004), and *Swimming in the Christian*

Atlantic: Judeoconversos, Afroiberians, and Amerindians in the Seventeenth Century (Leiden, the Netherlands: Brill, 2009).

120. I refer here not only to the distinctions made between themselves and the castas in the New World, but also to the exclusion of non-Sephardic Askenazi Jews from the Amsterdam Jewish community. See Yosef Kaplan, "The Self-Definition of the Sephardic Jews of Western Europe and Their Relation to the Alien and Stranger," in *Crisis and Creativity in the Sephardic World, 1391–1648*, ed. Benjamin R. Gampel (New York: Columbia University Press, 1997), 122–45.

121. AGN, trial of Sebastián de los Reyes, 1656, vol. 498, *expidiente* 5, f. 68. See the discussion in Solange Alberro, *Inquisición y sociedad en México, 1571–1800* (Mexico City: Fondo de Cultura Económica, 1988), 467–72; Schwartz, *All Can Be Saved*, 144.

122. See, for example, the case of Francisco Botelho discussed in Wachtel, *La foi du souvenir*, 161–228. The case involved an affair between a converso's daughter and a mestizo youth raised in the household.

123. Schorsch, *Jews and Blacks*, 303. See also Schorsch's expansive exploration of this relationship in *Swimming in the Christian Atlantic*.

124. Baroja, *Los judíos en la España moderna y contemporánea*, 3: 91–133; Jonathan Israel, "The Final Suppression of Crypto-Judaism in Spain and the End of the Sephardi World Maritime Networks," in Jonathan Israel, *Diasporas within a Diaspora: Jews, Crypto-Jews and the World Maritime Empires (1540–1740)* (Leiden, the Netherlands: Brill, 2002), 567–84.

125. Israel, *Diasporas within a Diaspora*, 1.

126. The process of assimilation is underlined in Juan Ignacio Pulido Serrano, "Antonio Domínguez Ortiz y el problema converso en su obra," *Historia Social* 47 (2003): 53–69. The historiography on the conversos in Latin America is narrowly focused on the seventeenth century. A full study of their actions, role, and contacts in the following century is lacking and would be particularly interesting in the Caribbean region—where by that time there were active Jewish communities in places like Barbados, Jamaica, and Curaçao, with which some of the conversos had relations.

127. Much of the rabbinic literature had long excluded conversos living as Christians from the Jewish community, although there was some dissent. Trivellato notes that when Jacob Carvaglio of Livorno prepared his will in the 1760s, he included as his heir any son that his son Abraham fathered

with a "woman of the Jewish nation of Spanish or Portuguese descent, born of parents living in Livorno, Venice, London, Amsterdam or Aleppo" (*The Familiarity of Strangers*, 41). This implies that conversos were not included. My thanks to Professor Trivelatto for pointing this out to me.

128. The original is: "l'oubli fait son œuvre." See Wachtel, *La foi du souvenir*, 330. Daviken Studnicki-Gizbert suggests that the concept of an ethnic trading nation was generally in retreat in the Atlantic, not only within the Hispano-Portuguese commercial network. See "La Nación among the Nations: Portuguese and Other Maritime Trading Diasporas in the Atlantic, Sixteenth to Eighteenth Centuries," in *Atlantic Diasporas: Jews, Conversos, and Crypto-Jews in the Age of Mercantilism*, ed. Richard L. Kagan and Philip D. Morgan (Baltimore, MD: Johns Hopkins University Press, 2008), 77).

129. Carlos González Batista, "Conversiones judaicas en Coro durante la época Española," *Croizatia* 1, no. 1 (1999): 8. On the conection of the Separdi merchants of Curaçao with Venezuela, see Wim Klooster, "Contraband Trade by Curaçao's Jews with Countries of Idolatry, 1660–1800," *Studia Rosenthaliana* 31, nos. 1–2 (1997): 58–73; Carlos González Batista, "Conversiones judaicas en Coro durante la época Española," *Croizatia* 1, no. 1 (1999): 15–22; Blanca de Lima, "Una red commercial sefardita en el eje Curaçao-Coro durante el siglo xviii," *Ler História* 74 (2019): 87–110; Linda Rupert, *Creolization and Contraband: Curaçao in the Early Modern Atlantic World* (Athens: University of Georgia Press, 2012). In 1816, a desperate Simón Bolívar and his sisters found assistance and housing among the Sephardi community of Curaçao, some of whom later enlisted in his revolutionary forces. After independence, Sephardi from Curaçao began to settle in Coro, Baranquilla, Bogotá, and Caracas where they lived under the religious liberty granted by the new republic of Greater Colombia. See Victor Mirelman, "Sephardim in Latin America after Independence," *American Jewish Archives* 44 (1992): 235–66.

130. The original is: "un monstruo de tantas especies cuanto son las castas inferiores." Quoted in Javier Jaramillo Uribe, "Mestizaje y diferenciación social en el Nuevo Reino de Granada en la segunda mitad del siglo xviii," *Anuario colombiano de historia social y de la cultura*, 3 (1965): 25–26.

CHAPTER 3

1. AHN, Inquisición, libro 1964 (Mexico), fs. 232v.-242. I have discussed this case previously. See Stuart B. Schwartz, *All Can Be Saved: Religious Tolerance and Salvation in the Iberian Atlantic World* (New Haven, CT: Yale University Press, 2008), 137–38. Plata, who served as confessor to the nuns of the convent of Santa Catalina, was denounced for lascivious contacts with the nuns and for his emphasis on interior mysticism associated with the *alumbrados*. For more on Plata, see Nora E. Jaffray, *False Mystics: Deviant Orthodoxy in Colonial Mexico* (Lincoln: University of Nebraska Press, 2004), 31–33. On the *alumbrados*, see Stefania Pastore, *Un'eresia Spagnola: Spiritualità conversa, alumbradismo e inquisizione (1449–1559)* (Florence, Italy: Leo S. Olschki, 2004); Mercedes García-Arenal and Felipe Pereda, "On the Alumbrados: Confessionalism and Religious Dissidence in the Iberian World," in *The Early Modern Hispanic World: Transnational and Interdisciplinary Approaches*, ed. Kimberly Lynn and Erin Kathleen Rowe (Cambridge: Cambridge University Press, 2017), 121–52.

2. Gerard Wiegers, "Fuzzy Categories and Religious Polemics: The Daily Life of Christians and Muslims in the Medieval and Early Modern Mediterranean World," *Common Knowledge* 19, no. 3 (2013): 474–88.

3. Robert H. Jackson, "Race/Caste and the Creation and Meaning of Identity in Colonial Spanish America," *Revista de Indias* 55 (1995): n. 203, 149–73. Jackson compared parish registers in Sonora and Cochabamba that demonstrate the shifting meaning and usage of casta labels. For a similar but somewhat stronger questioning of the reality of the casta divisions, see Tatiana Seijas, "Social Order and Mobility in 16th- and 17th-Century Central Mexico," August 2018, Oxford Research Encyclopedia: Latin American History, https://oxfordre.com/latinamericanhistory/view/10.1093/acrefore/9780199366439.001.0001/acrefore-9780199366439-e-359.

4. On the development of new colonial terminologies, see Eduardo França Paiva, *Dar nome ao novo: Uma história lexical da Ibero-América entre os séculos xvi e xviii* (Belo Horizonte, Brazil: Autêntica, 2015). On the role of the Caribbean influence on subsequent conquest patterns, see James Lockhart and Stuart B. Schwartz, *Early Latin America* (Cambridge: Cambridge University Press, 1983), 59–85.

5. Esteban Mira Caballos, "Una etnia conflictiva: Mestizos en las Antillas

en las primeras décadas de la colonización," in Esteban Mira Caballos, *Las Antillas mayores, 1492–1550: Ensayos y documentos* (Madrid: Vervuert Iberoamericana, 2000), 285–96.

6. Pilar Gonzalbo Aizpuru emphasizes the difference between this and the caste system of India, where caste was a fixed and immutable system supposedly unrelated to status, wealth, or other personal qualities ("La trampa de las castas," in La *Sociedad novohispana: Estereotipos y realidades*, ed. Solange Alberro and Pilar Gonzalbo Aizpuru [Mexico City: Colegio de México, 2013], 28–29).

7. For more details about this process of ethnogenesis, see Stuart B. Schwartz and Frank Salomon, "New Peoples and New Kinds of Peoples: Adaptation, Readjustment, and Ethnogenesis in South American Indigenous Societies (Colonial Era)," in *Cambridge History of the Native Peoples of the Americas*, ed. Frank Salomon and Stuart B. Schwartz, 34, part 2, *South America* (New York: Cambridge University Press, 1999), 443–501.

8. Jorge E. Delgadillo Nuñez, "The Workings of Calidad: Honor, Governance and Social Hierarchies in the Corporations of the Spanish Empire," *Americas* 76, no. 2 (2019): 215–40. One of the first studies emphasizing the importance of *calidad* is Robert McCaa, "Calidad, Class, and Marriage: The Case of Parral, 1788–90," *Hispanic American Historical Review* 64, no. 3 (1984): 477–501. In the twentieth century the anthropologists Charles Wagley and Marvin Harris, Wagley's former student, wrote about "social race," which was a malleable and contextualized concept much like *calidad*. See Charles Wagley, "On the Concept of Social Race in the Americas," *Acts: International Congress of Americantists*, 33 (San Jose, Costa Rica: Lehmann, 1959), 1:403–17; Marvin Harris, *Patterns of Race in the Americas* (New York: Norton, 1974).

9. Verena Stolcke, "Los mestizos no nacen sino que se hacen," in *Identidades ambivalentes en América Latina (siglos xvi–xvii)*, ed. Verena Stolcke and Alexandre Coello (Barcelona: Bellaterra, 2007).

10. "Instrucción dada por el Cardinal Cisneros a los frailes jerónimos (Madrid, 13 September 1514)," in Richard Konetzke, ed., *Colección de documentos para la historia de la formación social de Hispanoamérica (1493–1810)* (Madrid: CSIC, 1953), 1:64. This strategy depended on a supposed system of matrilineal descent among the Taino of the Greater Antilles, but its existenceis still debated in the anthropological and historical literature. For

more details on the early presence and status of mestizos in the Caribbean, see Mira Caballos, "Una etnia conflictiva."

11. Richard Konetzke, *El mestizaje y su importancia, en el desarrollo de la población hispano-americana durante la época colonial* (Madrid: Revista de Indias, 1947), 38–48.

12. The 1514 distribution of Indian laborers on Española known as the "Repartimiento de Albuquerque" listed 551 *encomenderos* on the island, 195 (35 percent) of whom were married men, and about a third of those were married to women "of the island," either Indians or mestizas. In the 1531 census of Puerto Rico by Francisco Manuel de Lando, of the sixty-eight married men listed, only 2.0 percent were married to Indian or black women, but 7.7 percent were married to women "of the land"—in this case, most likely mestizas. The Repartimiento de Albuquerque and the Lando census are discussed in Stuart B. Schwartz, "Spaniards, Pardos, and the Missing Mestizos: Identities and Racial Categories in the Early Hispanic Caribbean," *New West Indian Guide* 71, nos. 1–2 (1997): 8–11. See Julio Damiani Cósimi, *Estratificación social, esclavos y naborías en el Puerto Rico minero del siglo xvi* (Río Piedras, Puerto Rico: Universidad de Puerto Rico, 1994).

13. See, for example, Sara Guengerich, "Capac Women and the Politics of Marriage in Early Colonial Peru," *Colonial Latin American Review* 24, no. 2 (2015): 147–67. See also Eva Alexandra Uchmany, "El mestizaje en el siglo xvi novohispano," *Historia Mexicana* 37, no. 1 (1987): 29–47.

14. There have been a number of studies on the importance of gender in ethnic labeling. See, for example, Elizabeth Kuznesof, "Ethnic and Gender Influences on 'Spanish' Creole Society in Colonial Spanish America," *Colonial Latin American Review* 4, no. 1 (1995): 153–76; Karen Vieira Powers, "Conquering Discourses of 'Sexual Conquest': Of Women, Language, and Mestizaje," *Colonial Latin American Review* 11, no. 1 (2002): 7–32. Kathryn Burns showed how Spanish conquerors used convents to facilitate the acceptance of mestiza daughters as Spaniards ("Gender and the Politics of Mestizaje: The Convent of Santa Clara in Cuzco, Peru," *Hispanic American Historical Review* 78, no. 1 [1998]: 5–44).

15. Schwartz and Salomon, "New Peoples and New Kinds of Peoples," 471–73.

16. Pedro Carrasco, "Matrimonios hispano-indios em o primer siglo de la colônia," in *Familia y poder en Nueva España. Memoria del tercer simpo-*

sio de historia de las mentalidades (Mexico City: INAH, 1991), 11–21. See also Robert Schwaller, "The Importance of Mestizos and Mulatos as Bilingual Intermediaries in Sixteenth-Century New Spain," *Ethnohistory* 59, no. 4 (2012): 713–38; Caroline Cunill, "Un mosaico de lenguas: Los intérpretes en la Audiencia de México en el siglo xvi," *Historia Mexicana* 68, no. 1 (2018): 7–48.

17. See Stuart B. Schwartz, "Brazilian Ethnogenesis: Mestiços, Mamelucos, and Pardos," in *Le Nouveau Monde, Mondes Nouveaux: L'expérience américaine*, ed. Serge Gruzinski and Nathan Wachtel (Paris: Éditions de l'École des Hautes Études en Science Sociale, 1996), 13–15; Ronald Raminelli, "Da vila ao sertão: Os mamelucos como agentes da colonização," *Revista de história*, nos. 129–31 (1993): 209–19.

18. Letter of the viceroy of Peru, Conde de Nieva, to King Phillip II, May 4, 1562, in Roberto Levillier, ed., *Gobernantes de Perú, cartas y papeles, siglo xvi* (Madrid: Sucesores de Rivadaneyra, 1921–26), 1:423; letter of Governor García de Castro to King Phillip II, September 2, 1567, in ibid., 3:267. See the general discussion in Magnus Mörner, *La corona española y los foráneos en los pueblos de indios de América* (Stockholm: Almquist and Wiksell, 1970), 105–10.

19. Mörner, *La corona española*, 105–10.

20. Angel Rosenblatt, *La población indígena y el mestizaje en América* (Buenos Aires: Editorial Nova, 1954) 2:89–90.

21. Quoted in Thierry Saignes and Thérése Bouyusse-Cassagne, "Dos confundidas identidades: Mestizos y criollos en el siglo xvii," *Senri Ethnological Studies* 33 (1992): 14–15.

22. Quoted in Berta Ares Queija, "El papel de mediadores y la construcción de un discurso sobre la identidad de los mestizos peruanos (siglo xvi)," in *Entre dos mundos: Fronteras culturales y agentes mediadores*, ed. Berta Ares Queija and Serge Gruzinski (Seville, Spain: CSIC, 1997), 44.

23. Ares Queija, "El papel de mediadores," 46.

24. There is some debate whether these restrictions in Peru were racially motivated or were part of the ongoing competition between peninsular Spaniards and the American-born criollos in general. See Alexandre Coello de la Rosa, "De mestizos y criollos en la Compañía de Jesús," *Revista de Indias* 68, no. 245 (2008): 37–65. See also Sabine P. Hyland, "Illegitimacy and Racial Hierarchy in the Peruvian Priesthood: A Seventeenth-Century

Dispute," *Catholic Historical Review* 84, no. 3 (1998): 431–54. The Church's changing position on the formation of an Indian or mestizo clergy is presented in Magnus Lundbergh, "El clero indígena en Hispanoamérica: De la legislación a la implementación y práctica eclesiástica," *Estudios de historia novohispana* 38 (2008): 39–62.

25. The terms *genízaro* (used in Peru and northern New Spain) and *mameluco* (used in Brazil) were both drawn from contact with Islam in the Mediterranean, and both described people who had moved from Christianity to Islam. In the Americas the terms implied moving from one culture to another.

26. "Repartimiento de La isla Española (1514)," in Joaquín F. Pacheco, Francisco Cárdenas, and Luis Torres de Mendoza, eds., *Colección de Documentos Inéditos relativos al Descubrimiento, Conquista y Organización de las Antiguas Posesiones Españolas de Ultramar* (Madrid: Imprenta Española, 1864–84), 1:225.

27. AGI, Francisco de Barrionuevo to Carlos I, August 26, 1533, Santo Domingo, 77, ramo 111, document. 69. See also Konetzke, *El mestizaje*, 17. A slightly different version is quoted in Roberto Marte, ed., *Santo Domingo en los manuscritos de Juan Bautista Muñoz* (Santo Domingo, Dominican Republic: Ediciones Fundación García Arévalo, 1981), 292–93.

28. See Jacques Poloni-Simard, "Problèmes et tentatives d'identification des métis à travers la documentation colonial," in *Transgressions et stratégies du méstissage*, ed. Bernard Lavallé (Paris: Presses de la Sorbonne Nouvelle, 1999), 11–32. For an excellent and detailed study of mestizaje, see Joanne Rappaport, *The Disappearing Mestizo: Configuring Difference in the Colonial New Kingdom of Granada* (Durham, NC: Duke University Press, 2014). See also Robert Schwaller, *Generos de Gente in Early Colonial Mexico: Defining Racial Difference* (Norman: University of Oklahoma Press, 2016).

29. That observation was made by Pero de Magalhães Gandavo in 1576. See his *The Histories of Brazil*, trans. John B. Stetson (New York: Cortes Society, 1922), 34. I have previously presented more details on this process in Brazil. See Stuart B. Schwartz, "Brazilian Ethnogenesis: Mestiços, Mamelucos, and Pardos," in *Le Nouveau Monde, Mondes Nouveaux: L'expérience américaine*, ed. Serge Gruzinski and Nathan Wachtel (Paris: Éditions de l'École des Hautes Études en Science Sociale, 1996), 7–27.

30. The original is: "Que los españoles, mestizos y indios vagabundos sean

reducidos a pueblos." See *Recopilación de leyes de los reinos de las Indias*, 5th ed. (Madrid: Boix Editor, 1847), I, libro vii, título 4, ley iv, 319.

31. An alternative plan was to have lists made, giving people's age, marital status, property, and occupation, to make sure that no one would remain unemployed. See Juan de Matienzo, *Gobierno del Perú*, ed. Guillermo Lohmann Villena (Lima: Institut Français d'Études Andines, 1967), 85–86.

32. Severo Martínez Peláez, *La patria del criollo*, 4th ed. (San José, Costa Rica: Editorial Universidadi Centroameriocana Americana, 1976). See also Amos Megged, "The Rise of Creole Identity in Early Colonial Guatemala: Differential Patterns in Town and Countryside," *Social History* 17, no. 3 (1992): 421–40.

33. In 1609 the viceroy of Peru was asked by the king to consider creating towns for the various castas, which could provide a labor pool for the mines at Potosí. See Ann Wightman, *Indigenous Migration and Social Change: The Forasteros of Cuzco, 1570–1720* (Durham, NC: Duke University Press, 1990), 22.

34. Quoted in James Lockhart, *The Nahuas after the Conquest* (Stanford, CA: Stanford University Press, 1992), 384–85.

35. Baltasar Dorantes de Carranza, *Sumaria relación de las cosas de la Nueva España con noticia individual de los descendientes legítimos de los conquistadores y primeros pobladores españoles*, ed. Ernesto de Torre Villar (Mexico City: Porrua, 1987), 225.

36. Juan de Solórzano Pereira, *Política indiana* (Antwerp, Belgium: Henrico and CornelioVerdussen, 1703), book 2, chapter 30, 127.

37. Mörner, *La corona*, 106. For a discussion of the prohibitions of mestizos in Peru from holding *encomiendas* (1549), living in Indian villages (1565 and 1646), and holding the office of notary (1570); and those in Nueva Granada (Colombia) from serving as cacique in Indian villages (1576), see ibid., 121.

38. Adrian Masters, "A Thousand Invisible Architects: Vassals, the Petition and Response System, and the Creation of the Spanish Imperial Caste Legislation," *Hispanic American Historical Review* 98, no. 3 (2018): 377–406. The question about mestizo qualifications to be clergy is neatly summarized in Charles R. Boxer, *The Church Militant and Iberian Expansion, 1440–1770* (Baltimore, MD: Johns Hopkins University Press, 1978), 14–22.

See also Lundbergh, "El clero indígena," 54–61; Hyland, "Illegitimacy and Racial Hierarchy," 436–40.

39. AHU, Câmara of Natal to Conselho Ultramarino (1723), Rio Grande do Norte, *papéis avulsos, caixa* 3.

40. ANTT, Lourenço de Almeida to Conselho Ultramarino (April 20, 1722), Manuscritos. do Brasil 27.

41. Quoted in Rosenblatt, *La población indígena*, 114–15.

42. Martin Minchom, *The People of Quito, 1690–1810: Change and Unrest in an Underclass* (Boulder, CO: Westview, 1994).

43. Nicanor J. Dominguez discusses a revolt in a mining area in which the many mestizo participants were in fact acculturated Indians ("Rebels of Laicacota: Spaniards, Indians, and Andean Mestizos in Southern Peru during the Mid-Colonial Crisis of 1650–80" [PhD diss., University of Illinois at Urbana-Champaign, 2006]).

44. Alex Borucki, David Eltis, and David Wheat, "Atlantic History and the Slave Trade to Spanish America," *American Historical Review* 120, no. 2 (2015): 433–61.

45. Schwaller suggests that in sixteenth-century New Spain half of the mulattoes were actually the result of Afro-Indian mestizaje (*Generos de Gente*, 145–46).

46. The emphasis on the presence of Africans in the formation of the casta definitions can be seen in Ben Vinson III, *Before Mestizaje: The Frontiers of Race and Caste in Colonial Mexico* (Cambridge: Cambridge University Press, 2018), and María Elena Martínez, *Genealogical Fictions: Limpieza de Sangre, Religion, and Gender in Colonial Mexico* (Stanford, CA: Stanford University Press, 2008).

47. Viceroy Martín Enríquez to Philip II, January 9, 1574, in *Cartas de Indias* (Madrid: Ministerio de Formento, 1877), 2:298–99.

48. The audiencia of New Granada in 1594 considered the creation of an official position whose incumbent would keep mestizos, mulattoes, and urban Indians under control. See Santiago Muñoz Arbaláez, "Vagabundos urbanos: Las instrucciones para administrar indios, mestizos y mulatos en Santafé de Bogotá a fines del siglo xvi," *Anuario de historia regional y de las fronteras* 22, no. 1 (2017): 225–33.

49. The original is: "los malos mestizos, negros y mulatos, que son casta

sin Rey, y si libres más libres, y con quien se debe comer las manos el Corregidor. Y poco mas o menos, los tres géneros toda es un agua." Bartolomé de Góngora, *El corregidor sagaz: Abisos y documentos morales para los que lo fueren* (Madrid: La Sociedad de Biblófilos Españoles, 1960), 235.

50. The outstanding and roughly contemporary example is the mulatto Dominican lay servant Martín de Porres (1579–1639), whose charity, humility, and apparent healing powers made him a figure of popular piety in Peru. He was canonized in 1962. See Celia Cussens, *Black Saint of the Americas: The Life and Afterlife of Martin de Porres* (Cambridge: Cambridge University Press, 2014).

51. Góngora, *El corregidor sagaz*, 235.

52. See, for example, the many negative references and reports of black and mulatto crimes in Lima in Juan Antonio Suardo, *Diario de Lima (1629–39)*, ed. Rubén Vargas Ugarte, 2 vols. (Lima: Lumen, 1936); Fred Bronner, "La hispanidad de la temprana Lima barroca: Amerindios, morenos y marranos," in *El hombre y los Andes: Homenaje a Franklin Pease G.Y.*, ed Rafael Varón and Javier Flores Espinosa (Lima: Institut Français d'Etudes Andines, 2002), 1:915–28; Carlos Aguirre, *Breve historia de la esclavitud en el Perú* (Lima: Congreso del Perú, 2005), 43–48.

53. Solórzano Pereira, *Política indiana*, vol. 1, book 2, chapter 30. Solórzano Pereira was married to a criolla, and he was critical of Spaniards who defamed the criollos. He claimed that the advancement of criollos was impeded by people who feared their competition for civil and ecclesiastical offices and who claimed that the heavens and the climate of the provinces caused the criollos to degenerate, so that they lost whatever good came from Spanish blood, and thus became hardly worthy of the designation as rational beings.

54. Juan de Pineda, *Diálogos familiares de la agricultura cristiana*, 5 vols., ed. Juan Meseguer Fernández (Madrid: Biblioteca de Autores Españoles, 1963). For an overview, see Valerie Fildes, *Wet-Nursing: A History from Antiquity to the Present* (Oxford: Blackwell, 1988).

55. I have not encountered any early modern Hispanic sources that made the contrary argument that a mulatto or mestizo child who was nursed by a white woman acquired positive characteristics.

56. Martínez de Arce recorded these dreams and turned them over to the Inquisition of Mexico in 1699, concerned that their content might be hereti-

cal. He was admonished to stop recording them. See María Jordán Arroyo, *Entre la vigilia y el sueño: Soñar en el siglo de oro* (Madrid: Iberoamericana Vervuert, 2017), 165–85.

57. Jorge Cañizares-Esguerra, "New World, New Stars: Patriotic Astrology and the Invention of Indian and Creole Bodies in Colonial Spanish America, 1600–1650," *American Historical Review* 104, no. 1 (1999): 33–68; Rebecca Earle, *The Body of the Conquistador: Food, Race and the Colonial Experience in Latin America, 1492–1700* (Cambridge: Cambridge University Press, 2012), 187–216. Even cultural adaptations such as language acquisition were at times viewed as the Indianization of Spaniards residing in the Indies. See Martin Nesvig, "Spanish Men, Indigenous Language, and Informal Interpreters in Post Conquest Mexico," *Ethnohistory* 59, no. 4 (2012): 739–64.

58. Javier Sánchez makes the point that certification of purity did not in itself make one noble, but it was virtually a sine que non for acquiring noble status ("La limpieza de sangre en Nueva España, entre la rutina y la formalidad," in *El peso de la sangre: Limpios, mestizos y nobles en el mundo hispánico*, ed. Nikolaus Böttcher, Bernd Hausberger, and Max Hering [Mexico City: El Colegio de México, 2011], 113–36). See also, María Elena Martínez, "Interrogating Blood Lines: 'Purity of Blood,' the Inquisition, and Casta Categories," in *Religion in New Spain*, ed. Susan Schroeder and Stafford Poole (Albuquerque: University of New Mexico Press, 2007), 196–217.

59. I have discussed this in more detail elsewhere in relation to Brazil. See Stuart B. Schwartz, "A Colonial Slave Society," in Stuart B. Schwartz, *Sugar Plantations and the Formation of Brazilian Society: Bahia, 1550–1835* (Cambridge: Cambridge University Press, 1985), 245–63. António Manuel Hespanha provides the juridical foundation of the multiple statuses (*estados*) within the three orders (*História de Portugal moderno: Político e institucional* [Lisbon: Universidade Aberta, 1995], 42–50).

60. For the classic analysis of the tripartite division of society, see Georges Duby, *The Three Orders: Feudal Society Imagined* (Chicago: University of Chicago Press, 1980). Duby emphasized that the commoners were really divided into an urban patriciate of wealthy merchants and the "toiling classes," so that even at its birth the issue of class affected the concept of estates (ibid., 160–61 and 354–56). For a model study of the intersection of genealogy and corporate social status in the control of local government in a region of Castile, see Jerónimo López-Salazar Pérez, "Limpieza de sangre y división

em estados: El municipio de Almagro durante el siglo xvi," *Studia Historica: Historia Moderna* 12 (1994): 157–87.

61. In Spanish America only two noble titles were created in the sixteenth century: Hernán Cortés and Francisco Pizarro each became a marquis, as discussed below. The Spanish crown granted more titles in the next two centuries as its fiscal needs grew. The Portuguese rulers never created a titled nobility in Brazil prior to the nineteenth century. See Stuart B. Schwartz, "New World Nobility: Social Aspirations and Nobility in the Conquest and Colonization of Spanish America," in *Social Groups and Religious Ideas in the Sixteenth Century*, ed. Miriam Christman and Otto Gründler (Kalamazoo: Western Michigan University, 1978), 23–37. See also Ronald Raminelli, *Nobrezas do novo mundo: Brasil e ultramar hispânico: Séculos xvii e xviii* (Rio de Janeiro, Brazil: Editora FGV, 2015).

62. David Nirenberg, "Was There Race before Modernity? The Example of 'Jewish' Blood in Late Medieval Spain," in *The Origins of Racism in the West*, edited by Miriam Eliav-Feldon, Benjamin Isaac, Joseph Ziegler (Cambridge University Press, 2009), 233–64 (at https://www.medievalists.net/2013/01/was-there-race-before-modernity-the-example-of-jewish-blood-in-late-medieval-spain/).

63. Albert A. Sicroff, *Los estatutos de limpieza de sangre: Controversias en los siglos xvi y xvii* (Madrid: Taurus, 1985.

64. Jean-Frédéric Schaub, *Race Is about Politics*, trans. Lara Vergnaud (Princeton, NJ: Princeton University Press, 2019).

65. See Jeremy Mumford, "Aristocracy on the Auction Block: Race, Lords, and the Perpetuity Controversy in Sixteen-Century Peru," in *Imperial Subjects: Race and Identity in Colonial Latin America*, ed. Andrew B. Fisher and Matthew D. O'Hara (Durham, NC: Duke University Press, 2009), 39–60; Sergio Serulnikov, "Patricians and Plebians in Late Colonial Charcas: Identity, Representations, and Colonialism," in the same edited volume, 167–96.

66. Henry Kamen, "Uma crisis de conciencia en la edad de oro en España: Inquisición contra 'limpieza de sangre,'" *Bulletin Hispanique* 88, nos. 3–4 (1986): 347–49.

67. The literature on the topic is extensive. I have found particularly useful or suggestive María Elena Martínez, "Religion, Purity, and 'Race': The Spanish Concept of Limpieza de Sangre in Seventeenth-Century Mexico and the Broader Atlantic World" (International Seminar on the History of the

Atlantic World, 1500–1825, Harvard University, unpublished working paper no. 00–02, 2000); Carlos López Beltrán, "Sangre y temperamento: Pureza y mestizaje en las sociedades de castas americanas," in *Saberes locales: Ensayos sobre la historia de la ciencia en América Latina*, ed. Frida Gorbach and Carlos López Beltrán (Zamora, Mexico: El Colegio de Michoacán, 2008), 289–331; Jean-Paul Zúñiga, "Visible Signs of Belonging: The Spanish Empire and the Rise of Racial Logics in the Early Modern Period," in *Polycentric Monarchies*, ed. Pedro Cardim, Tamar Herzog, José Javier Ruiz Ibáñez, and Gaetano Sabatini (Eastbourne, UK: Sussex Academic Press, 2012), 126–45.

68. Solórzano Pereira, *Política indiana*, vol. 1, book 2, chapter 29, 126. See also the discussion of his position in Irene Silverblatt, *Modern Inquisitions: Peru and the Colonial Origins of the Civilized World* (Durham, NC: Duke University Press, 2004), 121.

69. Ronald Raminelli and Maria Fernanda Bicalho demonstrate that in Brazil nine Indian chieftains and a few free black military leaders were awarded knighthoods in the military orders for their services, but such rewards were exceptional ("'Nobreza' e 'cidadania' dos brasis: Hierarquias, impedimentos e privilégios na América portuguesa," in *O governo dos outros: Poder e diferença no império português*, ed. Ângela Barreto Xavier and Cristina Nogueira da Silva [Lisbon: Imprensa de Ciências Sociais, 2016], 387–408).

70. Martínez notes that the Mexico City Inquisition tribunal in 1576 denied a mestizo acceptance as a lay assistant (*familiar*) of the Inquisition because there was some suspicion that Indians might have Hebrew origins ("Interrogating Blood Lines," 210–11). But in 1624 it ruled that having one indigenous grandparent no longer disqualified applicants. This was a concession to the criollos, many of whom had some native ancestors.

71. Peter B. Villella, "'Pure and Noble Indians, Untainted by Inferior Idolatrous Races': Native Elites and the Discourse of Blood Purity in Late Colonial Mexico," *Hispanic American Historical Review* 91, no. 4 (2011): 633–64.

72. João de Figueirôa-Rego and Fernanda Olival discuss the question of black "purity" in the Portuguese empire ("Cor da pele, distinções e cargos: Portugal e espaços atlânticos portugueses [séculos xvi a xviii]," *Tempo* 30 [2011]: 115–45). Restrictions on people, including blacks or mulattoes, began only after 1615. Portugal's contacts with various African monarchs; its recep-

tion of African ambassadors; and other contacts through missionaries, diplomats, and commercial agents all merit further study in terms of the effects on ethnic and racial attitudes. See Cécile Fromont, *The Art of Conversion: Christian Visual Culture in the Kingdom of the Kongo* (Chapel Hill: University of North Carolina Press, 2014); Herman L. Bennett, *African Kings and Black Slaves: Sovereignty and Dispossession in the Early Modern Atlantic* (Philadelphia: University of Pennsylvania Press, 2019). For essays on related topics, see Francisco Bethencourt and Adrian Pearce, eds., *Racism and Ethnic Relations in the Portuguese-Speaking World* (Oxford: Oxford University Press, 2012).

73. Charles Boxer, *Race Relations in the Portuguese Colonial Empire, 1415–1825* (Oxford: Clarendon Press of Oxford University Press, 1963), 1–40. Portuguese monarchs occasionally awarded memberships in the military orders and other honors to Indian chieftains and *mestiços*, setting aside the usual deficiencies to reward military and other services. Similar royal awards to mulattoes and former slaves met with considerable bureaucratic and ecclesiastical opposition. See Raminelli and Bicalho, "'Nobreza' e 'cidadania.'"

74. Rebecca Earle, "The Pleasures of Taxonomy: Casta Paintings, Classification, and Colonialism," *William and Mary Quarterly*, 3d ser., 73, no. 1 (2016): especially 431–33.

75. I have discussed this issue in more detail elsewhere. See Schwartz, "New World Nobility," 23–36. Much newer work on the American nobility has appeared. On Brazil, see Ronald Raminelli, "Nobreza e principais da terra-América portuguesa, séculos xvii e xviii," *Topoi* 19, no. 38 (2018): 217–49. On Spanish America, see Christian Büschges, "Nobleza y estructura estamental entre concepto y realidad social: El caso de la Ciudad de Quito y su región (1765–1810)," *Jahrbuch für geschichte lateinamerikas* 33, no. 1 (1996): 165–86. For a comparative perspective, see Raminelli, *Nobrezas do Novo Mundo*.

76. Viceroy Marqués de Mancera reported in 1644 that there were thirty-four knights in Lima and twenty-seven more in the whole viceroyalty of Peru, from Quito to Buenos Aires. See Guillermo Lohmann Villena, *Los americanos en las órdenes nobiliarias (1529–1900)* (Madrid: CSIC, 1947), xxxv.

77. For the classic study of the Portuguese nobility, see Nuno Gonçalves Freitas Monteiro, *O crepúsculo dos grandes (1750–1832)* (Lisbon: Imprensa Nacional, 1996). On compensation for service against the Dutch in Brazil,

see Thiago Nascimento Krause, *Em busca da honra* (São Paulo, Brazil: Anna-Blume, 2012).

78. Jesús D. Rodríguez Velasco, *El debate sobre la caballería en el siglo xv: La tratadística caballeresca castellana en su marco europeo* (Valladolid, Spain: Junta de Castilla y León, 1996), and *Order and Chivalry: Knighthood and Citizenship in Late Medieval Castille*, trans. Eunice Rodríguez Ferguson (Philadelphia: University of Pennsylvania Press, 2010).

79. Thomas Gage, *The New World Society of the West Indies, 1648*, ed. A. P. Newton (New York: G. Routledge and Sons, 1928), 152. On the colonial propensity to seek honors, see "Consulta del Consejo de las Indias sobre la proposición de que se beneficien en las Indias ciento y cincuenta títulos de Castilla (19 July 1675)," in Richard Konetzke, ed., *Colección de documentos para la historia de la formación social de Hispanoamérica (1493–1810)* (Madrid: CSIC, 1953), vol. 2, part 2, 617. See also Emiliano Frutta, "Limpieza de sangre y nobleza en el México colonial: la formación de un saber nobiliario," *Jahrbuch für geschichte lateinamerikas*, 39 (2002), 217–35. For a useful discussion of mestizaje within a particular urban context, see Norma Angélica Castillo Palma, *Cholula: Sociedad mestiza en ciudad india* (Mexico City: Universidad Autónoma Metropolitana, 2001).

80. Konetzke, ed., *Colección de documentos*, volume 2, part 2, 152 and 158.

81. There was much criticism of the inflation of honors and rank in Spanish America. On the assumption of the honorific title of don as a mark of status, see Javier Jaramillo Uribe, "Mestizaje y diferenciación social en el Nuevo Reino de Granada en la segunda mitad del siglo xviii," *Anuario colombiano de historia social y de la cultura* 3 (1965): 21–48, especially 43–48. See also James Lockhart, *Spanish Peru, 1532–1560: A Social History* (Madison: University of Wisconsin Press, 1968), 39–41.

82. Aldair Carlos Rodrigues, "Inquisição e sociedade: A formação da rede de familiares do Santo Ofício em Minas Gerais colonial (1711–1808)," *Varia história* 26, no. 43 (2010): 197–216; James Wadsworth, *Agents of Orthodoxy: Honor, Status, and the Inquisition in Colonial Pernambuco, Brazil* (Lanham, MD: Rowman and Littlefield, 2007).

83. Douglas Cope, *The Limits of Racial Domination: Plebeian Society in Colonial Mexico City, 1660–1720* (Madison: University of Wisconsin Press, 1994), 161–63.

84. Ann Twinam, *Purchasing Whiteness: Pardos, Mulattos, and the Quest*

for Social Mobility in the Spanish Indies (Stanford, CA: Stanford University Press, 2015). Twinam presents a thorough study of the purchasing of whiteness by acquisition of a *gracias al sacar*—a document that formally removed the stain of ignoble birth and thus allowed the holder to advance socially and professionally. These documents appeared quite late in the colonial regime and were rare.

85. Fernanda Olival, "The Culture of Background Investigations (Portugal, 1570-1773)," *eHumanista/Conversos* 4 (2016): 112-27; Silvia Espelt-Bombín, "Notaries of Color in Colonial Panama: Limpieza de sangre, Legislation, and Imperial Practices in the Administration of the Spanish Empire," *Americas* 75, no. 1 (2014): 37-69.

86. AGN, Indiferente de Guerra (May 13, 1796), quoted in Juan Carlos Garavaglia and Juan Carlos Grosso, "Criollos, mestizos, y indios: Etnias y clases sociales en México colonial a fines del siglo xviii," *Secuencia* 29 (1994): 46. For an extensive discussion of the parish registers of Mexico City, see Gonzalbo Aizpuru, "La trampa de las castas," 65-100.

87. Vinson, *Before Mestizaje*, 152-60.

88. Arturo Grubessich, "Estructura social de Valparaíso durante el último cuarto de siglo xviii," *Notas Históricas y Geográficas* 4 (1993): 211-40.

89. Emilio Ravignani, ed., *Territorio y población, padrón de la compaña de Buenos Aires (1778)* . . . (Buenos Aires: Compañía Sud-americana de Billetes de Banco, 1919). There was also an underreporting of mestizos in the surrounding countryside and frontier outposts, where surely many of them lived. See Peggy Creider, "A Study of the Casta Population of Buenos Aires Based on the Census of 1778," undergraduate summa cum laude thesis, University of Minnesota, 1968. See also Carmen Bernand, "La plèbe ou le peuple? Buenos Aires, fin xviiie–xixe siècles," *Caravelle* 84 (2004): 146-68.

90. Jaramillo Uribe, "Mestizaje y diferenciación social," 25-26.

91. I base these observations on Kris Lane, "Betwixt and Between: A Preliminary Investigation of Mestizaje in the Audiencia of Quito, 1686-1781," (unpublished manuscript, University of Minnesota, 1993). Lane based his analysis of ninety-two cases in the National Historical Archive in Quito (AHNQ) in a series titled "Mestizos"). For a similar analysis, see Minchom, *The People of Quito.*

92. AHNQ, petition of Ignacio de Aguilar, 1771, Mestizos, caja 1, legajo 23. Lane ("Betwixt and Between") points out the disparity between the

25,528 persons (only 7.4 percent of the population of 342,739) listed as mestizos in the audiencia of Quito census of 1781 and the estimate that one-third of the region's inhabitants were mestizos, according to the earlier report made by Jorge Juan and Antonio de Ulloa (*A Voyage to South America*, 2 vols. [London: L. Davis and C. Reymers, 1758]). The petitions in this archive may have been mostly from poorer mestizos living among Indians and thus not able to pass as locally born criollo Spaniards—as many others apparently did.

93. Norma Angélica Castillo Palma, "Informaciones y probanzas de limpieza de sangre: Teoría y realidad frente a la movilidad de la población novohispana producida por el mestizaje," in *El peso de la sangre: Limpios, mestizos y nobles en el mundo hispánico*, ed. Nikolaus Böttcher, Bernd Hausberger, and Max Hering (Mexico City: El Colegio de México, 2011), 219–50.

94. Ann Twinam, "Purchasing Whiteness: Conversations on the Essence of Pardo-ness and Mulatto-ness at the End of Empire," in *Imperial Subjects: Race and Identity in Colonial Latin America*, ed. Andrew B. Fisher and Matthew D. O'Hara (Durham, NC: Duke University Press, 2009), 158–60.

95. Ilona Katzew, *Casta Painting: Images of Race in Eighteenth-Century Mexico* (New Haven, CT: Yale University Press, 2004); María Concepción García Sáiz, *Las castas mexicanas: Un género pictórico americano* (Milan, Italy: Olivetti, 1989).

96. *Ex voto* paintings are votive offerings usually presented in fulfillment of a vow made after praying for devine or saintly assistance. These images were often made by nonprofessional or "folk" artists, and the tradition of creating the images is particularly strong in the Catholic Mediterranean countries and Latin America.

97. The noteworthy exception is the painting of all the castas under the protection of the Virgin of Guadalupe by Luis de Mena (1750). See Sarah Cline, "Guadalupe and the Castas: The Power of a Singular Colonial Mexican Painting," *Mexican Studies/Estudios Mexicanos* 31, no. 2 (2015): 218–46.

98. Little contemporary evidence of reaction to these paintings has survived, but Efraín Castro Morales presents some interesting comments made around 1746 by the Mexican Creole Andrés Arce y Miranda, who objected to the casta paintings for portraying to Europeans "that which injures us, not which benefits us, that which denigrates us, not that which ennobles us (lo que nos daña, no lo que nos aprovecha, lo que nos infama, no lo que

nos ennoblece)" ("Los cuadros de castas de la Nueva España," *Jahrbuch für geschichte von staat, wirtschaft, und gesellschaft Lateinamerikas* 20 [1985]: 671–90).

99. *Chino* (or *china*) was used generically for Asians—Filipinos, Malays, Chinese, Indonesians, and people from India—most of whom arrived in Spanish America through Acapulco as slaves. Enslavement of *chinos* was abolished in 1672, after which they were legally considered Indians (indios) and thus subject to tribute payments. See Tatiana Seijas, *Asian Slaves in Colonial Mexico: From Chinos to Indians* (Cambridge: Cambridge University Press, 2014), 143–62. As indios neither by phenotype nor by clothing, *chinos* (Asians) cannot be identified in the casta paintings.

100. AGN, Census of Tepeaca, 1791, Padrones, vol. 38, quoted in Garavaglia and Grosso, "Criollos, mestizos, y indios," 47.

101. Leonardo León, "Entre la alegría y la tragedia: Los intersticios del mundo mestizo en la frontera," in *Historia de la vida privada en Chile*, ed. Rafael Segredo and Cristián Gazmuri, 4th ed. (Santiago, Chile: Taurus, 2007), 269–307.

102. Roxana Boixadós and Judith Farberman, "Clasificaciones mestizas: Una aproximación a la diversidad étnica y social de los llanos riojanos del siglo xviii," in *Historias mestizas en el Tucumán colonial y las pampas (siglos xvii–xx)*, ed. Judith Faberman and Silvia Ratto (Buenos Aires: Biblos, 2009), 79–114.

103. Quoted in Jorge M. Pedreira, "Mercantilism, Statebuilding and Social Reform: The Government of the Marquis of Pombal and the Abolition of the Distinction between New and Old Christians," *Journal of Levantine Studies* 6 (2016): 366–67.

104. On Pombal and the New Christians, see Jorge Martins, "A emancipação dos judeus em Portugal," *Cadernos de estudos sefarditas* 8 (2008): 63–845; Pedreira, "Mercantilism, Statebuilding and Social Reform," 357–83.

105. AMC, minutes of the Town Council (*vereação*, June 26, 1748), 1-I-36, fs. 82–83.

106. AHU, Bahia, *papéis avulsos, caixa* 66 (December 1, 1756), 1st series, uncatalogued; APB, governor of Sergipe to governor of Bahia (October 24, 1815), Cartas ao Governo 229. On pardos, see Schwartz, "Brazilian Ethnogenesis," 23–24, and the sources cited therein. For a useful summary, see Herbert Klein, "The Colored Freedman in Brazilian Slave Society," *Jour-*

nal of Social History 3, no. 1 (1969): 30–52. For a more recent study, see Raimundo Agnelo Soares Pessoa, "Gente sem sorte: Os mulatos no Brasil colonial" (PhD diss., Universidade Estadual Paulista "Júlio Mesquita Filho," Franca, 2007).

107. The limited effect of the casta restrictions has been effectively argued by Gonzalbo Aizpuru ("La trampa de las castas") and even earlier by Juan Carlos Garavaglia and Juan Marchena Fernández ("Mestizos y mulatos en la sociedad colonial," in *América Latina de los orígenes a la independencia*, ed. Juan Carlos Garavaglia and Juan Marchena Fernández [Barcelona: Crítica, 2005], 2:353–67). Seijas has forcefully made a similar argument in an excellent review of the literature ("Social Order and Mobility").

108. For examples, on Indian communities' defense of land titles (*títulos primordiales*), see Alex Hidalgo, *Trail of Footprints: A History of Indigenous Maps from Viceregal Mexico* (Austin: University of Texas Press, 2019); on mulatto military service and enlistment, see Ben Vinson III, *Bearing Arms for His Majesty: The Free-Colored Militia in Colonial Mexico* (Stanford, CA: Stanford University Press, 2001); on Indians and peoples of African origin and descent facing the colonial legal systems, see Brian Owensby, *Empire of Law and Indian Justice in Colonial Mexico* (Stanford, CA: Stanford University Press, 2011), and Michelle Mckinley, "Fractional Freedoms: Slavery, Legal Activism, and Ecclesiastical Courts in Colonial Lima, 1593–1689," *Law and History Review* 28, no. 3 (2010): 749–90; and on American Indians in lawsuits in Spain, see Nancy Van Dussen, *Global Indios: The Indigenous Struggle for Justice in Sixteenth-Century Spain* (Durham, NC: Duke University Press, 2015).

109. For the fullest study of the Real Pragmática, see Patricia Seed, *To Love, Honor and Obey in Colonial Mexico: Conflicts over Marriage Choice, 1574–1821* (Stanford, CA: Stanford University Press, 1988).

110. The statement is quoted and discussed in Ruth Mackay, *Lazy, Improvident People: Myth and Reality in the Writing of Spanish History* (Ithaca, NY: Cornell University Press, 2006), 179.

111. For an early recognition of this phenomenon, see Alberto Flores Galindo, *Aristocracia y plebe: Lima, 1760–1830: Estructura de clases y sociedad colonia*l (Lima: Osca Azul, 1984).

112. The quotation is from Luiz dos Santos Vilhena, a professor in Bahia (*A Bahia no século xviii*, ed. Braz do Amaral [Salvador, Brazil: Editora Ita-

puã, 1969], 3:919). I have previously discussed this theme at some length. See Stuart B. Schwartz, "De la plèbe au 'peuple' dans le Brésil du xviiie siècle," *Caravelle* 84, no. 1 (2005): 127–46.

113. Viceroy Juan Francisco de Güemes y Horcasitas, Conde de Revillagigedo, to Augustín de Ahumada y Villalón (October 8, 1755, quoted in Gonzalbo Aizpuru, "La trampa de las castas," 137–38. See also Thomas Calvo, "La plèbe à l'aune des vice-rois américains (xvie–xviiie siècles)," *Caravelle* 84, no. 1 (2005): 37–63, and "De l'indien à la plèbe: Les viages du réprimé dans la Nouvelle Espagne (xvie-xviiie siècles)," in *Conflicto, violencia y criminalidad en Europa y América*, ed. José Antonio Munita Loinaz (Bilbao, Spain: Universidad del País Vasco, 2004), 279–303. The latter work traces vicceregal complaints about the plebe in New Spain in the seventeenth and eighteenth centuries.

114. Patricio Hidalgo Nuchera, "El miedo de las élites a las clases bajas: Regulación de la pobreza legal y represión de la vagancia en España y Nueva España," *Revista Hispanoamericana* 8 (2018): 1-24. See also Pilar Gonzalbo Aizpuru, "Blancos pobres y libertos: Los colores de la pobreza en el virreinato de Nueva España," in *Historia general de América Latina*, ed. Josefina Zoraida Vázquez and Manuel Miño Grijalba (New York: UNESCO, 1999), volume 3, part 2, pp. 429–42.

115. Scarlett O'Phelan Godoy, "La construcción del miedo a la plebe en el siglo xviii a través de las rebeliones sociales," in *El miedo en el Perú: Siglos xvi al xx*, ed. Claudia Rosas Lauro (Lima: Pontificia Universidad Católica del Perú, 2005), 123–38. On Mexico, see Cope, *The Limits of Racial Domination*, 161–65.

116. In the original: "muchachos y muchachas, cholos y mestizos y gente de clase baja que andaban descalzos y usaban ponchillos." AGI, Audiencia de Lima, legajo 1052, quoted in O'Phelan Godoy, "La construcción," 126. *Cholo* is an Andean term of mestizaje. In Bolivia it is used for either acculturated urban Indians or mestizos, but in Peru and Ecuador it is used only for the former. In some instances the Andean rebellions of 1780–83 drove the castas to collaborate more closely and identify with the Spaniards. See Serulnikov, "Patricians and Plebians in Late Colonial Charcas."

117. The historian Jay Kinsbruner has raised objections to the use of the term "plebian" by historians of Latin America because of a lack of clear definition of what groups were included (*The Colonial Spanish American*

City: Urban Life in the Age of Capitalism [Austin, University of Texas Press, 2005]). He believed that the use of "plebian" (like that of "subaltern") as simply a synonym for "lower class" disguised more than it explained. His reservations centered on the inclusion of artisans and small shopkeepers as members of the plebian class.

118. For an excellent overview of the issues of race and inclusion debated at the Cortes of Cadiz, see Antonio Feros, *Speaking of Spain: The Evolution of Race and Nation in the Hispanic World* (Cambridge, MA: Harvard University Press, 2017), 232–61. As delegates to the Cortes of Cadiz in 1811 debated Spain's transition to a constitutional monarchy, some of the American delegates rose to the defend the castas as "the best part of the people," calling them "lively"; "fearless"; and artisans, workers, miners, and soldiers who made up "the robust spinal column of our defense and of the dominions of Your Majesty" (quoted in López Beltrán, "Sangre y temperamento," 330).

119. López Beltrán, "Sangre y temperamento," 330–31. The phrase comes from his discussion of statements made about the American population at the Cortes of Cadiz in 1811. Evidence of the legacy of the hierarchy of phenotypes and limpieza in the nineteenth century in Cuba is presented in Verena Martínez-Alier, *Marriage, Class and Color in Nineteenth-Century Cuba* (Cambridge: Cambridge University Press, 1974). Similar evidence in Puerto Rico is presented in María del Carmen Baerga, *Negociaciones de sangre: dinámicas racializantes en el Puerto Rico decimonónico* (San Juan, Puerto Rico: Iberoamericana Vervuert and Ediciones Callejón, 2015).

INDEX

Note: Page numbers with "n" or "nn" indicate endnotes.

Dom Antonio, 21
Duke of Linares, 101
Dutch Brazil, 48, 54

economics: corruption of faith and social divisions by, 52, 55–64; growth and social consequences, 106–9; Inquisition's corruption by, 56–59; trading networks, 45, 54, 60, 69–70, 136n19
Elvas, António Fernandes de, 60
emigration to the Americas, 15–16, 28, 45, 86, 137n21
encomenderos (holders of grants), 17–18, 47, 157n12
encomienda (grant of indigenous laborers), 17, 95
endogamy, 64, 98, 103
England, 21, 54–55
Enriquez, Martín, 86–88
Estebanico (Mustafa Azemmouri), 16–17
ethnogenesis, 76–77
ethnography, 19–20
evangelism, 20
exclusionary policies: in Americas, 72; based on blood, 103; and casta systems, 107; Christian theology of, 92; against conversos, 45, 50, 57; and discrimination, 43; effectiveness of, 16, 18; and expulsion of Jews, 41; justification for, 20; mestiços, 84; minority categories, 3–4; and race concept, 8; religious, 15, 68
expulsions: effects of, 35–36; of Jews, 41, 43–44; of mestizos, 81; of Moriscos, 21, 33, 63, 81; of Muslims, 18–19; and xenophobia, 119n13

falsified proof, 63
Fanshaw, Richard (wife of), 42–43

Ferdinand II, King of Aragon, 13–15, 126n55
Fernandes, Isabel, 68
1558 project, 83
1565 law (*cédula*) in Guatemala, 83
frontiers: calls for help against rebellions at, 124n45; conversos at, 48; mestizos at, 82, 104; slavery debate over inhabitants of, 23; and tendency to religious inconstancy, 31–37

Gage, Thomas, 96
Gallen, Francisco, 65
García-Arenal, Mercedes, 21–22
gender, 5–6, 31, 77–78, 157n14
genealogies, 4, 7, 53, 64, 80–82, 88, 94, 105
gentilismo (repression of Asian religious influence), 45, 136n20
globalization, Sephardi influence on, 59
Goa, 75
Goa Inquisition, 44–45, 136nn19–20
Gomes Solis, Duarte, 52, 55–56
Gómez, Juan, 67, 152n115
Gonçalves, Cosmé, 65
Góngora, Bartolomé de, 87
Granada, 1–2, 13–16, 22–24, 28
Greeks, 20, 29–30, 92
Griego, Jorge, 30
Guanajuato, 98
Guerrero, Gonzalo, 31–34

Haitian rebellion (1791), 108
Haitian Revolution (1792–1804), 39
Hapsburgs, 44, 47, 50, 54, 138n27
Herrera, Sebastian, 28–29
Hess, Andrew, 21
Hidalgo, Miguel de, 70–71
hidalgos (gentlemen), 7–8, 10, 40, 90, 94–96, 107

Hispanic orientalism, 14
Hispanic societies, 6–8, 16, 50–51,
    78–79, 83–84, 85–87
Hispaniola rebellion (1498), 46
hombres de la nación (the men of the
    nation), 51, 59–60
hombres de negocio (large-scale mer-
    chants, etc.), 48

identity: and belief, 24; Christian,
    29–30; converso, 43, 61; corporate,
    109; Jewish, 41, 64; mestizo, 78;
    racial, 5, 74; religious, 61, 68
idolatry, 93
illegal trade, 49–50, 63
immigration, 45–47, 63, 72
Indian laborers, 17, 80, 157n12
Indies. *See* Spanish Indies
indigenous peoples: African slaves
    as labor replacements for, 85–86;
    Araucanians (later Mapuche), 20,
    23, 35, 36–37, 104; and conversos,
    48–49; cultural crossovers, 34–37;
    European colonial plans for, 3–4,
    13; extirpation of religious prac-
    tices, 72; impracticality of lim-
    pieza de sangre restrictions, 92–96;
    Maya resistance, 31–34; and mes-
    tizo status, 77–79, 99; *moros y cris-
    tiano*, 14; multiple characteristics
    in identity markers, 74–75, 97–99;
    negotiated status of, 92, 93, 99,
    105–6; religious and ethnic con-
    texts for status of, 2–3; social inter-
    action with other groups, 103–4;
    Spanish fears of potential Muslim
    influence, 20; status vs. Jews, 69
inherited characteristics, 9, 32–33,
    42–43, 61, 88, 91, 110
Inquisition: agents of, 62–63, 104; in
    Americas, 16, 28, 49–50; in Brazil,
    46, 49–50; and conversos, 51–54;

crypto-islamism, 16; economic cor-
    ruption of, 56–59; in Goa, 44–45,
    136nn19–20; Gómez's experience
    with, 67; for indigenous peoples,
    2; and Jews, 50–51, 65, 69–70; in
    Lima, 16, 28, 47, 58–59, 62, 64,
    120n15; and limpieza de sangre re-
    strictions, 7, 96; and mestizos, 74,
    165n70; in Mexico City, 16, 47,
    165n70; and Muslims or Moriscos,
    18–19, 26–30, 33, 120n15; and New
    Christians, 44–48, 65–66; purity
    laws, 92; religious syncretism, 2;
    and slavery, 15–17; Zapata's experi-
    ence with, 24–25
integration, 52, 61, 64, 69, 74
Isabella, Queen of Castile, 13–15
Islam, 14–16, 20–27, 31, 33, 36–37,
    126n55, 132n89, 159n25. *See also*
    Moriscos; Muslims
Israel, Jonathan, 70
Italy, 26, 30, 44

Jesuits, 22, 46, 79–80
Jews and Judaism: Catholic Church's
    shifting relationship to, 50, 69;
    Christianity and Judaism, 133n4;
    expulsions of Jews, 41, 43–44;
    and Inquisition, 50–51, 65, 69–70;
    methods for thriving in Iberian
    Atlantic, 59–61; Sephardi, 50,
    54, 59–60, 64; as threat to Por-
    tuguese empire, 136n19; as threat
    to Spanish empire, 54–55. *See also*
    conversos
judaizante (baptized Christian re-
    verted to Judaism), 42–43
Judaizing, 45, 57, 141n48
"judíos en suley" (Jews in their reli-
    gion), 62–63
juridical model, 2, 4, 9, 52, 74, 89–90,
    97–98, 106

knighthoods, 43, 61, 89, 95–97, 104, 165n69

labradores (commoners), 89–90
Latrubesse, Amalia, 36–37
Laws of Burgos, 77
Lezcano, Juana de, 17
Lima, Luis de, 48
Lima Inquisition, 16, 28, 47, 58–59, 62, 64, 120n15
limpieza de sangre (purity of blood): casta paintings, 102–4; and casta system, 73, 76; and Christian conversion, 41–43; in colonial denunciations, 18; conversos, 69, 92–93; Creoles, 88–89; genealogies, 81; historical context, 90–100; and inheritance, 32–33; nobility, 7–9, 163n58; and origins of racism, 7–8; and power of money, 57–58; and *raza* (race), 133n3; in Spain, 52
linajudos (genealogists), 53
Loyola, Martín de, 63

mala inclinación (inclined to evil), 79
malones (raids), 36–37
mamelucos (Mamalukes), 33–34
Mamil Mapu, 37
Mapuche, 35–36, 104
Mapuche (Araucanians), 20, 23, 35, 36–37, 104
Marqués de la Conquista. *See* Pizarro, Francisco
Marqués del Valle de Oaxaca. *See* Cortés, Hernán
Marqués de Mancera, 49, 58–59, 166n76
Marqués de Pombal. *See* Carvalho e Melo, Sebastião de
marriages, 53, 63, 68, 75, 77–78, 95–96, 106–7
Martínez, María Elena, 94

Maya resistance, 31–34
Mayo, Carlos, 36–37
medieval society, 2, 6–10, 30, 42, 50, 76, 89–90, 94
Mediterranean, 20–23, 25–32, 34–38, 44, 59, 86, 124n45, 159n25
mercantilism, 50–51, 55, 69–70
Mercedarians, 21, 36
merchant class, 55–60
mestizos, 72–110; 1558 project, 83–84; Africanization of, 86–87, 97; Bourbon-era censuses of, 98–99; burdens of lineage, 80–81, 85–89; in Caribbean, 80–82; casta paintings, 101; colonial categories, 73–77; Creoles, 85, 89; defined, 4; earliest generation, 78; ethnogenesis, 76; exclusionary policies, 84, 110; and Inquisition, 74, 165n70; juridical social structure and religious purity, 89–106; and mulattoes, 86; in Peru, 79, 82–84; social organization changes of 18th century, 106–10; status and societal context, 77–84. *See also* casta system
Mestre Andrea, 28
Mexico, 22, 54, 77–79, 82, 162–63n56
Mexico City, 16, 47, 51, 59–61, 108, 120n15, 165n70
Minas Gerais, 84
miscegenation, 10, 43, 74
missionaries, 1–2, 14, 20–22, 72, 77
money. *See* economics
Moors. *See* Muslims
Morales, Pedro de, 65
Moreno, Pedro, 19–20
Moriscos (converted Muslims), 13–39; casta paintings, 102; Christian skepticism about, 16; cultural boundary crossing, 74; dealing with renegades, 25–31; expulsion,

180   INDEX

81; and Inquisition, 18–19, 26–30, 33, 120n15; visual representations, 42. *See also* Muslims

moros por naturaleza (born Muslims), 26

moros por profesión (Muslims by choice), 25–26

moros y cristianos, 13–14, 118n3

Moura, Cristóvão de, 56

mulattoes, 32–33, 83–84, 86–88, 91, 102–4, 161n45

Muslims (moros): American fears of, 20–25; and Christian Iberia, 13–20; colonizers' fears of, 20–25, 31–37; and conversos, 42–44; discrimination, 52; expulsion, 18–19; medieval representations of, 42; and Native American contact, 20, 22; Oran, 122n35; and reality of Muslim threat in 19th century, 38–39; renegades, 27–28; slavery, 132n87, 132n89; West African politics, 38–39

Natal, 84

national sovereignty, 50

Nativ, 86

Native Americans. *See* indigenous peoples

negros libres (free blacks), 88

New Christians: along Río de La Plata, 64; in Brazil, 49–50, 104; conversion as cultural as well as religious, 2; discrimination against, 60, 67, 104; emigration, 137n21; Goa tribunal, 136n19; indigenous peoples as, 93; and Inquisition, 44–48, 65–66; limpieza de sangre, 135n13; and Old Christians, 68; in Portugal, 44–48, 146n74

New Granada, 18, 82, 99–100, 161n48

New Spain. *See* colonial society

New World colonies. *See* colonial society

Nicolas, Juan, 30

nobility, 7–10, 40, 43, 55–56, 60, 89–98, 164n61

nobreza da terra (members of a local nobility), 96

non-Muslim Africans, 86

Noronha, Fernão de, 45

North Africa, 15–16, 20–21, 127n63

Nueva Galicia, 20

Old Christians: and conversos, 42, 43, 63–64, 67–69; exclusion of Muslims by, 18; intermarriages, 66–68; Marqués de Pombal, 104; and non-Muslim Africans, 86; Portuguese, 47, 60, 65, 146n74; purity laws, 92–93; and social difference, 4

Olivares, Count-Duke of, 55, 57–58, 146n77

oradores (clergy), 89–90

Oran, 21–22, 122n35

Ottoman Turks, 14, 18, 20–22, 24, 28–30, 39

Oviedo, Gonzalo Fernández de, 32

paganism, 49

pardo, 4, 82, 105. *See also* mestizos

pardon, 57, 67, 146n74

Paul IV (pope), 50

Peralta, Juan Suárez de, 18, 22

Pérez, Manuel Baptista, 58

Pérez, Manuel Bautista, 60–61

Peru: casta paintings, 100; concubinage, 77; fear of religious enemies, 20; Greeks in, 30; hidalgo status, 95; Indian laborers, 17; indigenous nobility, 92; and Inquisition, 47–48; mestizos, 79, 82–84;

and Muslims, 15; restrictions in, 158n24; uprisings in, 108

peruleros (illegal or gray-area trade with South America), 50

phenotypes: casta system, 69–70, 89, 97–99; and discrimination, 3, 43, 52; for Jews and conversos, 68; mestizos, 76, 80; religious purity's loss in defining status, 94; in social hierarchies, 62, 73, 110

Philip II, King of Spain, 21, 47, 52, 144n65

Philip III, King of Spain and Portugal, 57

Philip IV, King of Spain and Portugal, 57

Pizarro, Francisco, 13, 17, 30, 95, 164n61

Plata, Juan, 72–73

plebe, 71, 84, 90–91, 97, 107–9, 172–73n117

pluralism, 74

Ponce de León, Juan, 18

Portugal: and concept of race, 133n3; discrimination in, 3–4, 40, 52, 109; exclusion policies, 32; expulsions of minorities, 36; Jews and conversos in, 40, 41–42, 49–51, 52–54, 55–64, 65–66, 135–36n16; and mamelucos, 33; mestizos as challenge for, 70–71, 72, 73–75; missionary enterprise in Americas, 1–4; New Christians in, 44–48, 146n74; nobility for colonial minorities, 95, 165–66n72; reforms of 18th century, 106, 109; relations with other European powers, 21; social foundation in colonies, 6–10; sovereignty over emigrants, 143n59; and Spain, 53–55, 144nn65–66

Portuguese Brazil. *See* Brazil

Potosí, 13, 18, 49, 62–63, 139n32, 160n33

privilege: based on medieval juridical model, 89–90; blood criterion as stability for, 43; local nobility status, 96; and marriage laws for elites, 106–7; religious affiliation basis vs. blood, 9–10

probanzas (certificates), 52–53

prosopography, 59–60

Protestantism, 20, 21, 24, 49

Puerto Rico, 80, 157n12

Pulido Serrano, Juan Ignacio, 65, 147n84

purity. *See limpieza de sangre*

Quevedo, Francisco de, 56

Quiroga, Jerónimo de, 37

Quito rebellion, 79, 99–100, 169n92

race: defined, 100; and difference, 9; discrimination based on, 8, 100; and distinction, 99; exclusionary policies based on, 8; and ideology, 7, 91; labels, 103, 109; racial identity, 5, 74; taxonomies, 73–74; theories of, 8–9. *See also* phenotypes

racism, 6–8, 10, 40, 94, 115n20

Real Pragmática of 1776, 103, 106–7

rebellions, 23, 46, 48–49, 54, 64, 79, 99–100, 108, 169n92

reconciliados (recently converted), 15

reconciliation, 27, 32, 61

religion. *See* Christianity; Islam; Jews and Judaism

religious contamination, 26–27, 31, 42

religious fidelity, 90–91

religious identity, 61, 68

religious purity, 9–10, 44, 94, 102

religious syncretism, 2, 72, 112n6

renegades, 19, 25–37